Revolution
at the
Checkout Counter

Wertheim Publications in Industrial Relations

Established in 1923 by the family of the late Jacob Wertheim
"for the support of original research in the field of industrial cooperation"

Revolution at the Checkout Counter

Stephen A. Brown

Distributed by Harvard University Press
Cambridge, Massachusetts and London, England 1997

PRINTED IN THE UNITED STATES OF AMERICA

10   9   8   7   6   5   4   3   2   1

This book is printed on acid-free paper, and its binding materials have been chosen for strength and durability.

Library of Congress Cataloging-in-Publication Data

Brown, Stephen A. (Stephen Allen), 1938–
    Revolution at the checkout counter / Stephen A. Brown.
        p.   cm. — (Wertheim publications in industrial relations)
    Includes bibliographical references and index.
    ISBN 0-674-76720-9
    1. Product coding — United States — History.   I. Title.
II. Series.
    HF5416.B77   1997
    658.7'8'0285642 — dc21   97-2776
                                                                CIP

Dedicated to the members of the
Symbol Selection Subcommittee

"Remember, there are three kinds of people here."

Contents

Preface / xi

Prologue / xiii

Introduction / 1

One The Ad Hoc Committee / 39

Two The Symbol Selection Subcommittee / 57

Three UGPIC / 94

Four Public Policy / 123

Five Distribution Codes, Inc. / 131

Six Symbol Technical Advisory Committee (STAC) / 139

Seven UPCC—On Its Own / 148

Eight Electronic Data Interchange (EDI) / 163

Nine Beyond Retail / 174

Ten Coupons—Quid Pro Quo? / 184

Eleven Spreading the Word / 194

Twelve Formal Challenges / 211

Thirteen UCC—A Broader Vision / 224

Appendix A Giants of the Revolution / 247

Appendix B The Board of Governors of Uniform Code Council, Inc. / 269

Appendix C The U.P.C. Symbol / 281

Acknowledgments

The U.P.C. and its people have been a major part of my life for more than twenty-five years. As checkout scanning became accepted, there was a clear need to document this remarkable achievement in which company executives came together and put the needs of efficiency, productivity, and consumer satisfaction ahead of their company interests. It has taken longer than expected to do so.

While any errors are my responsibility, the book could not have been completed without the help of many people. Those associated with the U.P.C. and the Uniform Code Council have given me unflagging support and assistance.

There are three individuals whom I must call out for special mention. Alan Haberman, Chair of the Symbol Selection Committee, long-time UCC Board member, and first Chair of SC 31, has provided information, kept up my spirits when the project seemed endless, and reviewed the draft of the book. Barry Franz, who also served on the Symbol Committee and the Board, has done the same. The late Hal Juckett, UCC President, also helped enormously. More important, Hal only asked that I tell the story honestly. These men are much more than sources, they are also dear friends.

I am pleased to acknowledge the assistance of Susan Hayes in preparing the manuscript for publication and the decision of the Wertheim Publications in Industrial Relations, Harvard University, Professor John T. Dunlop, Editor, to accept the manuscript for publication.

Professor John Dunlop not only made publication a reality, he has honored me by providing an introductory chapter, placing this "revolution" in an economic context.

My daughter, Elizabeth Bradley, willingly gave me large chunks of her time to help with the index. She did it so cheerfully, she made me feel like she actually enjoyed it.

Finally, my deepest debt and gratitude go to my wife Nancy, who has shared most of this story with me. She has been a constant support, even when I came down with the "Sundays," and thought the project simply could not be done. She has also brought her professional editor's pencil to the text, making it sound less like a lawyer wrote it. I love you.

Preface

The development and successful implementation of the Universal Product Code by the US grocery industry is a remarkable achievement. Those ubiquitous black and white lines found on virtually all consumer products have been described as the most significant productivity improvement in the industry since the introduction of the supermarket. Few industry projects can match its success.

Yet for all its success, the U.P.C.'s origins and processes are little understood and even less heralded, even within the industry that spawned it. The limited knowledge that does exist continually erodes as the original participants fade from the scene.

If ever an undertaking deserved a history, the U.P.C. story does. I have been privileged to be a witness to all of the events, serving as counsel to, among others, the Ad Hoc Committee, the Symbol Selection Subcommittee, the Grocery Manufacturers of America, and the Uniform Code Council.

The development of the U.P.C. was a significant technological achievement. I leave to others, however, the technical aspects of the effort. This will be a more human story, focussing on the people and events that made the U.P.C. happen.

Hajo Holborn, a professor at Yale, says that "we study history, not only to be more clever today, but to be wiser forever." If we can understand how the grocery industry came together and looked beyond narrow corporate interests to devise something that both improved productivity and enhanced competition within the industry, we might find a model for future endeavors. Such is my hope.

Stephen Brown
Alexandria, Virginia
November 1996

Prologue

In the late 1960s, the Carousel Inn in Cincinnati was a sprawling motel with little to differentiate it from a number of other such institutions in the northern suburbs. In the motel's restaurant, the menu writer's skills far surpassed the chef's.

In September 1969, members of the Administrative Systems Committee of the Grocery Manufacturers of America (GMA) came here to meet with their counterparts from the National Association of Food Chains (NAFC). The purpose was to discuss an "inter-industry product code." The grocery industry was the largest in the United States. In 1972, retail grocery sales volume exceeded $100 billion, and over 1.5 million people were employed in the industry. The GMA's members included the major manufacturers of branded products sold through grocery stores, while NAFC represented the principal supermarket chains.

Systems professionals of both groups had independently reached the conclusion that productivity could be improved if a standard method of identifying products were developed. Even greater efficiency was possible if the method of identifying products could be represented by a machine-readable symbol. This, however, was about all that the two groups could agree upon.

The GMA Committee had concluded that the ideal

solution was a product-identification code eleven digits in length, with each digit having a specific meaning. This is called a "significant" code. A primary advantage of this approach, from the manufacturers' point of view, was that it could be implemented by GMA members with only minor adaptations of existing product codes already adopted by individual companies. NAFC members, on the other hand, while agreeing that a standard code was both feasible and desirable, argued that the industry standard should be but seven digits long, with no particular meaning attributed to any digit — in other words, a "non-significant" code. This would minimize the complexity of computer programs and memory capacity required at the checkout counter.

At the Carousel meeting, as had happened in the past, one group said, "eleven digits, significant," the other responded, "seven digits, non-significant." After staring at each other for a time, the groups adjourned the meeting and went their separate ways.

This was not the first time a standard product identification method had been discussed. It was seen as a sine qua non for an automated checkout counter. In 1932, a graduate student at MIT had made this subject the topic of his master's thesis. That student, Wallace Flint, was a staff officer of NAFC in 1969. Some work on automating the checkout was going on in Europe, and a little bit of research was underway in this country.[1] For the most part, however, the computer industry did not see a viable market for computerizing the front end of grocery stores, certainly not a market to justify the

---

[1] RCA established a partnership with the Kroger Co. in early 1967. This marked the first serious supermarket automation explorations between major US companies.

Prototype electronic checkout systems were demonstrated at the 1969 GMA Annual Meeting. Fully implemented, savings of $25,000 a year were predicted "Electronic Systems May Rev Up Checkers," *Supermarket News*, Nov. 17, 1969, p 1.

research and development required to make an automated checkout a business reality.

Nonetheless, the grocery industry refused to give up on the idea. From the retailer's viewpoint, an automated checkout offered the potential of speeding up the checkout process, reducing the labor required at the front end, and making automatic reordering procedures feasible. Some even believed that there were other, as yet unknown but surely large, benefits that would flow from such a system.

The grocery manufacturers' interest was more defensive: if a standard product code did not exist, individual customers might demand that different product-identification schemes be placed on their products by the manufacturer to satisfy the needs of different automated checkout systems. This might require multiple symbols on the can or box, or the segregation of inventory by customer. Both would be tremendously inefficient. There was also a concern that granting a customer's request for a nonstandard symbol would cause significant legal problems. The requirements of the Robinson-Patman Act forbade giving one customer preferential treatment.

Accordingly, the leaders of the associations decided to make one last effort despite the previous lack of success. In January 1970, Clarence "Clancy" Adamy, the staff head of the National Association of Food Chains, invited his counterparts from the other major grocery industry associations to meet. Present were George Koch, president of the Grocery Manufacturers of America, Frank Register, head of the National Association of Retail Grocers in the United States (NARGUS — the association of the smaller independent grocers), Jerry Peck, president of the National-American Wholesale Grocers Association (NAWGA), and Earl Mason, president of the Cooperative Food Distributors of America (CFDA). Adamy told the others he could also speak for Mike O'Connor, president of the Supermarket Institute (SMI).

Clancy Adamy looked like a politician, acted like a politician, was a politician. The association he headed was the lobbying arm of the supermarket industry. Adamy had a reputation for efficacy, and he reveled in his job. Turning his skills to inter-industry affairs, Clancy sold the U.P.C. project to the other associations. Perhaps the greatest mark of his skill was his willingness to stay in the background and make no attempt to direct the project, or even to claim credit for its success.

At this meeting in the Mayflower Hotel in Washington, DC, the association presidents recognized the impasse reached by the companies' system experts over a standard grocery industry product code. Adamy also pressed hard on the importance of the adoption of such a code. He intimated that if the industry could not agree, NAFC would take it upon itself to begin issuing code numbers to grocery product manufacturers and establish a de facto standard.

No one, including Adamy, thought that was an acceptable solution. The earlier meeting had been of technical experts, mid-level managers within their companies. The association heads concluded that the major problems were political, not technical. Obviously, trade-offs would have to be made. Company information systems executives lacked the authority to "give up" an advantage of their employers, but company presidents could. Accordingly, the Mayflower group decided to bring together a small, but representative, committee of chief executive officers to focus on a universal product code.

Its charge would be to rise above parochial company issues and focus on what is best for the whole industry. If an industrywide code was feasible, they should recommend one; if it was not, then the industry should be told and move on to other issues.

The associations represented at the Mayflower also

agreed to provide this committee with the funding necessary to complete the project.

The stage was set. The Ad Hoc Committee on a Universal Grocery Product Identification Code was about to come into existence.

Revolution
at the
Checkout Counter

Introduction*

John T. Dunlop and Jan W. Rivkin

The Universal Product Code (U.P.C.) is now so commonplace that few pause to notice or to ponder it. The small rectangle of black and white bars that embodies the U.P.C. adorns virtually every item we purchase in the supermarket, the discount store, or the shopping mall, and we take it for granted. Yet twenty-five years ago, the U.P.C. was no more than an idea shared by a small cadre of manufacturing and chain store executives.[1] In this volume, Stephen Brown, the legal counsel of those pioneering executives, traces the origins and development of the U.P.C.

This introductory chapter provides a background and setting for Brown's insightful narrative. It first documents the diffusion of the Code and identifies the U.P.C.'s widespread economic consequences. When coupled with information and communication technologies, the U.P.C. sparked a revolution that started at the supermarket checkout counter, spread throughout domestic retailing, moved around the globe, and is now taking place in sectors far removed from retailing. Having established the significance of the U.P.C.,

*John T. Dunlop is Lamont University Professor, Emeritus at Harvard University and Jan W. Rivkin is completing a Ph.D. degree in Business Economics at Harvard, a joint program of the Harvard Department of Economics and the Graduate School of Business Administration. The Introduction was written under the auspices of the Harvard Center for Textile and Apparel Research supported by grants from the Alfred P. Sloan Foundation.

1

the chapter turns to historical context. It sketches the technological, economic, regulatory, and labor-management setting of the late 1960s and early 1970s, the period of the Code's birth, with an emphasis on the food sector.

The chapter also identifies a number of current issues in economics that are informed by the history Brown records. The development of the U.P.C. illustrates the process of setting industry standards without government intervention, raises questions about the contractual relations between firms, and shows how systems of complementary technologies evolve. A final section of the chapter briefly contemplates the future of the U.P.C. and product coding. Bar coding and related distribution technologies are clearly among the great innovations of the last quarter of this century, and the full impact of these technologies is yet to be felt. The past that Brown recounts is prologue to a fascinating future.

The Diffusion and Significance of the Universal Product Code

The history of the U.P.C. is significant for at least three reasons. First, the sheer success of the Code should make this account of interest to those who would understand technology and business, to industrial economists, and to managers and public policy advocates who aim to enhance successful innovation. Second, the Code is a cornerstone of a technological system that is now transforming production and distribution, and economic relations, in numerous industries. This makes it doubly important to understand the U.P.C.'s origins. Finally, the U.P.C. succeeded in the face of an immense coordination challenge. The story of how it did so deserves the close attention of scholars and policy-makers who examine coordination and industry standards.

Explosive growth. Dissemination of the Universal Product Code has been widespread. As Figure 1 shows, growth of the U.P.C. has been explosive and shows no sign of abating even twenty-five years after the Code's introduction.[2] By 1994, the body that administers the U.P.C. had issued over 110,000 manufacturer-specific identifying numbers,[3] and by January 1997 the number had increased to 177,000. Because of the way the U.P.C. is configured and administered, no one knows precisely how many *products* carry the U.P.C. bar code. The standard Code consists of two parts: one half that identifies the product manufacturer and one half that specifies the product. (Additional digits identify the sector of the product and verify the accuracy of the scanning.) Only the first half of the Code is administered centrally. Any enterprise that registers with the Uniform Code Council (UCC), a small non-profit organization based in Dayton, Ohio, can receive a unique permanent designation for the first set of digits. The enterprise can then assign the second set to its individual products as it sees fit.

It is the cumulative number of registrations with the Council, the number of unique enterprise designations, that Figure 1 records. The explosive growth is especially striking when contrasted with the expectations held by the executives who pioneered the Code. As Brown recounts, some U.P.C. founders were confident that there would never be more than 6,000 registrations. Even the strongest advocates of the U.P.C. did not foresee fully what they were unleashing.

The pioneers underestimated the spread of the U.P.C. in part because they were focused on a subset of the economy, the grocery and chain store sector. The committee that set the U.P.C. in motion was established by six grocery trade associations, one representing manufacturers and five representing retailers. This Ad Hoc Committee was manned by top executives of firms such as Heinz, General

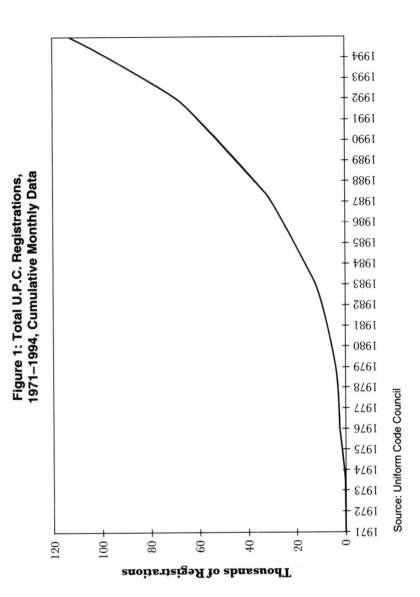

Figure 1: Total U.P.C. Registrations, 1971–1994, Cumulative Monthly Data

Thousands of Registrations

Source: Uniform Code Council

Mills, Bristol Myers, General Foods and retail and whole-sale executives from Kroger, A&P Tea Company, Wegman's, First National Stores, and Super Valu Stores. Thus the U.P.C. was adopted first and most thoroughly in the grocery and chain store sector (Figure 2). The first item bearing the U.P.C. symbol, a package of Wrigley's gum, crossed the scanner at Marsh's Supermarket in Troy, Ohio, in June of 1974. By April of 1976, 75 percent of the items in the typical supermarket carried a U.P.C. symbol.[4] Indeed, the vast majority of U.P.C. numbers in the early years were issued to manufacturers of food and beverages. (Compare Figures 3 and 4.) Installation of scanners in supermarkets proceeded much more slowly than placement of symbols on packages, but the U.P.C. was soon firmly established in the food industry.

Interest in the U.P.C. did not stop at the borders of the food sector. Mass merchants such as KMart and Wal-Mart, who operated high-volume checkstands and carried some grocery items, noted the benefits of uniform product coding. As part of larger efforts to improve productivity, they soon began to demand that their vendors adopt the U.P.C. Consequently, the U.P.C. symbol has become prevalent on consumer goods ranging from apparel to toys, newspapers and consumer electronics. Since 1982, food and beverage manufacturers have accounted for the minority of new U.P.C. registrations. A recent survey of 84 apparel manufacturers gives one indication of how quickly and widely the U.P.C. has spread beyond the grocery industry. By 1992, the surveyed apparel firms reported that over 60 percent of their product volume carried a U.P.C. bar code at the level of the stockkeeping unit (SKU). As recently as 1988, the figure was only 22 percent.[5]

As Brown records, the U.P.C. has moved beyond even retailing and consumer goods in recent years, reaching into commercial, industrial, and government sectors.

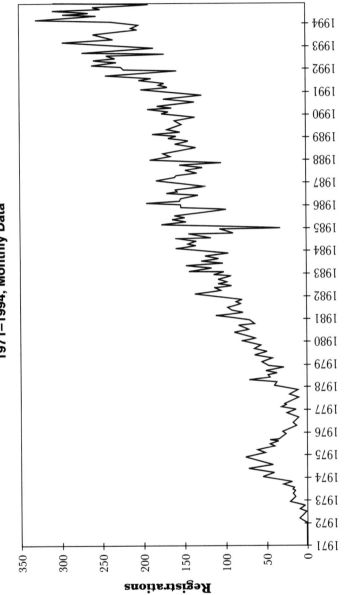

Figure 2: Food & Beverage U.P.C. Registrations, 1971–1994, Monthly Data

Registrations

Source: Uniform Code Council

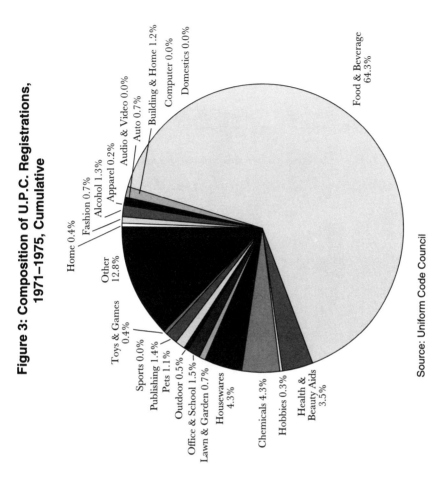

Figure 3: Composition of U.P.C. Registrations, 1971–1975, Cumulative

Food & Beverage 64.3%

Domestics 0.0%
Computer 0.0%
Building & Home 1.2%
Auto 0.7%
Audio & Video 0.0%
Apparel 0.2%
Alcohol 1.3%
Fashion 0.7%
Home 0.4%
Other 12.8%
Toys & Games 0.4%
Sports 0.0%
Publishing 1.4%
Pets 1.1%
Outdoor 0.5%
Office & School 1.5%
Lawn & Garden 0.7%
Housewares 4.3%
Chemicals 4.3%
Hobbies 0.3%
Health & Beauty Aids 3.5%

Source: Uniform Code Council

Figure 4: Composition of U.P.C. Registrations, 1971–1994, Cumulative

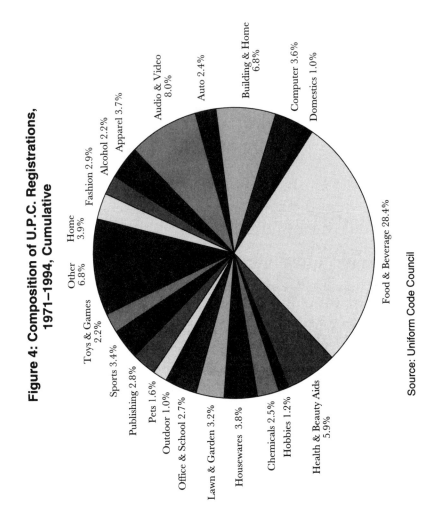

Other 6.8%

Home 3.9%

Fashion 2.9%

Alcohol 2.2%

Apparel 3.7%

Audio & Video 8.0%

Auto 2.4%

Building & Home 6.8%

Computer 3.6%

Domestics 1.0%

Food & Beverage 28.4%

Toys & Games 2.2%

Sports 3.4%

Publishing 2.8%

Pets 1.6%

Outdoor 1.0%

Office & School 2.7%

Lawn & Garden 3.2%

Housewares 3.8%

Chemicals 2.5%

Hobbies 1.2%

Health & Beauty Aids 5.9%

Source: Uniform Code Council

Similarly, interest in the U.P.C. did not stop at the borders of the United States. A European numbering system EAN, based on the same principles as the U.P.C., was set in motion in 1974 and has grown rapidly. When the U.P.C. system of product identification was adopted by EAN, a digit was added to the product code. The additional digit was needed to identify Numbering Organizations throughout the world. This enabled the U.P.C. system to reach beyond North America and become a global system. Over 80 countries now have organizations similar to the Uniform Code Council that issue numbers compatible with the U.P.C.[6]

The Universal Product Code has also facilitated the development of other code systems, albeit indirectly.[7] Not all machine-readable bar codes conform to the U.P.C. numbering system or symbology. The Uniform Code Council, the organization that administers the U.P.C., supports additional codes and symbols for particular applications. For instance, the Council recommends symbologies known as ITF and Code 128 for the marking of multi-pack and shipping containers. In addition, certain niche applications employ altogether different bar coding systems. The U.S. Postal Service, for instance, uses a code known as Postnet. Federal Express and operators of blood banks have adopted the Codabar symbology. Code 39, PDF417, Datamatrix, and Code 6 have been popular in the automotive, transportation, chemical, and electronics industries. Codes have proliferated both because they must be tailored to specific applications and because, once established in a setting, they are hard to change. Although different from the U.P.C., these other codes have gained indirectly from the U.P.C.'s pathbreaking success. The U.P.C. proved the feasibility and benefits of standardized, machine-readable product coding, and its success spurred equipment manufacturers to produce reliable, inexpensive bar code readers.

Machine-readable product coding may not stop even at

the boundaries of the earth. Recounting the docking of the space shuttle Atlantis to the space station Mir, the *New York Times* reported on September 19, 1996 that one astronaut "has been trained to work a bar code inventory management system that was designed to keep track of the many items that are to be transferred between the shuttle and the space station."[8] Perhaps the "universal" in U.P.C. is not hyperbole.

A cornerstone technology and managerial system. The U.P.C. is a significant innovation not merely because it has spread so far. The Code lies at the heart of a new management system that is transforming economic relations in a broad range of sectors.[9] At the retail level, the system operates as follows: When a consumer purchases an item, say a man's shirt at one of Federated's department stores, the bar code scanner at the checkout register reads the U.P.C. symbol on the item. The point-of-sale register uses the Code to look up the item's current price from a database in an on-site or central computer. At nearly the same time, the information that the shirt has been sold is relayed to Federated's buyers. There, the information is used in two ways. First, it provides Federated with immediate and precise knowledge of what is selling and what is not. Buyers can use this knowledge to adjust their purchases from vendors. Second, it triggers a process of replenishing the stock of a particular fabric, size, color, and style of shirt at the store.

The replenishment process employs two additional technologies: electronic data interchange (EDI) and automated distribution centers. EDI establishes standard electronic forms for documents related to purchases. It thereby permits retailers and vendors to exchange the information that is required to generate a purchase electronically, efficiently, and automatically. Automated distribution centers ensure that products move rapidly and smoothly through Federated's distribution network. Items often move directly from vendor trucks at a distribution center's incoming loading dock, across the center on conveyors, onto trucks at an outgoing loading dock, and directly to the appropriate store, never pausing in a Federated warehouse. The entire cross-docking symphony is conducted by bar code scanners mounted along the conveyors; by reading a variant of the U.P.C. symbol that is printed on shipping containers or a shipping label affixed by the manufacturer, these scanners route each box of merchandise to the appropriate truck.

The retailer's purpose in employing this suite of technologies is straightforward. Thanks to the U.P.C., bar code scanners, low cost microprocessors, and low cost electronic communications, the retailer can collect and process information concerning consumer demand, as expressed in thousands of transactions, inexpensively. The retailer can then use this information to reduce its exposure to market demand risk. It does so both by adjusting its orders quickly in response to shifts in demand and by minimizing the amount of inventory it holds. A retailer that deploys this technological system may enjoy higher product availability, reduced inventory levels, a better match between supply and demand, less product obsolescence, and lower distribution costs.

Of course, the effects of this technological system do not stop at the boundary between retailer and manufacturer. Rather, changes in the retail sector are calling forth a series of technological changes and investments among manufacturers. At the simplest level, manufacturers are taking basic steps to facilitate the new retail strategy. They are affixing U.P.C. symbols to products and similar bar codes to shipping containers, developing EDI capabilities, and so forth. At a deeper level, manufacturers are developing their own capabilities to respond rapidly to shifts in consumer demand. If they did not do so, they would have to hold the inventory and bear the market demand risk no longer accepted by retailers. To avoid this, manufacturers are investing in a series of technologies that enhance their own responsiveness: flexible production equipment, computer-aided manufacturing, computer-aided design, just-in-time logistical systems, and so forth. Manufacturers are also altering their work practices, the way they organize and reward production, and relationships with their suppliers in order to improve responsiveness.

The greatest efficiencies from the new technology are achieved when retailers and manufacturers integrate their systems and flows of information fully. Take, for instance, the partnership between Wal-Mart and Procter & Gamble.[10] When a bottle of P&G shampoo passes the bar code scanner at a Wal-Mart checkout counter, the information that the item has been sold is relayed directly to P&G, each day. P&G then initiates the replenishment process, alerts Wal-Mart of incoming shipments, and bills Wal-Mart without any purchase order being created. Moreover, P&G uses the data from Wal-Mart to adjust its manufacturing schedule. The entire transaction, from the transfer of the scanner data to the final transfer of funds from Wal-Mart to P&G, is performed electronically. Similarly, apparel manufacturers are increasingly using the new technologies to ship "floor-ready merchandise" to retailers. Such merchandise can be moved directly from the loading dock to the store floor, with little or no tagging, pressing, and re-hanging.

The ramifications of this technological and managerial system are profound and numerous, but three deserve special mention. First, the U.P.C. and its associated technologies have contributed to the pattern of *increasing concentration* we witness in the retail sector (Table 1). The innovations described above have made it possible to move goods through a retail network with unprecedented speed, accuracy, and efficiency. They have also permitted retail managers to monitor consumer tastes, learn from buying behavior, and respond to actual demand in a manner that would have been impossible in earlier times. The traditional buyer who relied primarily on an instinct for consumer tastes or a feel of the expected market this season has given way to a merchandizing executive who largely reads computer screens. Retailers such as Wal-Mart and Toys R Us have made substantial fixed investments to turn a technological possibility into a retail reality. Once in place, these investments can handle a much higher flow rate of goods than conventional systems, can reduce the shipment of items not desired by consumers, and hence can deliver goods at lower unit costs. Due to the lower marginal costs associated with the investments, managers of the new systems can reduce price in pursuit of greater volume. The combination of high volume, low costs, and low price have led to a cycle of concentration: high volume and low marginal costs produce profits, profits are reinvested to fuel expansion, and expansion leads to yet higher volume and lower marginal costs. The greater economies of scale associated with new retail technologies appear to have contributed to the striking pattern of increased concentration shown in Table 1, though other factors are also at work.

The second ramification of the new technological and managerial system concerns *product proliferation*. The technologies described above reduce the costs of managing variety in a retail network, both by lowering the inventory requirements and by automating the record-keeping tasks associated with variety. This change (coupled with others) has enabled a remarkable proliferation of products. The number of items in the typical supermarket has risen from 6,000 in 1960 and 9,000 in 1974 to between 40,000 and 61,000 items in 1994 for stores with 8 to 11 checkout counters and with an average weekly sales volume of $200–400 thousand.[11] This product proliferation has been associated with a considerable expansion in floor space and the number of specialty service departments. See Figure 5 for the size of new supermarkets, 1953–1993, and note the rapid increase in square feet after the mid-1970s. The extent of specialty service departments illustrates the power of the one-stop shop-

Table 1. Concentration in the Retail Sector, 1977 and 1992

SIC Code	Industry	Portion of sales (%) accounted for by the 50 largest firms			Portion of sales (%) accounted for by the 4 largest firms		
		1977	1992	Increase	1977	1992	Increase
52	Building materials and garden supplies stores	16.6	35.1	18.5	5.4	16.0	10.6
521	Lumber and other building materials dealers	23.0	45.7	22.7	8.3	23.2	14.9
523	Paint, glass, and wallpaper stores	39.9	51.3	11.4	24.1	29.5	5.4
525	Hardware stores	13.5	19.4	5.9	6.7	9.7	3.0
526	Retail nurseries, lawn, and garden supply stores	13.0	25.0	12.0	4.3	15.4	11.1
527	Manufactured (mobile) home dealers	14.0	21.1	7.1	3.4	9.7	6.3
53	General merchandise stores	77.3	91.8	14.5	37.7	47.3	9.6
531	Department stores	86.5	98.2	11.7	44.0	53.1	9.1
533	Variety stores	78.1	85.8	7.7	49.1	54.8	5.7
54	Food stores	40.7	47.6	6.9	16.3	15.4	−0.9
541	Grocery stores	43.5	49.9	6.4	17.4	16.1	−1.3
542	Meat and fish (seafood) markets	7.8	11.5	3.7	2.7	4.7	2.0
546	Retail bakeries	12.3	17.3	5.0	5.3	7.4	2.1
545	Dairy products stores	39.6	48.6	9.0	15.5	27.4	11.9
55	Automotive dealers	4.1	6.4	2.3	1.9	1.5	−0.4
551	New and used car dealers	3.5	5.9	2.4	1.4	1.5	0.1
553	Auto and home supply stores	24.0	39.6	15.6	13.1	15.5	2.4
555	Boat dealers	11.5	15.1	3.6	2.0	3.9	1.9
556	Recreational vehicle dealers	13.4	29.4	16.0	2.1	6.3	4.2
557	Motorcycle dealers	7.9	10.7	2.8	1.1	2.1	1.0
554	Gasoline service stations	18.4	28.3	9.9	5.1	7.2	2.1

56	Apparel and accessory stores	27.8	52.4	24.6	9.1	17.9	8.8
561	Men's and boys' clothing and accessory stores	24.2	48.6	24.4	8.5	20.0	11.5
562	Women's clothing stores	34.5	59.8	25.3	11.2	27.6	16.4
565	Family clothing stores	45.9	76.6	30.7	23.1	35.3	12.2
566	Shoe stores	48.6	68.2	19.6	22.8	38.6	15.8
57	Furniture and homefurnishings stores	11.8	26.8	15.0	4.5	9.7	5.2
5712	Furniture stores	16.0	22.6	6.6	5.3	6.8	1.5
5713	Floor covering stores	12.2	17.8	5.6	4.2	9.3	5.1
5714	Drapery, curtain, and upholstery stores	13.8	31.9	18.1	4.1	12.5	8.4
572	Household appliance stores	20.9	27.5	6.6	10.4	12.0	1.6
573	Radio, television, computer, and music stores	24.0	55.1	31.1	11.8	25.8	14.0
58	Eating and drinking places	15.7	21.3	5.6	3.9	7.9	4.0
5812	Eating places	17.8	22.6	4.8	4.5	8.4	3.9
5813	Drinking places	1.9	3.0	1.1	0.5	0.9	0.4
591	Drug and proprietary stores	45.2	61.5	16.3	14.0	24.7	10.7
592	Liquor stores	21.1	18.9	− 2.2	9.8	8.2	− 1.6
5941	Sporting goods stores and bicycle shops	15.3	29.7	14.4	6.8	12.8	6.0
5942	Book stores	37.2	55.8	18.6	19.2	41.3	22.1
5944	Jewelry stores	25.1	33.5	8.4	12.3	18.1	5.8
5943	Stationery stores	14.8	23.1	8.3	3.6	9.0	5.4
5945	Hobby, toy, and game shops	47.9	79.3	31.4	26.8	64.5	37.7
5946	Camera and photographic supply stores	21.1	49.5	28.4	4.1	25.4	21.3
5947	Gift, novelty, and souvenir shops	14.8	23.8	9.0	5.4	9.2	3.8
5948	Luggage and leather goods stores	46.0	61.4	15.4	24.3	21.2	− 3.1

Source: U.S. Bureau of the Census, Census of Retail Industries, 1977 and 1992
Note: Where industry designation has changed between 1977 and 1992, 1992 name is shown.

ping idea and the facilitating role of the U.P.C. Table 2 shows the percentage of supermarkets featuring such specialty service departments from 1988 to 1995.[12]

Table 2
Specialty Service Departments in Supermarkets

	Percentage of Supermarkets		
Department	1980	1986	1995
Deli	37.3	67.3	83.4
Postage stamps	N/A	N/A	75.3
Carry-out services	N/A	N/A	73.9
Scratch / bake-off bakery	27.7	49.8	73.5
Beer	N/A	70.9	71.5
Greeting cards	N/A	N/A	69.3
Photo service	N/A	40.5	61.7
Wine	47.3	57.9	58.5
Video sales	N/A	26.4	55.7
Floral / plant shop	19.2	45.9	53.9
Cosmetic center	N/A	20.0	52.6

N/A indicates that data point is not available

The expansion in size and scope of supermarkets and in the variety of products is facilitated by the checkout developments associated with the Uniform Product Code.

Product proliferation is not unique to the food sector. In the survey of apparel manufacturers cited above, the average respondent reported that the number of stock-keeping units in its product line rose from 3,871 in 1988 to 6,304 in 1992. At the same time, the average number of SKUs discontinued by the typical apparel business unit rose from 2,057 in 1988 to 3,050 in 1992. Thus, in each year a large portion of each business unit's product line consists of new products with little or no relevant demand history.[13]

The third ramification of the technological and managerial system relates to the relative *bargaining power* of manufacturers and retailers. Prior to the advent of the technologies, manufacturers tended to possess the best information concerning sales trends and shifts in demand. An individual retailer might not know the true state of sales until an end-of-month inventory, but a manufacturer would get a steady stream of signals from the numerous retailers it served, from market research, and from its sales force and brokers. A substantial portion of goods would be delivered and put on the shelves by manufacturer or distributor personnel, further concentrating information in the hands of suppliers. With the automatic, electronic collection of point-of-sale data, this situation changes. Now a large retailer can track the movement of goods continually and detect shifts in demand almost instantly. This alters the retailer/manufacturer relationship significantly. An agile retailer can, for instance, stock up on a popular item before its manufacturer realizes that it is in high demand. As Brown relates, the shift in information and therefore power engendered by the U.P.C. was one of its many unanticipated, yet profound, consequences.[14]

How much of the change documented in this section should we credit to the Universal Product Code alone? The systemic nature of the technologies makes it impossible to isolate the impact of the U.P.C. In many ways, the *primal* innovation concerned computing power whose declining cost made bar code scanning, EDI, automated distribution, computer-aided design and manufacturing, and rapid data communication feasible. Nonetheless, the development of the U.P.C. was clearly a vital, and early, milestone on the path toward a new way of doing business.

The story of change told in this section is reminiscent of the Second Industrial Revolution. In that earlier transition, the railroad and telegraph served as key technologies that transformed the industrial landscape. Together, these

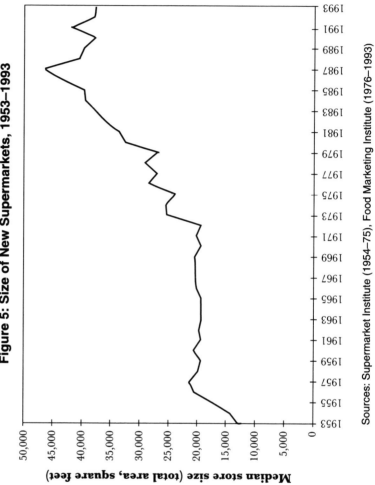

Figure 5: Size of New Supermarkets, 1953–1993

Median store size (total area, square feet)

Sources: Supermarket Institute (1954–75), Food Marketing Institute (1976–1993)

technologies created opportunities for truly national markets. The entrepreneurs who seized the openings sparked changes in the scale of production, the concentration of industries, the organization of work, the boundaries of firms, the balance of power in the economy, and so forth.[15] In the current revolution, the U.P.C. serves a role similar to that of Morse Code: as an economy-wide standard for communication, it enables innovative forms of coordination within and between organizations.

Coordination and incentive challenge. Beyond its role as a cornerstone technology and basis for new business relations, the Universal Product Code is significant for the way its founders approached a coordination challenge. The U.P.C. faced an immense hurdle in its first few years, rooted in the following chicken-and-egg dilemma: No supermarket wanted to invest in scanning technology until a substantial portion of groceries bore the U.P.C. symbol, but no manufacturer wanted to undertake the expense of changing packages and adding the symbol until a sizable fraction of retailers had scanners. Only by coordinating most of the grocery industry to adopt the U.P.C. *together* could the innovation achieve the critical mass to take hold. Indeed, the U.P.C. pioneers estimated that the benefits of the U.P.C. would match its costs only when 75 percent of all grocery items, representing 17 percent of the GNP, carried the symbol.[16] The Code very nearly foundered on this challenge. Manufacturers registered for numbers and put symbols on packages quickly, but supermarkets adopted scanners slowly. By 1976, *Business Week* was eulogizing The Supermarket Scanner That Failed.[17]

Despite its brush with failure, the U.P.C. did take hold as an economy-wide standard. Notably, it did so without any assistance from government bodies such as the Bureau of Standards which are often responsible for such standards. In fact, Brown suggests that the very lack of government involvement may have been critical to the Code's success. The U.P.C.

story tests conventional wisdom, as well as economic theory, concerning the establishment of standards. For this reason, the history contained in this volume deserves the attention of those interested in the standards-setting process.

The Setting of the Late 1960s and Early 1970s

In order to frame the problems and opportunities that confronted the initiators of the Universal Product Code, as Brown traces their activities, this section describes the technological, economic, regulatory, and labor-management environment of the period.

Technology. The development of the U.P.C. was shaped in part by technological forces of the era.[18] The 1960s and early 1970s were a period of extraordinary technical ferment, as progress in basic science and research efforts launched during World War II and the Cold War bore commercial fruit. Advances in electronics, optical technology, and computing were critical to making bar code scanning feasible and economical.

The operation of a bar code scanner mounted in a checkout counter is conceptually straightforward. The scanner produces a light beam, which is bounced off the bar code symbol on a passing product. White portions of the symbol reflect the beam and black portions absorb it. The reflected portion of the light signal is sensed by a detector on the scanner, and logical circuits "reconstruct" the code from the reflected pattern. An on-site computer matches the code to an item name and price, and the name and price are reported to the cash register at the checkout counter. The scheme is simple in concept, but making it work in practice presented at least three major challenges. To overcome each, equipment vendors such as RCA, IBM, and NCR had to harness cutting edge technologies.

The first challenge was posed by the light source: the

beam had to be intense enough to stand out even in a well lit supermarket, yet the source had to be compact and could not generate a great deal of heat. This encouraged the use of lasers, a young but fast advancing technology. The feasibility of lasers had been established only in the late 1950s, with the work of physicists A.L. Schawlow and Charles Townes.[19] Theodore Maiman of Hughes Research Laboratories constructed the first laser from a rod of ruby in 1960, with Bell Laboratories researchers following close behind that year with the first helium-neon laser.[20] GE and IBM announced the development of the semiconductor laser in 1962.[21] Within a few years, lasers were used to measure distances, track satellites, and conduct atmospheric research.[22] In 1970, a pocket-size, battery-operated laser became available.[23] By the time the U.P.C. was introduced, laser technology was well understood, but was not yet commonplace commercially. Indeed, a subcommittee of the Ad Hoc Committee remained concerned about the health and safety risks of the laser.

The second challenge concerned the reflection of the light beam back to the detector. A single beam of light would not return to the detector unless the checkout clerk held the purchased item at precisely the correct angle, and there was no assurance that the clerk would or could do so. Equipment vendors solved this problem by placing a holographic optical element, essentially a spinning wheel, in front of the outgoing beam. This split the single beam into many, virtually ensuring that one would reflect back to the detector. Such optical elements were as novel as the laser. The ideas behind holography dated back to 1947 and the work of Dennis Gabor at Imperial College, London.[24] Early work petered out, however, largely because coherent light was difficult to obtain. The invention of the laser resolved this difficulty and sparked pathbreaking work in holography starting in the early 1960s.

The final challenge was to process the signals that returned to the scanner, and to do so inexpensively. Thanks to advances in electronics and computing, the costs of logical processing plummeted during the post-war era. The advances that led to this decline are too numerous to catalog here, but important milestones include the following: the invention of the transistor in 1947 by John Bardeen, Walter Brattain, and William Shockley of Bell Laboratories; the invention of the integrated circuit by Jack Kirby of Texas Instruments and Jean Hoerni and Robert Noyce of Fairchild Semiconductor in 1958–1959; the launch of the first highly successful minicomputer, Digital Equipment Corporation's PDP-8, in 1965; and Intel's introduction of the microprocessor in 1971.[25] By 1970, one could purchase a minicomputer for roughly $20,000 that had as much processing power as a 1965 model, $200,000 mainframe.[26] Moreover, such a minicomputer could fit easily in a supermarket office. The first microcomputers lay only a few years ahead.

The 1960s witnessed not only a rapid reduction in processing costs, but also the introduction of real time, interactive computing. Computing in the 1950s consisted largely of batch processing; jobs were submitted to the computer and returned to the programmer in large lots. Clearly, transactions at the checkout counter could not be handled in such a mode. Interactive computing grew out of Project Whirlwind, Jay Forrester's brainchild at MIT during the 1940s and 1950s.[27] It saw its first large-scale application in the SAGE air defense system, fully deployed by 1963 at an estimated cost of $8 billion.[28] Commercial applications followed quickly, beginning with American Airlines' SABRE reservation system in 1964.[29] The stage was set for the real time computing inherent in bar code scanning.

In sum, the commercial revolution that Brown describes rested on equally radical technical changes. The U.P.C. system would have been prohibitively expensive, perhaps technically impossible, to implement a decade earlier than it was. ***Economic and regulatory setting.*** The U.P.C. was shaped as much by the challenging and volatile conditions of the food sector as it was by the forces of technology. The era was characterized by rapid price inflation. The consumer price index rose 16.3 percent from 1967 through 1970 and 27.0 percent in the years 1970–1974. Food prices in the CPI index rose 14.9 percent from 1967 through 1970 and 40.7 percent in the years 1970–1974. Wholesale prices of farm products rose 11.0 percent from 1967 through 1970 and an extraordinary 69.1 percent in the years 1970–1974, with 50.2 percent in the two years 1973–1974 alone.

These rates of inflation were unprecedented in the peacetime experience of the country. The extent of inflation was unforeseen by forecasters in the Department of Agriculture and in the private sector alike. The inflation was worldwide. It was highly sectoral, concentrated in food and energy, with OPEC leading the energy component.[30]

A confluence of events and developments are said to have contributed to the extraordinary agricultural and food price inflation of the early 1970s. World grain production in 1972 declined by 36 million metric tons (3.2 percent) compared to an annual increase of 34 million metric tons in the years 1961–1971. El Niño and the sudden disappearance of Peruvian anchovies contributed to a shortage of animal feeds. Corn blight played a role. A simultaneous boom in Japan, Western Europe, and the United States — for the first time since World War II — appreciably increased disposable income and the demand for feed grains and red meat. The devaluation of the U.S. dollar relative to other currencies increased the attractiveness of U.S. agricultural exports, including sales to the Soviet Union,[31] reduced substantial domestic buffer stocks, and raised prices at home.

On August 15, 1971 President Nixon imposed a wage and price freeze under the Economic Stabilization Act of 1970; there followed a series of phases and regulations that applied generally as well as to manufactured and retail food prices, but the authority to impose direct controls on primary agricultural prices was never delegated by the President to the stabilization authorities and was never invoked. In the manufactured and retail food sectors price controls consisted of margin controls over authorized costs without ceilings on primary agricultural products. Even with wage and salary standards, this structure of controls placed food manufacturers and retailers, including the U.P.C.'s pioneers, under serious cost pressures.

Retail food chains showed profits as a percentage of stockholders' equity of 5.2 percent in 1972 and 8.2 percent in 1973 compared with 10.9 percent for the period 1963–1970. They showed profits as a percentage return on sales of .5 percent in 1972, .7 percent in 1973, and .9 percent in 1974 compared with an average of 1.2 percent in 1963–1970.[32] Among food manufacturers profits as a percentage return on sales were unchanged, however, compared to the 1963–1970 period at 2.6 percent.

Low profitability in food retailing led industry leaders to search energetically for ways to improve productivity, and labor costs were a natural place to focus. Labor costs, especially wage levels, had a significant impact on the food industry's profitability. For food retail firms, in 1974 total payroll and fringe benefits constituted 67 percent of all expenses other than the costs of goods sold. In food wholesaling, the comparable figure was 56 percent. Non-supervisory workers accounted for almost 90 percent of all employees in the retail food industry. Retail food employees have been relatively high paid among retail trade sectors. In January 1973 average hourly earnings were $3.20 in grocery, meat, and vegetable stores compared to $2.78 in retail trade.[33] The economic case for the U.P.C. system was based in part on its ability to boost labor productivity in the hard-pressed food retailing industry.

Labor-management environment. Productivity improvements

were unlikely to be achieved, however, without the cooperation of organized labor. In early 1973[34] the stabilization program established a Tripartite Food Industry Wage and Salary
Committee. The Committee brought together union and
management representatives from the industry with neutrals
to administer the regulations in particular cases and to resolve disputes over the terms of collective bargaining agreements. The Cost of Living Council estimated that in 1974
seventy percent of production employees in the retail food
industry were under collective bargaining agreements.

On December 11, 1973 the Director of the Cost of Living
Council (the senior author of this Introduction) met with the
CEOs of the leading food chain stores and the presidents of
the national unions with major representation among food
chain store employees — butchers, retail clerks, teamsters
and bakery workers. This was the first occasion these management and labor officers had met each other. The stabilization
director proposed that wage and price controls be eliminated
from the food sector provided the parties agree, among other
items, to establish a joint labor-management committee to
seek to resolve a variety of common problems. The parties
accepted, and the food retail and wholesale sectors were
decontrolled on April 15, 1974.

The Joint Labor Management Committee of the Retail
Food Industry met for the first time on March 29, 1974,[35] and
adopted an agenda that included the development of improved wage and benefit data, a mechanism to mediate and
resolve collective bargaining disputes over the terms of agreements, and a forum for consideration of issues of technological change. (The Committee continues in operation in
1997.)

On April 28, 1975 the Committee formed an eight member subgroup to study the impact of the automated checkout
system with its electronic scanning system that reads the Universal Product Code. The tripartite subgroup, headed by

Wayne Horwitz, neutral chair of the Committee, was to have two functions: to develop accurate and impartial information on the checkout technology for collective bargaining purposes; and to design approaches to resolve disputes over the introduction of the technology.[36] On June 2, 1975 the Committee adopted unanimously a "Statement of Principles on UPC and Related Technology." The Committee was able to resolve all issues that arose over the automated checkouts in the course of negotiations over the terms of collective bargaining agreements.

But an issue related to the U.P.C. continued to create difficulties within the Committee. With the advent of the Code, and the printing of the item and price on a checkout tape for the customer, some retailers were eager to cease placing prices on each individual item on the shelf. At the same time some union leaders and consumer advocates were seeking state laws or city ordinances requiring the continued attachment of item prices on each product. A Public Policy subcommittee was created to treat this issue that moved into the legislative arena. This subcommittee sponsored a major research project by Dr. John Allen and Gilbert Harrell of Michigan State University and Dr. Michael Hutt of the University of Vermont, with the assistance of consumer groups, on the effects of item pricing removal.

In March 1976 a status quo understanding was reached between the labor and management of the Committee: Labor would not block the introduction of scanning systems and would not pursue item pricing legislation, and management would agree to leave prices on most retail products.[37] While the international unions ceased to grant funds to locals to lobby state legislation on item pricing, some retail clerk local unions continued to seek state legislation mandating item pricing. This controversy over state or locality legislation requiring item pricing appears never to have been formally resolved. By 1995 only five states required item pricing.[38]

The discussion among labor and management leaders in the late 1970s turned to a related topic. The industry for a number of years had been advocating an expansion in the size of chain stores to achieve "one-stop shopping" by including delis, pharmacies, bakeries, flower and plant departments, and other products beyond traditional groceries, meats, and produce. The automated checkout facilitated such expansion with economies at the front end of the stores. But hourly wages inside chain stores were typically higher than in competitive stores in these specialty product lines. The unions had an interest in added employment, and the automated checkout had apparently been introduced without job loss. The private discourse led to the understanding that the unions would be supportive of "one-stop shopping" expansions and would not initially insist on the same wage scale for clerks in new departments. The growth of store size was further encouraged. See Figure 5.

In sum, while technological advances provided the means to develop the U.P.C., economic and regulatory pressures supplied the urgent motivation. Severe volatility and constraints on profits in the food sector spurred industry leaders to work together in search of productivity gains, even at some risk of antitrust action, and to reach creative compromises with unions in the sector.

Reflections for Economic Analysis

Brown's chronicle of the U.P.C. raises a number of issues that are currently of special interest to academic economists. Three topics are particularly noteworthy: network externalities, contractual relations between firms, and complementarities. The discussion in this section links each topic to the U.P.C.'s history and suggests what economists can learn from the history.

Network externalities. In the past decade, a spate of

research — largely theoretical work — has considered the adoption of technology in the face of so-called network externalities.[39] Network externalities arise when the value placed on a new technology by a potential adopter depends on the number of other users who adopt compatible technology. Consider, for instance, the facsimile machine. A fax machine is worthless to an individual unless the people with whom he or she communicates purchase fax machines with compatible communication standards. The value of the machine rises steadily with the number of other adopters. A similar effect arises in hardware/software systems. An IBM-compatible computer is valuable largely because software suitable for the computer is widely available. The utility of the hardware rises with the prevalence of the software.

The network externalities associated with the U.P.C. were strong, as has been noted. Scanners, the hardware, had little value until the U.P.C. symbol, the software, was commonplace. Conversely, the symbol was of limited use unless scanners were installed. The system as a whole would not yield net savings, the pioneers believed, unless 75 percent of products bore the symbol and scanners were installed in nearly 8,000 supermarkets.

Economists have identified a number of phenomena that may arise when network externalities are strong. First, there is the specter of *excess inertia*. A technology from which all would benefit if all adopted might not get off the ground, simply because no user is willing to take the risk of adopting the new technology first. This threat is especially potent when users are unsure of others' taste for the new technology. A second possibility is *excess momentum:* users move as a herd to a new technology that may be socially inferior. Once the bandwagon toward the worse technology begins to move, no firm jumps off and risks being stranded with an incompatible technology. Third, technologies with network externalities tend to exhibit *lock-in*. Once a particular standard or technology is established in a community of users, it will be especially difficult to change. A widely cited example of this is the QWERTY typewriter keyboard.[40] The QWERTY keyboard remains locked in as an industry standard long after the rationale for this odd arrangement of typewriter keys has passed.

The self-reinforcing nature of technologies with network externalities accounts for a fourth feature of such systems, *multiple equilibria.* Take, for example, the early video cassette recorder industry, in which JVC and Sony championed the VHS and Beta standards, respectively. Users' desire to exchange tapes with friends and to rent tapes created strong externalities, and this made it likely that only one standard would prevail. *Which* standard would triumph was unclear. The VHS standard eventually won out, but a second equilibrium with Beta as the standard was equally viable from an economist's point of view. When multiple equilibrium outcomes are possible, further phenomena may arise. In such a setting, small, seemingly irrelevant historical accidents can have a permanent impact on which outcome arises. Expectations of users can also have a decisive effect; a new technology may fail simply because all users expect it to fail. Finally, sponsorship of a technology can matter a great deal. Users, firms, and others may have especially strong incentives to take action to ensure that the outcome they prefer is the one that becomes locked in.

What can a history of the U.P.C. contribute to the analysis of network externalities? The academic literature in this area consists largely of theoretical work, backed up by a handful of case studies of the QWERTY keyboard, the VCR industry, the emergence of certain telecommunications standards, and so forth.[41] At the most elemental level, the history in this volume provides an unusually detailed case study of the birth of a network technology. Those who view Brown's account through the lens of economic theory will see the forces mentioned above at play: inertia, momentum, bandwagons, lock-in, small but decisive accidents, influential expectations, and sponsorship.

At a deeper level, the history highlights the vital role played by actors and institutions that are usually omitted entirely from economic models. These include cooperative trade organizations, voluntary standards-writing bodies, consulting firms, and consumer unions. The history also illustrates tactics that industry leaders can employ to overcome the inertia associated with an immense coordination challenge. The ways in which the U.P.C. pioneers managed industry expectations, involved the very top layer of management, assured CEO commitment, drove to attain "critical mass" — all of these suggest that the pioneers had a visceral understanding of the network externality problem, even though they never used such an abstract term.

Finally, the history raises a challenge to conventional theory. The agents in customary models of the standard-setting process act in narrow self-interest. In contrast, the actors in Brown's history have a much more complex set of motivations. Zealous commitment to an idea, regard for industry-level productivity, and concerns about personal legacies all seem to have played influential roles. History shows that such motivations are important, but can economic theory incorporate them or shed light on them?

Contractual relations between firms. The earlier discussion emphasized how a suite of innovations, including the Universal Product Code, is transforming the practices of retailers and their suppliers. Firms at the forefront of this transformation have begun to employ certain arrangements that alter the relationship between retailers and vendors in a fundamental way. Traditionally, retail buyers and supplier salespeople hammered out prices, quantities, and terms in hard fought, arm's length transactions; each party kept its information carefully guarded in order to protect its bargaining leverage. Under new arrangements, information flows freely across the borders of the firms, and vendors manage inventory on behalf of retailers in the context of a long-term relationship. Wal-Mart, for instance, relays data directly from its checkout counters to Procter & Gamble. In this way, P&G learns precisely which of its products are selling at which Wal-Mart sites. P&G then chooses the quantity to ship to each Wal-Mart store and initiates replenishment even without a specific purchase order. Wal-Mart's POS (point of sale) data affect P&G's production schedule directly.[42] The upshot is a channel with a very unconventional allocation of information and decisions. Transactions that used to be carried out at arm's length are now conducted in long-term relationships almost as if they were occurring within a single, integrated enterprise.

How can economic analysis account for such new interorganizational arrangements? At a facile level, we can say that the arrangements have arisen because the new technologies make them more efficient than the traditional arm's length alternative. Theory may be able to offer more. Transaction cost theory emphasizes the role of vertical integration in encouraging investments in relationship-specific assets.[43] Without integration, a firm may hesitate to invest in assets that are specific to a relationship with a particular upstream or downstream firm, for fear that the benefits of such assets will be expropriated by the other firm. Vertical integration mitigates the threat of expropriation, alters bargaining positions, and thereby restores investment incentives.

Seen in this light, a significant feature of the U.P.C., EDI, and associated innovations is their *non-specific* character. Thanks to the setting of industry-level standards, firms can invest in these technologies, and engage in pseudo-integration with partners, without exposing themselves as much to the hazards of relationship-specific assets. They may readily change partners under widely utilized standards. Wal-Mart and P&G, for example, could conceivably have created their own product numbering and labeling scheme and their own communication protocols in order to carry through their partnership. The risks and costs of doing so, however, would be greater than those associated with employing industry standards. In this sense, industry standards such as the U.P.C. enable the new relationships between firms that we observe.

The evolution of a complementary system. The U.P.C., it was argued above, is part of a suite of new technologies. A retailer that wants to take full advantage of these innovations must modify a long list of its practices and investments. In the food industry, for instance, a supermarket must install scanners and electronic registers, develop new routines for posting and changing prices, establish electronic links with suppliers, automate its distribution facilities, acquire the ability to interpret demand information quickly, retrain virtually all of its employees, reconsider the scope of its product offering and its scale of operations, and so forth. These numerous changes are arguably far from independent. Rather, they may constitute a system of *complements;* the marginal benefit of adopting each change may rise as the others are instituted.

A growing economic literature focuses on the behavior of such systems. Paul Milgrom and John Roberts sparked this line of research by adapting mathematical tools from lattice theory to analyze systems of complements and by applying those tools to examine "modern manufacturing."[44] They showed how a decline in the costs of computing, communications, and flexible production equipment could account for a host of subsequent changes in product-line breadth, pricing, human resource practices, quality control, and vertical integration. Most importantly, they explained why we should expect to observe firms adopting such complementary changes in unison rather than piecemeal. Subsequent empirical research has attempted to document the presence of complementarities in a variety of settings.[45] The research of Margaret Hwang and David Weil in the apparel industry is especially pertinent here. They show that the diffusion of "modern manufacturing" practices in the apparel industry can be explained in part by the advantages to business units of adopting complementary sets of information, distribution, and manufacturing technologies in response to new methods of retailing that are built around the U.P.C. Their research documents the impact of the Code on the diffusion of complementary practices within and between the retailing and apparel manufacturing industries.[46]

The emerging research on complementarity is based on a set of comparative static results. Consequently, it is not surprising that the literature has relatively little to say about the dynamics of systems of complements. The theory tells us that firms make coherent bundles of choices in equilibrium. But the theory remains relatively quiet on how firms arrive at an equilibrium and how various bundles become technically feasible in the first place. The history told in this volume reports the emergence of a wholly new "coherent bundle." We can see how the leaders of individual firms both contributed to and responded to this evolution. The dynamic story deserves the careful attention of those who study complementary systems in equilibrium.

The Future

The revolution at the checkout counter recounted in this volume is still very much in process. The full potentials of machine-readable coding and scanning lie ahead, as a few examples illustrate. The development of two-dimensional symbology, 2-D, provides more digits and information in less space. (For instance, the Gettysburg Address can be represented in 2-D symbology by a 2-inch by 2-inch block of black and white squares.)[47] This makes it possible to record detailed information and a history of process related to individual production batches, which opens a variety of frontiers in a range of industries. Pills in the pharmaceutical industry or fabric in clothes, for example, can be given a symbol to provide a record of origins.

The transformation of production-distribution-retail channels with bar coding, EDI, and distribution centers is far from complete in many sectors and is only beginning in some industries as in health care. These innovations are influencing production processes and foreign sourcing and assembly as in parts of the apparel sector.

In the food sector, transponders are becoming inexpensive enough that they are starting to appear in some stores. A transmitter placed in the supermarket ceiling relays by radio signal a price for each SKU to small devices attached to shelves. Where state or local regulations do not prohibit, transponders are likely to provide further economies in distribution and more freedom for retailers to change prices frequently. Peak-load pricing might become feasible in supermarkets, for instance.

The growth in usage of individual customer cards facilitates the adjustment of store inventory to tastes and purchasing patterns of local customers. They also permit stores to tailor promotions to small segments or even individual customers. Such target marketing techniques show considerable promise to enhance marketing and sales, but they require considerable changes in the marketing organizations of food chain stores. They may also raise concerns about the privacy of information relating to individual customers.

From the perspective of the economy these developments continue the diminution of inventory per sales dollar and enhance the role of retailers with new relationships to suppliers. The unfolding future from the beginnings recounted in this volume warrants continuing attention.

Notes

[1] See Chapter 1 of this text. For an early account, see "Grocery Industry in the U.S.A., Choice of a Universal Product Code," Harvard Business School Case, 9-676-087, 1975; and "Choice of a Standard Symbol," Harvard Business School Case, 9-677-045, 1976.

[2] See, Tom Mahoney, "Revolution at the Checkout Counter," *The American Legion Magazine,* November, 1974, pp. 18–21; 40–48 that reports the early developments; also see Nick Walsh, "Evolution at the Checkstand," *California Grocers Advocate,* December 1972, pp. 19–23.

[3] Registration data for Figures 1–4 were kindly provided by the Uniform Code Council to the Harvard Center for Textile and Apparel Research and were analyzed by Peter Fisher.

[4] "UPC Progress Report," McKinsey & Company, 1976.

[5] F.H. Abernathy, J.T. Dunlop, J.H. Hammond, and D. Weil, "The Information-Integrated Channel: A Study of the U.S. Apparel Industry in Transition," *Brookings Papers on Economic Activity,* 1995, pp. 175–246.

[6] Minutes of UCC Board of Governors, November 15, 1996.

[7] The discussion of other codes and symbologies draws from Craig K. Harmon, *Lines of Communication: Bar Code and Data Collection Technology for the 90s,* Peterborough, NH: Helmers, 1994, especially chapters 3 and 4.

[8] Warren E. Leary, "Russia's Mir and a Shuttle are Flawless in Space Link," *New York Times,* September 19, 1996, p. A25.

[9] For further description, see Abernathy, Dunlop, Hammond, and Weil, *op. cit.;* P. Milgrom and J. Roberts, "The Economics of Modern Manufacturing," *American Economic Review* (80), June 1990, pp. 511–528. A detailed discussion of "lean retailing" is included in a forthcoming volume by Abernathy, Dunlop, Hammond and Weil.

[10] Nirmalya Kumar, "The Power of Trust in Manufacturer-Retailer Relationships," *Harvard Business Review* (74:6), November-December 1996, pp. 92–106. See especially the insert entitled "Two Tough Companies Learn to Dance Together."

[11] See, Food Marketing Institute, Inc., Washington, D.C., *The Food Marketing Institute Speaks,* 1977, Appendix Table 41; *The Food Marketing Industry Speaks,* 1995, p. 6.

[12] Food Marketing Institute, Inc., *loc. cit.,* 1996, p. 12. Food Marketing Institute, Inc., Washington, D.C., *The Food Marketing Institute Speaks: Detailed Tabulations,* 1981, p. 72. Food Marketing Institute, Inc., Washington, D.C., *The Food Marketing Institute Speaks: Detailed Tabulations,* 1987, p. 87.

[13] Abernathy, Dunlop, Hammond, and Weil, *op. cit.,* p. 191.

[14] It is interesting to note that the pioneers of the U.P.C. only rarely articulated the full economic revolution of which they were an integral part. As this volume makes clear, the founders of the Code were focused for immediate practical reasons on improving the productivity of checkout clerks and price-marking clerks. The so-called "soft savings" associated with better information and inventory management were

downplayed. In the late 1980s the food sector returned to issues of inventory management after the mass merchandisers had pioneered these developments earlier in the decade.

[15] See, Alfred D. Chandler, Jr., *The Visible Hand,* Cambridge: Harvard University Press, 1977.

[16] See, Alan L. Haberman, "Twenty Years of UPC," for an account of the early history. Also, see transcript of interview with Alan Haberman by F.H. Abernathy and John T. Dunlop, May 3, 1995. Both are available at the Harvard Center for Textile and Apparel Research at the Harvard Business School, Cambridge, MA.

[17] "The Supermarket Scanner That Failed," *Business Week,* March 22, 1976, pp. 52B–52E. Also see the negative concerns and cautious short-term predictions in Robin Neilson Shaw, "Universal Product Code Scanning Systems: The Retail Experience, 1974–1976," A Thesis Presented to the Faculty of the Graduate School of Cornell University in Partial Fulfillment for the Degree of Doctor of Philosophy, August 1977, Marquette Memorial Library, pp. 280–88.

[18] We wish to thank Professor Victor Jones for formative discussions concerning this subsection.

[19] M. Bertolotti, *Masers and Lasers: An Historical Approach,* Bristol: Adam Hilger, 1983, pp. 103–110.

[20] Henry B.O. Davis, *Electrical and Electronic Technologies: A Chronology of Events and Inventors from 1940 to 1980,* Metuchen: Scarecrow Press, 1985, p. 148.

[21] *Ibid.,* p. 162.

[22] *Ibid.,* pp. 162, 179–180.

[23] *Ibid.,* p. 221.

[24] *Ibid.,* p. 58.

[25] Martin Campbell-Kelly and William Aspray, *Computer: A History of the Information Machine,* New York: Basic Books, 1996. Davis, *op. cit.,* pp. 62, 129, 136–137, 220.

[26] Campbell-Kelly and Aspray, *op. cit.,* p. 222.

[27] *Ibid.,* pp. 157–164.

[28] *Ibid.,* pp. 165–169.

[29] *Ibid.,* pp. 169–176.

[30] For a fuller discussion see, John T. Dunlop, "Inflation and Income Policies: The Political Economy of Recent U.S. Experience," *The Eighth Monash Economics Lecture,* Monash University, Australia, September 9, 1974. For a detailed account of policies in the period, see John T. Dunlop and Kenneth J. Fedor, eds., *The Lessons of Wage and Price Controls — The Food Sector,* Cambridge, MA: Harvard University Press, 1977.

[31] See, Roger B. Porter, *Presidential Decision Making, The Economic Policy Board,* Cambridge: Cambridge University Press, 1980. Chapter 5 treats the U.S.–U.S.S.R. grain agreement of 1975 and provides background for the 1972–1973 years, p. 127. For the 1974–1975 events in more detail, see Roger B. Porter, *The U.S. – U.S.S.R. Grain Agreement,* Cambridge: Cambridge University Press, 1980.

[32] John T. Dunlop, "Lessons of Food Controls, 1971–74," in John T. Dunlop and Kenneth J. Fedor, eds., *loc. cit.*, p. 247.

[33] William M. Vaughn, III, "Wage Stabilization in the Food Industry," in John T. Dunlop and Kenneth J. Fedor, Eds., *loc. cit.*, pp. 148–49, 184.

[34] John T. Dunlop was chairman of the tripartite Construction Industry Stabilization Commission from its outset on March 29, 1971 and became Director of the Cost of Living Council on January 11, 1973.

[35] The agenda was prepared by John T. Dunlop in consultation with members of the Committee. See, The Joint Labor Management Committee on the Retail Food Industry, March 29, 1994, Twentieth Anniversary Banquet, for the text of the 1974 agenda.

[36] Joint Labor Management Committee of the Retail Industry, Release, April 28, 1975. Information that follows has been made available from the files of the Committee for the period.

[37] This understanding is reported in a memorandum dated August 9, 1978. Also see a summary letter of Phillip E. Ray, Executive Director of the Committee to Wayne H. Fisher, Chairman, Lucky Stores, Inc. dated July 23, 1979.

[38] *The Food Marketing Industry Speaks,* Washington, D.C., The Research Department, Food Marketing Institute, 1995.

[39] Major, early contributions include P.A. David, "Clio and the Economics of QWERTY," *American Economic Review* (75), May 1985, pp. 332–337; W.B. Arthur, "Competing Technologies, Increasing Returns, and Lock-in by Historical Events," *Economic Journal* (99), March 1989, pp. 116–131; M. Katz and C. Shapiro, "Network Externalities, Competition, and Compatibility," *American Economic Review* (75), June 1985, pp. 424–440; J. Farrell and G. Saloner, "Standardization, Compatibility, and Innovation," *RAND Journal of Economics* (16), Spring 1985, pp. 70–83; and J. Farrell and G. Saloner, "Installed Base and Compatibility: Innovation, Product Pre-announcements and Predation," *American Economic Review* (76), December 1986, pp. 940–955. For a survey, see M. Katz and C. Shapiro, "Systems Competition and Network Effects," *Journal of Economic Perspectives* (8), Spring 1994, pp. 93–115.

[40] David, *op. cit.*

[41] David, *op. cit.;* M. Cusumano, V. Mylonadis, and R. Rosenbloom, "Strategic Maneuvering and Mass-Market Dynamics: The Triumph of VHS over Beta," *Business History Review* (66), Spring 1992, pp. 51–94; and S. Besen and L. Johnson, *Compatibility Standards, Competition, and Innovation in the Broadcasting Industry,* RAND Corporation R-3453-NSF, 1986.

[42] See N. Kumar, *op. cit.*

[43] O. Williamson, *Markets and Hierarchies,* New York: Free Press, 1975, and B. Klein, R. Crawford, and A. Alchian, "Vertical Integration, Appropriable Rents, and the Competitive Contracting Process," *Journal of Law and Economics* (21), October 1978, pp. 297–326. S.J. Grossman and O. Hart, "The Costs and Benefits of Ownership: A Theory of Vertical and

Lateral Control," *Journal of Political Economy* (94), August 1986, pp. 297–326.

44 P. Milgrom and J. Roberts, "Communications and Inventories as Substitutes in Organizing Production," *Scandinavian Journal of Economics* (90), 1988, pp. 275–289. P. Milgrom and J. Roberts, "The Economics of Modern Manufacturing," *American Economic Review* (80), June 1990, pp. 511–528. P. Milgrom and C. Shannon, "Monotone Comparative Statics," *Econometrica* (62), 1994, pp. 157–180. P. Milgrom and J. Roberts, "Complementarities and Fit: Strategy, Structure, and Organizational Change in Manufacturing," *Journal of Accounting and Economics* (19), 1995, pp. 179–208.

45 C. Ichniowski, K. Shaw, and G. Prennushi, "The Effects of Human Resource Management Practices on Productivity," 1996, mimeo. E. Brynjolfsson and L. Hitt, "Information Technology and Organizational Architecture: An Exploratory Analysis," 1996, mimeo.

46 M. Hwang and D. Weil, "Production Complementarities and the Diffusion of Modern Manufacturing Practices: Evidence from the U.S. Apparel Industry," 1996, mimeo.

47 B.J. Feder, "For Bar Codes, An Added Dimension," *New York Times,* April 24, 1991; M. Alpert, "Building a Better Bar Code," *Fortune,* June 15, 1992, p. 101.

1
The Ad Hoc Committee

It took several months to put together an inter-industry committee. Each association walked around the proposal several times to be sure the other groups were not using the proposal to obtain an unfair advantage. More important, it is not easy to persuade chief executive officers to commit to an industry project that, so far at least, seemed insoluble. This was compounded by the need to assure that the committee represented all facets of the industry.

The industry fear of a multiplicity of incompatible checkout systems requiring different product coding schemes seemed very real. It gave a sense of urgency to this project. In early 1970, two small high tech companies held highly publicized demonstrations of automated checkout counters. There were also reports that a major computer firm was also working on a system. These tests required a product-identification code.

At least the committee members would not have to pay for the honor of serving.[1] GMA and the Supermarket Institute (SMI) each agreed to put up $50,000 to fund the committee's work. In addition, NAFC had sponsored considerable work on the subject by an independent consultant. This, too, was made available to the committee.

[1] That is not quite true. Each member's company not only volunteered the executive's time; it also paid his out of pocket expenses. By the time the project was completed, this was a significant contribution.

The Ad Hoc Committee would cost considerably more before its work was completed. The Grocery Manufacturers of America would contribute another $85,000 while a fund-raising drive by retailers would add almost a million dollars before 1973.

The associations agreed that the committee had to be representative, but small. They settled on a committee of ten chief executive officers. Five would be grocery manufacturers, appointed by GMA. The five distributor associations would each designate a single member. Each CEO would be allowed to bring a technical expert from his company to the meetings.[2] The five manufacturers included large processors, small processors, frozen food, canned food, packaged food, and health and beauty aids. The distributors were two chains, a wholesaler, an independent, and a cooperative.

The original members of the Ad Hoc Committee and their technical experts were:

R. Burt Gookin, President H. J. Heinz. Gookin, the first nonfamily member to run the Heinz organization became the Ad Hoc Committee's chairman. He became the embodiment of the committee. Physically, he resembled the stereotype of the company bookkeeper, which he once was. His looks belied his youth as a boxer and gave no hint of his prodigious golfing ability. No meal, breakfast, lunch, or dinner, would pass without Burt asking for "some of that good Heinz ketchup."

John Hayes, General Manager, Marketing Services, H. J. Heinz, in some ways sacrificed his career to the U.P.C. This lanky Englishman was Gookin's technical support. His service to the Ad Hoc Committee became so consuming that he lost his place within the Heinz organization and never returned to his original job.

---

[2] The technicians were not intended to be members of the committee. In practice, however, they were treated as equals, and some of them became leaders of the committee.

Art Larkin, CEO of General Foods, attended few Ad Hoc Committee meetings, but his technical advisor, Bob Stringer, Vice President Distribution, became one of the group's leaders. Stringer was to lead the effort to devise a satisfactory code-management scheme, an undertaking that ended in the creation of the predecessor to the Uniform Code Council.

Bob Aders, Vice Chairman of the Kroger Company, had a major role at the outset, then stepped into the background. Jack Strubbe, Kroger Vice President, on the other hand was a tower of strength, particularly in the crucial early years of the U.P.C.'s implementation.

J. P. MacFarland, CEO of General Mills, had a spotty involvement with the Ad Hoc Committee, but was always there when it counted. In addition, both he and Burt Gookin held leadership positions in the GMA and proved invaluable as communicators and salesmen to that vital constituency.

MacFarland's advisor on the Committee was Tom Nelson, Vice President-Controller of General Mills. Nelson provided financial expertise to the Ad Hoc Committee and later to the Uniform Grocery Product Code Council.

Don Lloyd, President of Associated Food Stores of Salt Lake City, represented cooperatives on the Ad Hoc Committee. A devout Mormon, he devoted himself to his church after retiring from Associated. Later, Lloyd was given the task of figuring out how to apply the U.P.C. to coupons, an assignment that proved to be considerably more difficult than was originally thought.

The remaining members of the Committee were Gordon Ellis, President of Fairmont Foods, and his advisor, Bill Logan, Vice President, Administration; Gavin MacBain, Chairman of the Board of Bristol Myers, and Fred Butler, Vice President, Operations; W. J. Kane, President of A&P; James Wyman, President of Super Valu Stores; and Earl Madsen, President, Madsen Enterprises. Ellis represented small manufacturers and MacBain health and beauty aids companies, while Kane, like Aders, headed a chain. Wyman headed a major grocery wholesaler, and Madsen was the representative of independent retailers.

This, then, was the Ad Hoc Committee on a Uniform Grocery Product Code. Considering the other commitments of its members, it would remain remarkably intact until it finally faded away in 1975. There were, of course, some changes in membership — Gordon Ellis and Jim Wyman would die, and as the committee passed from code to symbol issues, there would be some additions. The group that began the project was, by and large, the group that saw it through to completion. No committee member was lost to hostile takeovers or leveraged buyouts. This was the start of the 1970s, not the end of the 1980s.

The Ad Hoc Committee held its first meeting on Tuesday, August 25, 1970, at the O'Hare Inn in Chicago. The setting quickly dispelled any notion that this was to be anything other than a "roll up your sleeves and work in the trenches" group. The O'Hare Inn was one of the first of the now ubiquitous airport hotel/motels catering to business meetings of short duration. It possessed precious few amenities. A sprawling two-story building, it had neither trees nor grass and it abutted the end of a runway.

In this spot, the trade association executives sat with their chosen committee members. Unofficially led by Clancy Adamy of NAFC, they first explained the potential, then described the impasse. The committee members were charged to rise above their concerns as company representatives or even as representatives of their associations. Instead, they were urged to make their decisions based upon total system efficiencies and what was best for the industry as a whole.

Five questions were assigned the Committee by the trade associations: (1) is a standard industry product code worthwhile even if it is not feasible to devise a standard symbol?

(2) If so, what should that code be? (3) How can widespread acceptance of the industry standard be obtained? (4) How shall the code be managed? (5) Should there be a standard symbol representing the code, and if so what should it be?

Having given the Ad Hoc Committee a financial base and its marching orders, the trade association presidents declared their work done and withdrew from the room. The Committee was on its own.[3] Kroger's Bob Aders was designated Chairman Pro Tem. Clancy Adamy of NAFC had been the driving force behind calling the meeting, and Kroger not only was a major NAFC member, but had been actively investigating technological improvements at the checkout counter.

The first order of business was to elect a permanent chairman. Burt Gookin of Heinz was nominated and quickly elected by acclamation. The next item took a little longer, but not much. The group needed to find out if they shared the belief that it was worthwhile to search for a standard industry product-identification code. Quickly, the group concluded the effort to find such a code was worthwhile. Potential productivity improvements could be engendered by a standard product code.

It was also apparent that the Ad Hoc Committee lacked the time and the ability to conduct the basic research necessary. The demands of running a company made it impossible for the CEOs on the Committee to do the work. While some of the Committee members' technical advisors might be

---

[3] It was at this moment that I officially obtained representation of the Ad Hoc Committee. As counsel to GMA, I had attended this meeting. When the trade association executives walked, I remained, saying that "at GMA we have a rule against this kind of a group meeting unless counsel is present. I plan to stay, unless I am told to leave." Bob Aders, sitting as Chairman Pro Tem, responded, "You can stay, so long as you represent *all* of us." (The GMA "Rule" came from a healthy respect for the antitrust laws and a recognition that the Federal Trade Commission often focussed on the grocery industry.)

released from their corporate responsibilities to do the research, their independence would undoubtedly be questioned. The Committee agreed that a consultant should be retained to do the work.

Anticipating that the Ad Hoc Committee would desire a consultant, four firms were prepared on that August day to submit a proposal: Arthur Andersen & Co.; Booz Allen and Hamilton; Logicon, Inc.; and McKinsey & Co. McKinsey, however, had a significant advantage. Under contract to NAFC, McKinsey had already been considering the issues.

It required little debate for the Ad Hoc Committee to select McKinsey as its consultant. Burt Gookin appointed a subcommittee of Jim Wyman, Gordon Ellis, Jack Strubbe, and Bob Stringer to work with the consultant to refine the proposal so that actual work could begin as quickly as possible.

The initial meeting of the Ad Hoc Committee was brief, but momentous. In a little more than an hour, the group picked its leader, concluded that the task it had been set was worth the effort that would be required, and selected a consultant to guide its work.

While the choice of a consultant may have seemed obvious, in retrospect it may have been the most important decision the Committee ever made. McKinsey & Co was far from a disinterested, neutral observer in the process. It saw its role as that of leader and advocate, and was not shy about exercising it. In Tom Wilson, the principal, and Larry Russell, the manager on the project, McKinsey had assembled an ideal team. Wilson understood the politics and nuances of the industries involved and was superb in developing the right tone and program to market the Committee's decision, while Russell was a brilliantly creative individual who thoroughly understood the issues involved and delighted in unraveling their complexity. This team would eventually split apart, but while together, they were virtually unstoppable.

McKinsey's task was to identify a coding structure that could be used as a standard for item identification by grocery manufacturers, distributors, and retailers, yet require the minimum changes to existing coding structures. An economic case would have to be built that the benefits to the industry as a whole, and to each segment of the industry, could justify the expense of making whatever changes were required to existing codes.

A uniform grocery product-identification code ("UGPIC") should also be conducive to a symbolic representation that could lead to the automation of the checkout process. Finally, the ideal code would be structured in such a way as to convey the maximum amount of information in the minimum amount of space. In that connection, an alphanumeric code, combining letters and numbers, would allow a great deal of information to be compressed into a small number of digits. On the other hand, such a code would force a great many companies to change their coding systems at considerable trouble and expense.[4]

Each proposal had to be analyzed on an economic cost/benefit fulcrum. From the outset, McKinsey insisted on a rigorous, conservative approach to economics. Benefits were classified as "hard" or "soft." "Hard" savings could be quantified and tied specifically to the adoption and implementation of the code. Potential savings or savings that might be facilitated by a code but not necessarily directly flow from the code were defined as "soft" savings.[5] In measuring costs and

[4] Human factors studies by AT&T convinced the Ad Hoc Committee that alphanumeric codes were more difficult for humans to handle without error.

[5] Hard savings were derived from increased productivity at checkout, reduced checkout errors, reduced checker training, elimination of price marking and remarking, and inventory reduction. Soft savings were categorized as improvements in shelf-space allocation, determination of departmental profitability, labor scheduling, shrink control, evaluation of advertising, better pricing decisions, new item evaluation, reduction of out of stock, selection of product mix, and compilation of statistical data.

benefits, McKinsey would only allow hard savings to be considered; the others were considered too speculative. McKinsey used as its model for economic analysis a supermarket with sales of $40,000 per week, almost at the industry average.[6]

The consultant's task was first to estimate the cost to the industry to move to a standard code and then to articulate how the code could most effectively be used. Lastly, it was to provide leadership to help assure the benefits would be realized.

By December 15, the McKinsey team was ready to provide a progress report to the Ad Hoc Committee. For the second (and last) time, the group returned to the O'Hare Inn. After McKinsey presented, Burt Gookin once again asked if the Committee should abandon the project, now that they had the benefit of three and one half months of work. No member of the Ad Hoc proved faint of heart; all voted to continue.

At this meeting, Larry Russell addressed for the first time a theme that would often recur. Emphasizing the importance of the Ad Hoc Committee, he pointed out that the various equipment companies had gone about as far as they could go in a vacuum. If the automation of the checkout process was to take place, the grocery industry was going to have to exert the leadership. The Ad Hoc Committee's decisions were, in effect, the key to future progress.

In order to maximize their effectiveness, and to prevent the spread of misinformation, or insider information, the members of the Ad Hoc agreed at this meeting to hold all information confidential. While they recognized a need to have McKinsey provide the sponsoring associations with progress reports, they directed that those reports be confined to general statements, omitting specific details.

By the Committee's next meeting, six weeks later,

[6] That analysis, based on hard savings alone, showed that for the industry to break even, at least 1500 stores had to participate.

McKinsey was ready with what it called its "semi-final" recommendations. The Ad Hoc Committee met three times in March 1971, including one meeting to brief the sponsoring trade association executives. The boards of directors of the associations also received status reports that an industry standard product-identification code appeared feasible, with implementation taking place over several years.

At the first March meeting, the technical advisors to the members of the Ad Hoc Committee assured their principals that they had reviewed the data on which McKinsey was relying as a basis for its conclusions. These technicians were satisfied with the integrity of that data and indeed believed that some of the data, such as the assumptions on labor rates, was so conservative that the industry savings from a standard code might well be considerably greater than projected by McKinsey.

Accordingly, on March 31, 1971, the Ad Hoc Committee on a Uniform Grocery Product Identification Code made its first major decision. It did so in an unusual manner. It stated its decision in the form of the answers to eight questions:

1. *Should the grocery industry have a U.P.C.?* We recommend adopting a Universal Product Code, but not solely for the purpose of optimizing the use of code scan checkout systems.

2. *What should the structure of the code be?* We believe a ten-digit, all numeric mixed code is the most pragmatic solution to the code structure problem. A check digit will also be required for communication and key punching, but not for front-end use.

3. *Should the Committee adopt a standard symbol?* We recommend the Committee stop short of picking a standard symbol, but proceed to adopt tentative guidelines for standardization.

4. *What approach should be taken to ensure acceptable symbol standards?* We recommend using the symbol guidelines as a framework for getting agreement on a standard among users and equipment companies of a standard symbol.
5. *What should be done about code management?* We recommend a code management subcommittee look into the operational requirements for code management.
6. *What time period should be set for conversion?*
7. *What should the Committee do to ensure continued technological development?*
8. *What continuing role should the Committee play?* We recommend a continuing role for the Committee, with conversion to a U.P.C. as soon as possible, but conversion to symbol should be scheduled after store tests. The . . . implementation plan with store tests and guidelines approach to symbols should ensure continued technological development.

These tentative guidelines for development of a standard symbol had already been developed by Larry Russell. They had been reviewed by the equipment manufacturers and appeared workable.

The Ad Hoc unanimously adopted the conclusions embodied in the answers to the eight questions, but the path to get to this point had not been perfectly smooth. One significant problem surfaced early, and would continue to plague the Ad Hoc throughout its existence. No matter how much the Committee accomplished or how rapidly, the industry's expectations outpaced them. As early as January 28, 1971, Bob Aders reported that some members of the Supermarket Institute were convinced that the Ad Hoc was much closer to making a decision than was in fact the case.

There were technical considerations as well. The Committee wanted a code that was long enough to cover all products sold in a grocery store, short enough to achieve productivity gains, simple enough to administer, and compatible with other codes such as the National Drug Code. The code should be flexible and place minimum costs upon product manufacturers. From this standpoint, an eight digit, limited structure, all-numeric code appeared to be best. However, it had one staggering drawback — such a code would have to be administered totally, at an annual cost of millions of dollars.

Most grocery manufacturers used all numeric codes of six digits or less. This led to a focussing on a two-part code, with the first part identifying the manufacturer. Such a code structure would enable the costs of management to be brought down to a more manageable annual cost of two to three hundred thousand dollars, since only the manufacturer prefix needed centralized control.[7]

Meetings were held with the Food and Drug Administration to assure compatibility with the National Drug Code and the National Health Related Items Code, but commitment from the government was not easy to come by. Many months would pass before the possibility of incompatibility with these codes faded as an issue.

Although McKinsey early on focussed on a ten-digit code, there was considerable support, especially among grocery manufacturers for an eleventh digit. An eleven-digit code would significantly diminish the change in systems required for many grocery manufacturers. It could ensure compatibility with the coding system employed in the drug industry, and the eleventh digit could be used as a check digit. On the other hand, the extra digit would increase the total cost from an overall industry standpoint. At least one equipment

[7] See Chapter 3.

manufacturer was telling Larry Russell that its technology could not handle a code of that length.

Another problem would reoccur with each new advance by the Committee. It was a classic "chicken and egg" dilemma: why would a retailer invest in scanning equipment until a significant amount of his product was source coded? Why should a manufacturer go to the trouble of source coding product if there were no retailers prepared to scan it?

Some feared that jealousy and the "not invented here" syndrome would plague the Committee's efforts. One of the earliest manifestations was a fear that a study conducted by Arthur Andersen & Co. for the Supermarket Institute on factors relevant to the economics of the automated checkout counter would "confuse and mislead" readers. McKinsey was concerned especially since, in its view, the Andersen study was much less complete than the work McKinsey was doing.

Several, including Mike O'Connor of SMI and Clancy Adamy of NAFC, were concerned that the McKinsey rigidly conservative approach grossly understated the soft savings that could be realized from a universal product code (U.P.C.). They feared the result would be a weakened response to a U.P.C. and a serious threat to the viability of the entire project.

Nor were all groups positive about the Ad Hoc Committee and its work. On March 31, for example, Tom Wilson reported that the American Meat Institute was opposed to the development of a U.P.C. He further reported that the National Association of Wholesalers, an umbrella trade group, was attempting to develop a coding system that would be compatible for all products.[8]

The Ad Hoc Committee also talked about consumer concerns, but not much. They early on agreed that consumer

[8] Wilson said the NAW scheme involved a six-digit code prefix (two-digit commodity code and a four-digit company code), which would be controlled by NAW.

interests must be considered in any final decision and that an implementation strategy must emphasize the consumer benefits of the U.P.C. However, the Committee concluded that, at the outset, their contacts should be limited to the office of Mrs. Virginia Knauer, the consumer advisor to the president. A number of consumer groups had become public policy activists, and some members of the Ad Hoc Committee had had unpleasant experiences with them. Accordingly, they chose to avoid bringing any of the activist groups into their confidence.

Even though there was talk of maximizing consumer benefit, there was an air of unreality to the discussion. It was clear to the Ad Hoc that U.P.C.'s impact was directly and almost exclusively on the distribution of product and the internal systems of manufacturers and distributors in the grocery industry. In the eyes of the Committee, the U.P.C.'s effect on consumers was all positive — checkout would be faster and more accurate. It came as a great shock when, four years later, consumers expressed fear and outrage at the removal of prices on the item, made possible by the U.P.C. A massive effort was then launched to address consumers in an intense and serious way.

By far the most serious issue facing the Ad Hoc Committee members in the winter of 1971 was how to achieve their goal without a government challenge alleging a violation of the antitrust laws. The grocery industry had considerable experience with antitrust. Indeed, the growth of supermarket chains in the early 1930s had led directly to the passage of an antitrust law, the Robinson-Patman Act. The Federal Trade Commission (FTC) had antitrust lawyers and economists who specialized in the grocery industry.

On the other hand, there was a belief that government involvement in the project, while it might insulate against antitrust liability, would unreasonably complicate and delay the Committee's work. The Ad Hoc members feared that

most bureaucrats whose advice was sought would first equivo-
cate and then give the most conservative answer conceivable.
However, to conduct a major inter- and intra-industry productivity project while ignoring the government seemed the
height of folly and irresponsibility. The government was
known to ask for jail terms for some executives named in
antitrust prosecutions.

Slowly, the Committee evolved a strategy for dealing with
the antitrust issue, which went a long way toward minimizing
the risk. In January 1971, as counsel to the Committee, I was
authorized to approach the Federal Trade Commission on an
informal basis to sound them out on the antitrust issues
raised by the Ad Hoc's work.

This led to a meeting with Basil Mezines, then Executive
Director of the FTC, in early March.[9] After hearing my story,
Mezines told me (to my relief) that he saw no significant legal
problems in the project. He cautioned, however, that his
opinion did not constitute a clearance on which we could
rely. Mezines suggested that we discuss our situation further
with Joseph Martin, General Counsel of the FTC.

The Ad Hoc agreed, and a meeting with Martin was
arranged for Burt Gookin, Tom Wilson, Larry Russell, and
me. The meeting was extremely productive. It opened a
channel of communication to Martin's successors, and,
through them, the Commission itself. Our meetings continued throughout the life of the Ad Hoc. Our approach was as
follows:

> We don't want a formal advisory opinion on our
> activity because we know it would take a long time to
> get and you would have to give us the most conserva-
> tive answer possible. We do want you to know what we

[9] My meeting was facilitated by my senior partner and mentor,
Frederick M. Rowe, a top FTC practitioner, and the author of the
leading treatise on the Robinson-Patman Act, *Price Discrimination Under the
Robinson-Patman Act* (1962).

are doing and we want to respond to your questions. We recognize that you remain free to take any action that seems appropriate to you. The Ad Hoc Committee hopes, however, that if the FTC receives complaints about our work, or develops a concern about it, the Commission will discuss the concerns or complaints with the Committee before taking formal legal action.

This hybrid policy of formal and informal communication was highly successful. There have been no serious antitrust challenges to this day.

The Ad Hoc Committee made its decision for a ten-digit, all-numeric universal product code at the end of March 1971. It was time to see if the grocery industry would accept the recommendation and make it work.

The first step toward implementation occurred even before the final decision was made on a code. Assuming that a decision would be forthcoming, on March 9, the Ad Hoc Committee created two subcommittees. One was the Symbol Standardization Subcommittee, comprised of non-Ad-Hoc Committee members from the grocery industry who were computer experts who could work with equipment companies to develop a symbolic representation of the still unborn U.P.C. The second was the Code Management Subcommittee, composed of four of the technical advisors to the Ad Hoc. This group had the responsibility of determining how the U.P.C., once selected, would be managed.

The Ad Hoc meeting with the trade association heads in early March was a dress rehearsal of the implementation program. If that sympathetic audience was not sold, there would be little point in attempting to sell it to the members of the industry who would have to make the investment to make the U.P.C. a success. Successfully passing the checkpoint with the trade associations, the Ad Hoc chose to use the SMI convention in Dallas in early May to make the public announcement of the U.P.C.

The SMI convention was the biggest single event in the grocery industry. It was both meeting and trade show, and almost all members of the industry, both manufacturers and distributors, participated. In addition, the convention was well covered by both the trade press and the general press. Some positive momentum could be generated to "sell" the program.

Tom Wilson and Larry Russell persuaded the Ad Hoc Committee that it was not enough to decide the format for a universal product code. The Committee would also have to assume responsibility for the adoption of the U.P.C. by a "critical mass" of manufacturers and distributors. This mass was never precisely defined, but it was seen to consist of the leaders of the industry, by virtue of their size or prestige.

To woo these leaders, McKinsey proposed a series of briefings, some on a one-to-one basis, others in small groups. The briefings would be conducted by McKinsey and someone from the Ad Hoc Committee. At the briefing's end, companies were asked to agree in principle to the U.P.C., and manufacturers were asked to commit to convert to the new code.

This strategy obviously involved a greater role for McKinsey. It also meant additional funding, which the Ad Hoc did not have. On March 12, the Ad Hoc asked the trade associations for an additional $150,000. The association executives refused to commit on the spot, but agreed to study the problem. Later, the funding problem was solved by a major fund-raising campaign by retailers. For now, however, the Ad Hoc — and McKinsey — moved ahead on faith that their need for cash would somehow be met.

Even as private briefing sessions were held, any public announcement was to be delayed until the views of "Washington" were clearer. Our meetings with Basil Mezines and

Joe Martin of the FTC seemed to provide the Committee an acceptable comfort level. A Washington strategy committee was formed to advise on future dealings with the government. It was composed of Wilson, Russell, Jim Wyman, and Gavin MacBain (from the Ad Hoc), George Koch (GMA), Clancy Adamy (NAFC), Henry Bison (counsel to NARGUS), and me.

The public announcement of the U.P.C. was scheduled for early May at the SMI convention in Dallas. The Ad Hoc redoubled its efforts to obtain the commitment of the "critical mass" of manufacturers and distributors prior to Gookin's speech at SMI. The public unveiling of the U.P.C. could be accompanied by a chorus of endorsements from industry leaders if the Committee were successful. A package of materials explaining the Ad Hoc's rationale for a ten-digit, two-part U.P.C. was developed and utilized quite successfully in the efforts to reach a "critical mass."

By the Ad Hoc meeting on June 24, there had been twenty-five individual meetings with manufacturers, and over one hundred companies represented at group meetings. Thirty retailers had been seen individually, and hundreds had been briefed in group meetings, including presentations at the SMI and NARGUS conventions, and to the SMI, NAFC, and CFDA Boards. There was no significant opposition. The trade association boards were working toward formally endorsing the U.P.C. Some manufacturers, especially canners, were concerned over the cost of applying a U.P.C. symbol to their products, but they too embraced the code.

Leaping the first major hurdle, the Ad Hoc Committee decided to move on to the next, considerably more difficult, task of determining if a symbolic representation of the code were feasible. The first step was to name Alan Haberman, CEO of First National Stores and Chairman of the Symbol Standardization Subcommittee, a member of the Ad Hoc Committee.

By June 1971, Larry Russell reported at least six store tests of potential symbols were set for 1972. Kroger and RCA were set to test in a supermarket in the Kenwood Shopping Center, near Cincinnati, Ohio. Texas Instruments, Sweda, TRW, IBM, NCR, Scanner Inc., and Pitney-Bowes-Alpex were all looking for retailer test partners.

For the next two years, the Symbol Selection Subcommittee would be at center stage.

2
The Symbol Selection Subcommittee

The opportunity to join a group of other talented individuals in the development of something totally new is exhilarating. Such was the experience of the Symbol Selection Subcommittee. The whole was truly greater than the sum of its parts. Without this group of seven or eight, there would have been no U.P.C. symbol. Like bees busy pollinating flowers, the members of the committee buzzed among the computer equipment companies, challenging technologies and spreading the message that there was a market for a grocery industry product symbol and equipment to scan it.

The Ad Hoc Committee created the Symbol Selection Subcommittee on March 31, 1971. Two years later to the day, the Committee fulfilled its charge and went out of existence. It was an extraordinary two years.

Alan Haberman, Executive Vice President of First National Stores, was named chairman of the committee and was also made a member of the Ad Hoc. His committee, like the Ad Hoc, representing both grocery manufacturers and retailers, included John Hayes of Heinz, Burt Gookin's technical expert, Eric Waldbaum, President of Greenbelt Consumer Services, a consumer cooperative in the Washington, DC area, Bill Galt, Assistant Controller of Del Monte, Barry Franz, an EDP Manager from Procter & Gamble, and representatives of Winn-Dixie and General Foods, who changed several times over the period. Vern Schatz of Jewel was originally on the committee but quickly resigned when it became clear that certain inventions of his placed both Schatz and his company in a potential conflict of interest situation. Fritz Biermeier of Red Owl joined the Symbol Committee in late 1972, but still made a significant contribution to the Committee's work. Larry Russell staffed the committee.

The Committee was young, intense, brilliant, and committed to their charge. Committee meetings were electric as idea fed upon idea. While still holding their regular jobs, each devoted great chunks of time to the project. Although pleased with their handiwork, most were sorry to see it end because of the intensity and creativity involved.

Assisted by McKinsey, the Ad Hoc Committee was able to give specific guidance to the Symbol Committee. Was it feasible to develop a machine-readable version of the universal product code? This symbol needed to be an omnidirectional, binary symbol with better than 99.99 percent accuracy of scanning and reading. Systems using this symbol should be capable of detecting a "no read" 99.99 percent of the time and allow for the possibility of scanning two identical symbols simultaneously. It was critical that the symbol be able to be read in the environmental conditions found in the typical supermarket — through ice, stains, moisture, and so forth. The maximum label area that could be occupied by a symbol was defined by the Ad Hoc as 5 square inches. The print specifications must be consistent with current packaging requirements and compatible with all containers currently in use or predicted for use. It must be possible to print the symbol in the supermarket at a reasonable cost. Finally, it was critical that the symbol be human, as well as machine-readable.

When the Symbol[1] Committee first met on June 1, 1971, it was presented (courtesy of Larry Russell) with a formal charge and a set of operating procedures from the Ad Hoc Committee. These "Operating Principals [*sic*] for Universal Product Code Symbol Standardization" directed the Committee to develop criteria for store tests of proposed symbols and then to ensure there would be enough tests in 1972 to provide worthwhile data.

The Symbol Committee was to follow these key criteria:

- The symbol is to be selected on the basis of overall industry economics;
- It shall not place an undue competitive burden on any segment of industry;
- All negative points of view must be answered;
- All requests for information will be honored; and
- Consumer interests are to be recognized.

The work of the Symbol Committee was enormously aided by its positioning under the protection of the Ad Hoc Committee. The Ad Hoc's stature and the respect it enjoyed throughout the industry proved invaluable in obtaining company commitments to adopt the U.P.C.

The Ad Hoc Committee took three actions to preserve its strength in September 1971. Some of the original Ad Hoc participants had retired from the Committee. Chairman Gookin was given the authority to renew the Committee by appointing new members. Counsel was authorized to demand financial information from Committee members in order to short-circuit any potential conflict-of-interest problems. The Committee also looked to its financial health. The

[1] For all of the precision of its standardization work, nomenclature was sometimes fuzzy. Thus, the Ad Hoc Committee was sometimes referenced as the Ad Hoc Council; the Symbol Selection Subcommittee also answered to the Symbol Standardization Subcommittee; and was it the "universal" or "uniform" product code?

GMA pledged an additional $85,000. Retailers organized such a successful fundraising effort led by Robert Wegman of Wegman's, an upstate New York grocery chain, that it would eventually raise almost a million dollars to fund the work of both the Ad Hoc Committee and its child, the Symbol Selection Subcommittee.

Establishing the Symbol Committee, the Ad Hoc called for a final recommendation within two years, or by April 1, 1973. In the opening phase, 1971, the Committee determined how to go about its work, develop guidelines, and get the word out. Data collection and testing in 1972 led to the ultimate phase — the actual selection of a symbol.

Minutes of the meetings of the Symbol Committee present a sense of urgency and clock watching. There would be regular checks on how close the Committee held to the timetable. "On schedule" was almost always the reply. The Ad Hoc continued to reenforce urgency by emphasizing the importance of the deadline.

The schedule was not just an internal guide. Companies began to plan against the promised symbol decision date of April 1, 1973. The publicized date of selection strongly reenforced adherence to the timetable. Committee members were among the real "comers" in the grocery industry. They did not accept failure and vowed that they would be successful.

Pressure to move expeditiously was paired with equal or greater insistence to do the job well. In selecting a code, the Ad Hoc Committee had deliberately avoided the elaborate procedures of the American National Standards Institute. They feared correctly that the ANSI process, while exquisitely fair, would so elongate their task that success would almost certainly be foreclosed. The Symbol Committee's "Operating Principles" made clear that they were very concerned that their decision not only be arrived at fairly, but be perceived as a fair process as well. Nonetheless, they too rejected

ANSI as a viable process, for to go the ANSI route would make it impossible to meet the deadline.

As the Committee began, it chose as its beginning hypothesis that a single symbolic representation of the U.P.C. code would be its ultimate recommendation two years later. Yet it agreed to consider seriously all possible alternatives and to reject nothing out of hand. The Committee also vowed not to put a cut-off time on data reception: "If a proposal is written on the back of an envelope and slipped under the door at midnight the night before our decision, we will consider it. Of course, it will receive only the consideration possible in the time available."

This oft-conveyed outlook generated a sense of participation in the process by a wide group of players. One onlooker observed that the Symbol Committee sought help "aggressively" from anyone who could help.

At its first meeting, in June 1971, the Committee identified its key tasks:

1. Develop alternate agreements to license and/or put selected symbol in public domain;
2. Visit key equipment companies
   - Modify guidelines as appropriate
   - Agree on relationships for store tests
   - Get agreement on license/public domain issue
3. Initiate and coordinate special studies:
   - Canners
   - Beverage Council
   - Label makers
   - Container manufacturers
4. Contact other affected groups, e.g.,
   - Printers
   - Scale manufacturers
5. Develop test parameters and format

6. Develop environmental guidelines
   - Overlay book for discoloration, etc.
   - Temperature, humidity
7. Interview and decide on special consultants, e.g.,
   - Optical
   - Magnetics
   - Printing
8. Develop press release

Even at the outset, the Committee recognized the conundrum: Retailers were unwilling to purchase scanning equipment until they could be assured the system worked *and* there were source-marked products to scan. But grocery manufacturers had little interest in placing symbols on packages unless someone was prepared to scan them. A coincidence at almost the precise moment of symbol selection broke this impasse. The Food and Drug Administration adopted regulations for nutritional labeling of food products in 1973. This meant that a significant percentage of food labels had to be redesigned. Since there were to be new labels anyway, the incremental cost to product manufacturers of adding the newly-selected U.P.C. symbol was minimal.

There were also legal concerns. The Committee was particularly sensitive that they not be accused of a conspiracy to force smaller competitors out of the marketplace. Legal research was commissioned to provide legal pathways for conducting the work of the Symbol Selection Subcommittee. McKinsey also launched economic studies designed to show the cost of source-marking product to be small enough that all manufacturers could afford to do it, and that the benefits of scanning would make it desirable and feasible for even the smaller retailer.

The publicity surrounding the Committee and its work persuaded some companies to begin thinking about the development of a symbol. One of the reasons symbol development had lagged was that the high technology companies had not seen a significant market for equipment in the grocery industry. Now, these companies began to assign serious talent and financial resources to the problem.

The awakening of the technology industry, however, raised the issue of confidentiality. To encourage invention and creativity, companies wanted to be sure the Committee would hold in confidence data revealed to it. In order to make an informed choice, the Symbol Committee needed to understand each proposal in detail. The ability to explain and defend its choice, however, was every bit as important as making the correct selection. This meant that the Committee could not agree to hold company data confidential.

Once again, the Committee opted for a pragmatic solution. While committee members refused to sign confidentiality agreements, they did agree to treat sensitive information with "appropriate discretion." Privately, they assured technology companies that such data would be made public only if it was absolutely necessary to explain, justify or defend the Committee's decision. In addition, Larry Russell, the Committee's consultant, was authorized to sign an assurance of confidentiality if it was the only feasible means of obtaining necessary information.

This transferred the dilemma to the companies. While concerned over the possible publication of secret information, they saw a prize well worth taking some risks for. Therefore, with greater or lesser reluctance, technology companies determined to accept the Committee's posture.[2]

Larry Russell and Tom Wilson initiated contacts with companies, responded to requests for information about the committee's process, and acted as provocateurs, initiating dialogues and posing questions that forced the submitter of

[2] IBM, apparently motivated by antitrust decrees, steadfastly refused to disclose data unless a confidentiality agreement was in place. Consequently, Larry Russell had the best knowledge of IBM's position.

data to rethink, refine, and expand its position. These meetings began over the summer and would continue, often augmented with all or part of the Committee, until a symbol was chosen.[3]

By the end of August 1971, McKinsey was able to report on some specific activities of equipment companies. Litton/Sweda was said to have a test of scanning equipment underway in Sweden, but the planned tests by Zellweger in the Migros stores in Switzerland had been delayed. According to Larry Russell, one company was experimenting with a holographic solution. It had little or no interest in the grocery industry, however, because of the costs involved. Another company was experimenting with voice scanning. The Kroger Company and RCA were already deeply involved in the exploration of front-end scanning. And now, Russell reported, meetings were scheduled with IBM and NCR.

Chairman Haberman, Eric Waldbaum, John Hayes, and Russell made a European swing in early September, visiting Zellweger, Anker, and Olivetti. Barry Franz met with Canadian and Mexican interests, and Creighton Peet had the task of contacting other affected groups.

The Committee also adopted several documents to guide its deliberations. Larry Russell presented "Retailer Guidelines on Relationships with Equipment Manufacturers," Bob Head offered "Environmental Guidelines" that a proposed symbol must meet, while Waldbaum, Hayes, and Russell advanced a "Symbol Evaluation Process."

The "Retailer Guidelines" were straightforward and even a bit simplistic. Retailer members of the Symbol Committee agreed to disclose plans for testing a proposed symbol but did not have to forego testing. Equipment companies could

[3] Folk wisdom as taught by Larry Russell: In a strange city, ask the hotel bellman for the location of the "second best restaurant in town." He is probably under orders to recommend a particular place. By asking for the second best, you get his honest opinion.

come to the Committee for assistance in finding testing partners. No member of the Committee would invest in a system requiring source-marked symbols prior to the Committee's decision, nor would a Committee member agree to a test with a company that would not release necessary information to the Committee.

The "Environmental Guidelines" set forth, in seventeen points, an unvarnished statement of the real world conditions in the supermarket and declared that a successful symbol would operate satisfactorily in the worst of those conditions. These included heat and humidity, power fluctuations, and scuffing or staining of the symbol. A successful symbol would resist tampering to change it to a lower-priced item. If a wand scanner was used, dropping the wand on a concrete floor could not render it inoperative.

The Committee viewed store testing of candidates symbols as important for two reasons. Many believed that this was the only way to obtain reliable data on the symbol's technical and economic viability. Credibility was equally important. The Committee was convinced that a symbol chosen by testing under laboratory conditions only would not persuade supermarket management teams to make enormous capital-investment decisions.

The "Symbol Evaluation Process" was designed to establish comparability of store test data. It insisted that data collection focus on "hard" savings and costs, and pay less attention to "soft" savings. The impact of scanning on checkout labor, checker training, price marking, cost of capital, symbol marking, and maintenance costs were among the items for which the Committee sought data.

The Committee also knew that it must decide on the basis of a total system, not just the efficacy of a scanner and a symbol. They began to initiate contacts with scale manufacturers, printers, producers of packaging material, and so forth.

U.P.C. work already completed and underway was starting to be recognized. The Supermarket Institute awarded its highly prized Albers Award to Ad Hoc Chairman Burt Gookin. The Committee's work in selecting a universal product code and spearheading the search for a symbolic representation of that code was a major reason.

The Symbol Committee not only had to demonstrate the economic and technical viability of a symbol, but it had to be satisfied that the symbol was legally feasible as well. The Symbol Committee built upon the relationship created by the Ad Hoc with the Federal Trade Commission.[4]

The FTC would be concerned with the committee's fairness in choosing a symbol. Legal troubles would arise if it appeared that an unfair competitive edge would be given someone by the symbol. Viewed by many as the devil's advocate, I attended virtually all of the Committee's meetings and was responsible for pointing to the dark side of contemplated actions. I was to stand up and refocus the discussion when the group was tempted to stray from the Operating Principles.

In addition, we kept the FTC fully informed of our progress, anticipating potential concerns, and responding to the Commission's questions. The Committee was concerned the FTC might see all of this activity as a plot by the big companies in the grocery industry to squeeze out the little. A lot of work went into demonstrating this was not the case. Counsel was directed to prepare the program's legal defense, focussing on its availability to all. McKinsey studied the economics of scanning in smaller volume stores.

The small store study was extraordinarily difficult to complete because McKinsey had a hard time gathering sufficient data. This proved to be the only item off schedule. Completed, the small store study was anticlimactic in every way. The study results supported the thesis that scanning would be economically feasible for smaller stores but was not as conclu-

[4] See Chapter 1.

sive as desired. However, the FTC seemed satisfied that the search for a symbol was not anticompetitive, and would not exclude others from the marketplace.

The Committee maintained contact with the FTC, keeping the Commission fully informed and responding promptly and thoroughly to any questions. The line of communication went to the FTC's General Counsel, but the five Commissioners raised numerous questions. The Committee, following the example of the Ad Hoc, did not seek a formal blessing. This could both take too long and result in an overly conservative opinion. Instead, the Symbol Committee relied successfully on its policy of openness and communication.

However, other threats of a legal challenge would arise over time, but none materialized. Two of the small proposers of symbols, Resources for Lawyers and Charecogn, expressed concern that the Committee's requirement that any proposed symbol be available publicly would penalize them unfairly. The concerns diminished after Larry Russell noted that only the symbol had to be publicly available; equipment to read it could be proprietary. But still the Committee worried over the disparity in resources available to symbol proposers. The Committee bent over backward to help and encourage small companies, but the depth of the resources available to the large companies was awesome, once they committed to the project.

The Symbol Committee also heard legal chains rattling by organizations who feared their members would be harmed by the selection of a symbol. The Paperboard Packaging Council, for example, feared symbol marking would require expensive changes in cardboard. The National Canners Association worried that a bottom-marking requirement would require stick-on labels for cans, increasing costs, and decreasing the appeal of cans as a packaging medium. Both organizations muttered about legal damage, but were calmed by assiduous courting and communication by the Committee, and especially Larry Russell.

The 1972 scanning test at a Kroger store in Kenwood, Ohio outside Cincinnati, involved the removal of prices from some of the items scanned. Test results showed little if any consumer resistance to price removal, and neither the Ad Hoc Committee nor the Symbol Committee spent much time on the subject. Ironically, item price removal later proved the most significant consumer concern with scanning.

It was a mindset issue. These grocery industry leaders simply could not imagine the consumer concern. If the distribution system were improved, benefits would, of course, redound to the consumer. Consumer groups proved more skeptical, as we shall see.[5] Ultimately, item price removal became the major issue.

The heart and soul of the Symbol Committee's work, however, was the testing program it encouraged, defined, and in some cases sponsored. Decisions on source marking and capital equipment purchases would not be made on theory alone. Real world experience was needed, and this could only be obtained in tests in actual supermarkets.

The Committee was a catalyst. It wanted supermarkets to negotiate with equipment companies and test equipment designed to fit their operating environments. It rejected the setting up of test stores by the Committee. Such a suggestion was also totally unrealistic financially. In late 1971, neither the Ad Hoc Committee nor the Symbol Committee could be confident of funding to complete the project.

No sooner was one dilemma resolved than another arose. The Committee held real world tests of candidate symbols to be an indispensable part of the decision framework. A successful test required both the symbol proposer and a retail partner who could test in stores. The best potential test partners were the retail members of the Symbol Committee.

[5] See Chapter 4.

Testing companies would also learn valuable things in arriving at a symbol decision.

On the other hand, it was unthinkable that the decision could be made by a group that included members with an actual or perceived conflict of interest. The Committee went for the best of both worlds. It created a separate class of non-decisionmaking consulting members for those retailers who were to test scanning systems. An existing committee member automatically became a consulting member when it agreed with an equipment company to test; other retail test stores were invited to join the Committee as consulting members. The first Symbol Committee meeting with consulting members was held in November 1971.

In November 1971, Larry Russell reported that McKinsey was developing a store test manual setting forth general guidelines for tests so that different tests could be compared. He asked the consulting members of the Committee to critique the manual. In addition, the Symbol Committee prepared a Memorandum of Understanding among the Committee, testing retailers, and their equipment company partners. Included in this document was the assurance that the symbol tested would be in the public domain or available on a reasonable license basis.

Not everyone agreed with the Committee in its commitment to store tests as a sine qua non of symbol selection. Both NCR and IBM argued vigorously, but fruitlessly, that store tests were not necessary. NCR campaigned constantly to convince the industry that the search for a symbol was premature at best and most likely totally unnecessary.

NCR (the modern name of the National Cash Register Company) was facing a number of challenges to its business, and the Symbol Selection Committee's work was one of the most serious. For years, the National Cash Register mechanical machines had had a virtual monopoly. By 1971, however, the mechanical cash register was becoming obsolete, and

NCR was facing serious competition from electronic cash register manufacturers.

NCR's own entry in the field of electronic registers was promising, and company officials were confident that the company's position would remain secure. The universal product code helped the marketing of electronic registers. However, NCR faced the possibility that a scannable symbol would render the electronic register obsolete before the development costs could be recovered, and sales of electronic registers would slow while customers waited for the development of scanners. NCR would be forced to expend massive resources to develop a scanner so that it could stay in the market.

NCR preferred to avoid all this, claiming that scanning would add little or nothing to the productivity gains that could be achieved by using electronic registers and a universal product code. Yet the company needed to stay close to this project. If the supermarkets moved to scanning, NCR had to be there. The grocery industry was a major source of NCR business. And so NCR participated throughout the process, but its participation was different from other companies'. It offered no candidate symbol. NCR criticized proposals and kept trying to persuade the committee to drop the project. Yet they were prepared to act once a symbol was selected, and this strategy paid off.[6]

IBM's antipathy to store tests had a different genesis. IBM was eager for the Symbol Committee to succeed and went out of its way to cooperate. The supermarket front end represented a major new market for IBM. They were excited by the opportunity to get a foothold. Nonetheless, they tried to convince the Symbol Committee that candidate symbols

[6] Indeed, after the adoption of the U.P.C. symbol, the first store to scan U.P.C. symbols was a Marsh Supermarket in Troy, Ohio, in 1974. This supermarket had NCR scanners.

could be evaluated adequately through laboratory tests and mathematical analysis.

IBM, by virtue of its position in other markets and past difficulties with the antitrust laws, operated under a number of consent decrees that prohibited it from disclosing a new product unless it intended to offer the product for sale. IBM had kept competitors at bay by strategic public disclosures of research that dampened enthusiasm for the competitor's products.

The Symbol Committee continued to reenforce the need for store tests. In early May 1972, the Committee was told that at least four store tests of candidate symbols were likely in 1972 and that some nontesting equipment companies (IBM) were serious contenders. On July 3, 1972, the first test monitored by the Committee started in a Kroger store in Kenwood, Ohio, a suburb of Cincinnati. This was a test of RCA equipment and utilized a bull's-eye-shaped symbol.[7]

The test not only showed productivity gains of 44 percent, but also demonstrated that product scanning worked in the supermarket. On August 10, 1972, the Committee saw the future when it visited the Kenwood store. In retrospect, the Kroger-RCA Kenwood test has even more significance. Data was limited from other store tests of candidate symbols because of logistical and other difficulties.

In lieu of store tests, IBM had proposed a program called PIDAS (Pictorial Information Dissector and Analyzer). This program would analyze printing requirements and capabilities by analyzing the letter "t." All package graphics contained the letter "t" in "Net Weight." IBM argued that a strict mathematical analysis of candidate symbols in light of printing capabilities would clearly demonstrate the symbol that should be selected.

[7] One part of this test involved the scanning of coupons. This would be enormously important later in defeating a patent-infringement suit against the UCC. See Chapter 12.

Although skeptical, the Symbol Committee agreed to a PIDAS program, but declined to retreat from its insistence on store tests as well. McKinsey, IBM, and the Graphic Arts Technical Foundation began the collection and analysis of data collected from supermarket shelves. In early January 1972, Barry Franz reported that, somewhat to his surprise, the PIDAS program might be more viable than it seemed at first.

PIDAS became a meaningful part of a testing program, as did laboratory tests of candidate symbols, at the Battelle Institute. That circular symbols would suffer greater distortion than rectangular ones was one PIDAS conclusion of significance. PIDAS also contributed to developing a print specification for the U.P.C. symbol.

Still, on November 12, 1971, Committee Chairman Haberman reported to the Ad Hoc Committee that store tests must be pressed because the symbol decision is more than an analytical problem. Laboratory tests and analyses would ensure that data is comparable. However, he noted the economic viability of a proposed symbol could be the most important measure of success. The cost estimates for source-symbol marking might well determine whether or not product manufacturers would affix a symbol at point of labeling.

The Symbol Committee was flexible, allowing companies to participate in development at different levels of commitment. The Committee also wanted those industries particularly affected by a segment of the test program to underwrite that segment. The Committee saw its responsibility to encourage maximum data from as many companies as possible. It recognized, however, that each company would submit what it chose, and the committee would decide based on the total amount of data it had.

At the Battelle Institute, in Columbus, Ohio, a full-scale supermarket checkstand was built to test the candidate symbols under controlled laboratory conditions. Seven companies participated in the laboratory tests. Battelle tested both perfect symbols and scuffed symbols. Recognition of a trade-off between print quality and the scanner was an important conclusion — a tighter symbol print specification could mean a simpler scanner. The lab tests were encouraging in other ways. They confirmed that scuffed symbols would scan, speeds of up to one hundred inches per second were acceptable, and that scanning could increase checker productivity by almost 40 percent.

On the other hand, performance in the laboratory did not always correlate perfectly with performance in the field, and each phase of the testing program contributed significantly to the committee's final decision.

The Committee also worried about its own makeup: an early agenda contained an item identified as "Caesar's wife." The issue was the appropriate relationship of Committee members, especially retail members, with companies involved in the testing of symbols and the equipment to read them. After two meetings, Vern Schatz, a Vice President of Jewel Food Stores, resigned because of interests he and his company had with the development of electronic cash registers.

In September 1971, the Ad Hoc authorized the Symbol Committee to create a two-tier membership scheme. Retailers testing equipment could become nonvoting members of the Committee, provided they agreed to disclose the results of their testing to the Committee. Including the testing companies as nonvoting members was considered important in validating methodology and building consensus.

This structure led to different kinds of meetings: open meetings, attended by anyone interested in the Committee's work; meetings attended by regular members and consulting members; and meetings for regular members only. Some meetings included all three. At open committee meetings, I would introduce the antitrust invocation by saying,

"Remember, there are three kinds of people here." It got to be a catch phrase, oft repeated by Committee members.

At least one company, Safeway, began as a regular member and in late 1972 became a consulting member as it reached an agreement to begin a test. Consulting members critiqued drafts of the store test manual to make sure that it made sense in the real world. The Committee would receive status reports as the test at a consulting member progressed.

In the end, seven companies submitted candidate symbols: Litton/Sweda, IBM, RCA, Scanner Inc., Singer, Pitney Bowes, and Charecogn. Six of the symbols had at least some store test data available for analysis, and IBM submitted a mathematical analysis of its proposal. Well over twenty companies had expressed interest in the project at some time during the life of the Committee, and nineteen had attended a meeting sponsored by the Ad Hoc in November 1971.[8]

A Swiss company, Zellweger, was the first to actually run a store test of a bottom-scanning laser in January 1972 with the Swiss grocery company Migros. Zellweger also announced its intention to test in the United States with Stop and Shop. On October 5, 1972, Zellweger (who had joined its efforts with those of Litton and Sweda) reported to the Symbol Committee that the Migros test had met its objectives.

Even the two major reluctant cooperators were viewed positively. Barry Franz learned that NCR continued to develop equipment that could be used for point-of-sale scanning, and had even applied for patents on some of its technology. As John Hayes put it in a report to the Ad Hoc Committee, "NCR continues to believe that the time is not

---

[8] Other companies included Threshhold Technology, Texas Instruments, Data Source Corp, NCR, Zellweger, E. M. Harwell & Co., TRW, Maddox Readers, Inc. ADS Anker Corp., Bonner & Moore, Fisher-Stevens, Recognition Equipment, Resources for Lawyers, Olivetti, Electronic Systems Design, and Quikount.

ripe for selection of a symbol. Nonetheless, they are cooperating with us."[9]

Indeed, a delegation from the Symbol Committee met with NCR scientists at a private NCR facility for a woodshedding on the Committee's understanding of the technical issues involved in scanning. In this way, the Committee learned where more information and study were required before any irreversible decisions were made.

Another Symbol Committee subgroup visited the IBM facility in Rochester, Minnesota. There they agreed to hold confidential whether or not the group had seen devices that demonstrated the readability of IBM's proposed symbol. They were able to say that IBM asserted that its symbol would be both slot scannable and wandable. Other companies would, in IBM's opinion, be able to develop equipment that could read the symbol.

The Committee, however, was concerned with IBM's totally mathematical and statistical evidence. The printability of the IBM symbol at the store level was a major concern. IBM also appeared to be creating its own interpretations of the Committee's guidelines. The absence of store test data made it all the more difficult to evaluate these concerns.

Nonetheless, the Committee agreed — with some trepidation — to circulate a white paper by IBM on its symbol. The Committee both withheld from endorsing the IBM proposal, and encouraged others to develop position papers to explain the choices inherent in their symbol proposals.

In early January 1973, the Symbol Committee met in San Francisco[10] to hear presentations from seven of the eight

[9] Minutes, Ad Hoc Committee, May 9, 1972, p. 2.

[10] On this trip, another of the Symbol Committee's legends was born. None of us were familiar with San Francisco, so Barry Franz undertook to be our guide. Following a street map, he led us up and down San Francisco's legendary hills to get from hotel to meeting room. We were exhausted upon reaching the McKinsey offices. Only later did we learn that we could have reached the meeting by walking *around* the hills rather than *over* them.

companies then considering symbol proposals. On January 4 and 5, the Committee sat in marathon sessions listening to progress reports from Dymo/Data General, IBM, RCA, Pitney-Bowes-Alpex, Singer, Scanner Inc., and Litton. On January 6, the Committee held an open session to provide a status report to all interested persons.

A religious cult claimed the world was going to end at 9 A.M. January 4, 1973. We were just beginning our sessions on the forty-eighth floor of the Bank of America building in the heart of San Francisco's financial district. If the world had ended, our last views would have been of one of the world's most beautiful sights, San Francisco Bay.

The principal discordant note to come out of the presentations was a threat by RCA to drop out of the market if the RCA "bull's eye" was not selected as a symbol. The Committee was eager to have many suppliers of scanning equipment. Competition would both improve the efficiency of scanners and lower the price of the equipment. RCA had been the pioneer in this field, moving into the market with research and equipment when no one else would. The Kroger Kenwood test of the RCA symbol was the source of much of the data. If RCA dropped out of the market, it could raise apprehensions throughout the grocery industry and damage the chances for success.

The Committee was relieved to learn in early March that RCA was encouraged by the results of both the store tests and tests of symbol printability. In the end, however, the bull's eye was not selected, and RCA did, in fact withdraw from the market. Whether this contributed to the relatively slow adoption of scanning remains unsettled.

Charecogn, a small, Massachusetts-based company, elected to report to consultants retained by the Committee at MIT instead of presenting at San Francisco. This special consideration typified the Committee's efforts to reject no proposal, and to be especially receptive to the creativity and proposals of smaller companies.

John Essarian, founder and President of Charecogn had developed a universal product coding and scanning system before the appointment of the Ad Hoc Committee. An executive at the National Association of Food Chains had suggested the project. Charecogn had developed a prototype that included a tabulator, a memory bank, a teletype, and an electronic scanner. Essarian demonstrated his machine to US Department of Agriculture officials and others, including the press, in the summer of 1970.

Both Charecogn and another small company, Resources for Lawyers, were acutely aware of the advantages the larger companies had. They made sure the Committee was aware of their unease and even muttered the dreaded words, "legal problems." The Committee, in turn, went out of its way to ensure that the smaller companies were given full consideration.

Proprietary rights was a most difficult issue. The Committee was adamant that the symbol ultimately selected had to be either in the public domain or available for reasonable royalties. This was essential if there were to be multiple suppliers of scanners and the resulting benefits from competition. Charecogn and Resources for Lawyers felt, however, that their proprietary material was all they had; if they could not reap the rewards of their inventions, why bother?

This led to delicate (and unresolved) discussions with the Committee over what was meant by "reasonable royalties." Fortunately, the Committee's work and its documentation convinced both companies that other proposals were stronger than theirs.

The whole issue of patents and proprietary rights seemed to be in a perpetual state of confusion and vague dissatisfaction. The main goal of the Committee was never in doubt. The symbol ultimately selected must be in the public domain, and it must be possible for multiple suppliers to develop equipment that could scan the symbol at a reasonable cost. If the optimal symbol was not in the public domain and the inventor was not willing to dedicate it to the public, the licensing terms must be reasonable enough to make the use of the symbol economically viable. A precise definition of "reasonable" never was given, and the Committee had great difficulty explaining how its policy would work.

Early on, a subcommittee was appointed to develop a standard approach to licensing. Working with outside patent counsel, we developed a "patent policy," given to anyone who expressed any interest in proposing a symbol. The policy went through innumerable revisions. Each equipment company in turn submitted a letter to the Committee stating its intentions with respect to patents and licenses.

In the end, we believed the U.P.C. symbol recommended by the Committee was in the public domain. However, two expensive patent lawsuits,[11] neither of which involved any of the proposers of a standard symbol, arose later. In hindsight, it would probably have been wise to apply for a patent on the symbol. If a patent had been issued, the Committee could have dedicated it to the public. If the symbol had been rejected as unpatentable, we would have had a ruling from the patent office to that effect.

Almost four hundred grocery manufacturers and symbol proposers met in October 1972 to discuss printing specifications. About the same time, eighty-five people met with the Symbol Committee to receive a status report and to ask questions of Committee members. In the midst of the project, Larry Russell was receiving over one hundred calls a day, and McKinsey had so many requests for meetings that some had to be turned down.

To manage the inquiries and to make sure that all public statements were consistent, the Symbol Committee decided that all questions, even if directed to an individual member of the Committee, were to be referred to either McKinsey or

[11] See Chapter 12.

Steve Brown. There was concern that at least one internal committee document had received a broader circulation. The Committee feared that this could undermine the success of the project.

Meanwhile, it appeared in May 1972 that grocery manufacturers were adopting the universal product code at a more rapid rate than retailers. The Supermarket Institute approached the Symbol Committee about building the 1973 SMI convention in May around the U.P.C. and the symbol. The Committee agreed to be a part of the program but warned SMI of its December checkpoint. The Committee might determine that a symbol was not feasible at that time.

In October 1972, Alan Haberman told the Ad Hoc that the March 30, 1973, deadline still appeared feasible. He cautioned that there was no "pad" left and any untoward event could make it impossible to meet the appointed time. The Committee reached out in many directions for help. In addition to the store tests and the Battelle laboratory tests, the Paperboard Packaging Council, the National Canners Association, the Graphic Arts Technical Foundation, the National Soft Drink Association, the US Brewers Association, and the National Flexible Packaging Association were all doing research related to symbol development. The Committee was also successful in persuading these associations to do the research at no cost to the Committee.

The store and lab tests would determine the technical feasibility of a U.P.C. symbol, but the Committee also had to determine the economic viability of a symbol. As a draft Harvard Business School case study put it, the core of the economic evaluation was the projection of the cost of symbol marking at the point of production. In 1971, the Ad Hoc had posited an annual cost of $28 million for placing the symbol on the natural bottom of packages. The Symbol Committee, however, estimated the cost to be in excess of $130 million, while source-marking in the least-cost position on the product package was still expected to be in the $65 to 70 million range.

Many product manufacturers cooperated fully with the Committee's request for data on source-marking costs; however, the data was biased on the high side. There was simply no incentive to guess low. The survey of estimated source-marking costs revealed that costs did not vary significantly by symbol proposal, although printing costs could be reduced if variable-size symbols were acceptable.

In October 1972, the Symbol Committee reported to the Ad Hoc Committee (with fingers crossed for good luck) that the cost of product scanners might be significantly lowered once equipment companies went into full production. Once again, Ad Hoc debated the question of which should come first: the installation of scanners in supermarkets or source marking of symbols on products. One event would clearly pace the other. The cost of a scanner was obviously much greater than the cost of changing a label. However, a manufacturer probably had many more products than a retailer had check-lanes. More important, the potential benefits of scanning were much larger and much more immediate for retailers.

As the results of the survey of projected source-marking costs began trickling in, the Committee's premonitions proved correct. Source-marking on the natural bottom, Larry Russell reported, might be ten times as costly as other locations for some products. Overall, the costs reported were nearly five times previous estimates.

Moreover, both the Paperboard Packaging Council and the National Flexible Packaging Association were telling the Committee that achieving the required tolerances for the printed symbol did not seem technically feasible, especially if the symbol was circular.

As 1973 began, the Symbol Committee had reached some significant conclusions. The cost of scanning equipment was estimated to be between $50,000 and $250,000 for a supermarket with $60,000 a week in sales. "Hard" savings — those that could be quantified — from scanning appeared to justify the investment required if 50 to 75 percent source symbol-marking could be attained. And the "soft savings," which the committee continued to not consider, were projected to be at least equal to the hard savings. McKinsey estimated savings in the $40 million plus range attributable to scanning by the mid-1970s. This could triple if there were at least 7000 scanning stores.

All of the estimates of savings attainable through the scanning of U.P.C. symbols were based on the hypothesis that items would no longer be price marked. Item price removal would later become a major issue with consumer groups and lawmakers. But the store test data was equivocal. The Kroger Kenwood store had gradually eliminated price-marking while simultaneously conducting heavy consumer education. While the overall consumer reaction to price removal was positive, the test was not conclusive. Ultimate consumer reaction was uncertain.

Most important, the Committee agreed that there was no economic justification for requiring symbol-marking on the bottom of cases and glass. This led to a position that symbols should be placed on the natural bottom if practicable, but other locations could be acceptable. This decision was critical in making source-marking palatable to manufacturers. Without it, progress would have been slowed dramatically. The project might even have failed. The Symbol Committee decided to give this decision full, immediate, and widespread publicity not only to allay fears, but to build support for the Committee's work.

Fritz Biermeier urged the Committee to act to reduce the costs of printing the symbol. The Committee concluded that a variety of symbol sizes would give the printers flexibility to enable them to minimize their costs. This factor rose in significance as the day of symbol decision neared.

A number of external events arose during the Committee's life. The most obvious externality was nearly thirty potential vendors of scanning equipment. The Committee and McKinsey had vigorously fanned tiny sparks of interest to the point where at least seven companies established a formal relationship with a grocery retailer, and it appeared that seven or eight companies would actually offer scanning equipment for sale.

Prior to the advent of the Symbol Committee, only RCA had expressed an interest in automating the front end of the supermarket. In the mid 1960s RCA had seen a substantial business opportunity if the cost of scanning equipment could be kept low enough. RCA sought to achieve this with a circular symbol.

The Committee recognized RCA's unique contribution, and as the disadvantages of a circular or semicircular symbol became more obvious, the Committee struggled, in vain, to persuade RCA to stay in the field. At the time, RCA's response seemed an attempt to intimidate the Committee into choosing the RCA bullseye. When the now ubiquitous oversquare symbol was chosen, RCA made good on its threat and abandoned the field.

NCR also continued its efforts to short-circuit the Committee's work by suggesting the Committee turn its work over to the National Bureau of Standards or the American National Standards Institute to finish the job. Alan Haberman politely thanked NCR, but said the Committee would finish what it had started.

As the grocery industry became aware of the Committee's work, various segments began to act to protect their own interests. In the fall of 1971, for example, the National Canners Association[12] held a seminar on the application of symbols to bottles, cans, and glass. Bill Galt reported to the

---

[12] Now the National Food Processors Association.

Committee that the canners were very concerned with a potential requirement for the application of a pressure-sensitive label bearing a symbol to the can bottom. It bore both a high cost and error potential. Canners (and the National Soft Drink Association) argued vigorously for symbol placement on the natural label.

The Distilled Spirits Institute and the US Brewers Association were concerned because the Distilled Spirits Institute was contemplating adopting for its members a twenty-one-digit product code that would be incompatible with the U.P.C.

The relationship between the grocery industry and other branches of retailing often sputtered and misfired. When Larry Russell proposed an overture to the National Retail Merchants Association[13] ("NRMA") at a Symbol Committee meeting in August 1971, he was told to stick to the grocery industry. Nine months later, however, the Ad Hoc Committee asked Burt Gookin and Tom Wilson to contact the NRMA. NRMA was also attempting to establish a product-identification code and symbol but was not making any significant progress. Major retailers had been purchasing incompatible systems. In addition, NRMA had decided to follow the ANSI procedures in establishing its standard symbol, and this meant it would take many years.

Accordingly, the NRMA went its own way. The Ad Hoc asked McKinsey to open unofficial communications with general merchandise retailers, who also sold their goods over high volume checkstands.

As discussed earlier, Vern Schatz of Jewel Tea had been one of the original members of the Symbol Committee, but had resigned almost immediately over conflict-of-interest issues. During 1972, Jewel raised a number of issues to challenge the wisdom of the Committee's work.

On March 14, 1972, Tom Wilson told the Ad Hoc

[13] Now the National Retail Federation.

Committee that Jewel believed the incremental advantages of scanners over electronic registers (in which Jewel had a significant investment) were insufficient to justify a symbol at this time. Wilson added that McKinsey was not persuaded by the Jewel contentions.

At the direction of the Ad Hoc, Wilson prepared a tactful, but forceful, response to Don Perkins, President of the Jewel Companies. In addition to the assertion that electronic registers would provide a better return than scanners, Jewel contended that "a decision at this point in time runs the risk of freezing the industry on a solution that would be likely to be obsolete within a relatively short period of time."[14] Jewel also maintained adopting a U.P.C., and source-symbol marking and automatic reading within a narrow time frame would exceed the industry's "ability to accomplish fundamental change."[15] Finally, Jewel was concerned at the significant legal risk created by the endeavor.

The response acknowledged Jewel's concerns and praised the company for the responsible way in which the issues were brought before the Ad Hoc Committee. It then rebutted each of the concerns.

> We all recognize that technological innovation will inevitably continue. The question is simply, how long should the grocery industry wait? ... [W]e believe that the onus should be on you to specify what we should wait for, how long we should wait, and why.[16]

The letter concluded with a commitment to testing and evaluation. If the data proved the validity of any of Jewel's arguments, there would be no symbol decision.

Shortly after this exchange with Jewel, Larry Russell told the Symbol Committee that the company was more suppor-

[14] Letter from T. Wilson to D. Perkins, May 3, 1972, p. 1.
[15] Ibid.
[16] Id at p 4.

tive of the effort than it had been. Uncharacteristically, Russell was guilty of wishful thinking. At the peak of the Committee's development work, Jewel wrote NAFC and SMI, the trade associations of grocery retailers, raising seven concerns about the work:

1. Jewel argued that the ten-digit code would not stand the test of time;
2. Manual entry of the code at point-of-sale would not be a reasonable alternative;
3. The lack of compatibility with other codes would prove a significant weakness;
4. The feasibility of increasing the size of the code at a later date is doubtful;
5. The logic of the ten-digit code is based upon technology which is no longer relevant;
6. Basing a symbol decision on 1970 and 1971 technology means that the code and symbol will soon be obsolete; and
7. The total industry estimates of potential savings should be reconsidered.

Jewel urged the Symbol Committee to stop its work while the industry coalesced around a twelve-or-more-digit, structured code. Future efforts should be spearheaded by a group without a financial stake in the outcome, such as the President's Commission on Productivity. Alan Haberman, whose probing, professorial style did little to conceal the passion he brought to the project, responded calmly. "No good effort has ever come to fruition without substantial opposition," he told the Symbol Committee. They should be prepared for more challenges.

Two other external events spurred the Symbol Committee to complete its mission. Eight months after its creation, manufacturers representing more than 20 percent of retail sales volume had joined the Uniform Grocery Product Code

Council and had been assigned U.P.C. numbers. Then in March 1973, the Food and Drug Administration announced new regulations regarding the labeling of foods that made nutritional claims. A great many processed foods would be required to change their labels. If the Symbol Committee could complete its work on schedule, there would be a window of opportunity in which manufacturers could add a symbol to the package at a minimal cost.

Cost was a significant factor. As data came in from the various tests, it became clear that scanners would operate most efficiently if the symbol appeared on the natural bottom of the package. For some types of packaging, however, the cost of source-symbol marking this way would be so high that many product manufacturers would refuse to do it.

These and other decision trade-offs occupied the Committee in the beginning months of 1973 as intense communication between the Committee, its consultant, and symbol proposers continued. Symbol proposers amended their submissions as the brainstorming process created notions of hybrid solutions — some promising, some not.

By December 1972, the Symbol Committee was to advise the Ad Hoc as to whether it was economically, technically, and legally feasible to select a machine-readable version of the U.P.C. A "yes" would mean a commitment that a symbol recommendation would come next.

The Committee needed to weigh its choices carefully against criteria. Larry Russell urged that a positive macroeconomic impact on the grocery industry was indispensable. In addition, the symbol should be technically feasible today, be scannable on a variety of scanners, and have at least four number sets available to provide an adequate capacity for the system. These were "must have" features. There were also some "nice to have," such as the ability of the symbol to be read by a wand.

As the December checkpoint approached, Larry Russell

told the committee the task was simple, "measure the store-level savings, . . . examine the source-marking costs, . . . then pick a symbol."[17] It was, of course, far more complex. For example, a variable-size symbol would mean lower printing costs but higher equipment costs. The Symbol Committee was introducing the concept of quantitative measurement of print quality. To reduce the anxiety of printers, who feared being held to unmeetable standards, the Committee developed a printability gauge. This symbol tool was a "yes/no" determinant for printers to use.

The Committee began to explore the possibility of a hybrid symbol comprised of elements from different proposals. As the decision date approached, the Committee held a three-day session in Los Angeles designed to bring all of the data together. This was the last meeting at which consulting members and outsiders would be present. At this meeting, the Committee agreed for the final time to proceed to the ultimate task of selecting a symbol. Prodded by Larry Russell, they agreed that the alternatives could be narrowed, using a "McKinsey grid," so that the final choice would be rational.

The most significant decision made in Los Angeles was the adoption of this resolution:

> Whereas there has been great concern throughout the grocery and equipment industries over the location of a symbol on packages and the problems associated with the location of the symbol;
> Therefore, be it resolved that the Symbol Standardization Subcommittee [sic] intends to recommend to the Ad Hoc Committee that the guidelines for symbol application shall provide for no requirement that the symbol be located on the bottoms of cans, glass, plastic bottles, milk cartons and the like, and
> Be it further resolved that in view of the industry

[17] Minutes, Symbol Standardization Committee, Nov. 14, 1972, p. 1.

concern, this determination be publicized as quickly as possible and in advance of the symbol decision.

The Symbol Committee did not grasp the ironic contrast between the new frontiers of their work and their quarters in Los Angeles. The Committee met in the Biltmore, an old and somewhat dilapidated hotel in downtown, decaying Los Angeles.

By meeting's end, the group realized they sought a solution with the capability of handling multiple number sets and a varying number of digits. There were four symbol geometries to choose from: a wraparound bar code; a square bar code; a two-field bar code; and an omnidirectional code. A circular symbol would provide the best chance for quick implementation by scanner manufacturers, but a circular symbol would be the most difficult to print.

Before a final decision, Alan Haberman insisted on one more step. He had always been concerned that the Committee would misinterpret the future by selecting a symbol that would quickly be rendered obsolete. To avoid such a catastrophe, Haberman went to Jerome Wiesner at the Massachusetts Institute of Technology who put together a multidiscipline team under the direction of Murray Eden both to look over the Committee's shoulder and to brainstorm about what might happen in the future.

Eden and his team had concerns about all of the symbol proposals but never suggested the project be halted or even radically re-oriented. MIT did have one suggestion, which the Committee was quick to incorporate — they urged that the human-readable U.P.C. number be printed on the package in a specific type font, and recommended OCR-B for this purpose. This would, in Eden's view, make it possible for the symbol to fade away when technology made it unnecessary.

The Symbol Selection Subcommittee was acutely aware of the responsibility entrusted to it, and of the potential for change that could come from its activities. As someone put it at the time, it is like the introduction of the computer to business; everyone knew it was significant, but no one could foresee the varied applications of computers which later developed.

The Committee members prepared for the final decision-making meeting on March 29 and 30 with both anticipation and anxiety. The Committee had been talking for months about going away to an isolated location for this meeting and being free of outside distractions or attempts to pressure a particular solution. It had even become an inside joke. Alan Haberman said he knew a beer distributor who had a yacht harbored in Florida. The Committee talked of sailing into the Caribbean to make their decision on a symbol recommendation, but in the end, met at the McKinsey offices on Park Avenue in New York City, three blocks from Grand Central Station.

The final meetings opened with a review of the legal framework in which the decision should be made. This included a recital of those things — boycotts, conspiracies, and so forth — that would violate the antitrust laws. This was followed by a brief discussion of technical questions, reports on individual briefing sessions with equipment companies, and a review of the final data from the laboratory tests conducted by the Battelle Institute. There were no surprises.

Russell and Wilson then summarized McKinsey's input. The savings in stores doing at least $60,000 a week appeared firm, a requirement of bottom symbol-marking made the costs prohibitive, and a variable-size symbol would dramatically reduce the costs of printing the symbol. Then each symbol was reviewed and discussed in detail.

When the Committee reconvened on Friday March 30, they quickly achieved a consensus that the fundamental choice was between the bull's eye symbol proposed by RCA and Litton, and the oversquare proposal of IBM.[18] In

---

[18] Readers interested in a nontechnical description of the IBM symbol and its history should read Alan Green, "Big Brother is Scanning You" *Regardies* (Dec. 1990).

comparing these two, most factors were a wash; error detection capability and directional effects of printing favored the square symbol, while cost and the ability of multiple technologies to scan favored the bullseye.

Alan Haberman then startled the group with an unusual question. He wanted to take a straw vote, but he did not wish Committee members to reveal which proposal they favored. Rather, he wanted to know how sure they were of the vote they would cast. The poll revealed that the entire committee had over 90 percent confidence in their decision.

Thus it was that at 1:10 P.M. on Friday March 30, 1973, the Symbol Selection Committee cast its first and only vote for a U.P.C. symbol. It was emphasized that votes could be cast for any of the symbols proposed or any hybrid. Unanimously, the Committee voted for what the minutes of the meeting call the "IBM/Committee Final Proposal." This was described as

> a shorthand way of describing a solution developed by the Committee in conjunction with IBM's technical staff. Although the geometry parallels that of the IBM proposal, all other aspects differ. This proposal combines the experience of the Symbol Standardization Subcommittee, the work of other manufacturers, and IBM's expertise. This solution had not been made publicly available and had been reviewed only by the Committee.[19]

Murray Eden, the Committee's MIT consultant, noted this was the first enterprise with which he had been associated in which an industry group chose a cost for itself in order to benefit the economy as a whole.

Pleased as it was with this praise and satisfied that the

An IBM engineer, Joe Woodland, had patented the basic idea for a linear bar code in 1949 while still a student. Another IBMer, George Lauer, was one of those primarily responsible for refining the idea for use by supermarkets.

[19] Minutes, Symbol Standardization Committee, Mar. 30, 1973, p. 5.

decision was correct, the Committee nonetheless recognized that its decision would probably be misunderstood and second guessed. None of the proposed symbols had been ideal, and by opting for the oversquare symbol instead of the bullseye, the Committee may have dramatically slowed the pace of implementation.

On this subdued note, at 2:45 P.M. the fourteenth and next-to-the-last meeting of the Symbol Selection Subcommittee adjourned with a commitment by all to absolute silence on the decision until the meeting of the Ad Hoc Committee on Tuesday, April 3.

On that Tuesday morning, every member of the Ad Hoc Committee and most of the members of the Symbol Selection Subcommittee gathered at the McKinsey offices. The Symbol Committee's recommendation was presented by Tom Wilson and Larry Russell. The following discussions focussed heavily on the return on investment that could be expected at various levels of symbol implementation.

The Symbol Committee emphasized that a symbol was economically, technically, and legally feasible. The heavy cost to product manufacturers of printing the symbol would be substantially ameliorated because of the ability to vary the symbol's size. Through Larry Russell, the Committee noted if its recommendation were accepted, a deadline of May 1 should be set for the development of printing specifications.

As I had done with the Symbol Committee, I proceeded to provide the Ad Hoc the legal framework within which it should make its decision. The Committee began its discussions by focussing on some of the unknowns surrounding its decision.

They were concerned about whether the National Bureau of Standards or the National Retail Merchants Association would publicly attack the standard grocery industry symbol. The federal government was considering regulations covering laser-emitting devices, and many of the planned symbol scanners used lasers as a light source. Would the regulations foreclose the implementation of scanning? Additionally, just how much label space would the FDA's nutrition labeling regulations take; would there be enough room for a U.P.C. symbol? And, the most significant imponderable of all, would retailers make the enormous capital investment required to purchase scanning systems?

Slightly discomfited by the realization that, like all decisions, the symbol choice would be made on imperfect information, the Ad Hoc prepared to listen to one last presentation by the symbol proposers. Six companies took advantage of the offer, and each was given about thirty minutes before the Committee's horseshoe table to make one last plea for its proposal. Companies used that time variously. Litton/Zellweger emphasized that it would be a good sport; regardless of which symbol was selected, Litton intended to produce equipment to scan it. This was important and welcome news for it guaranteed multiple suppliers.

NCR continued to bad-mouth the project, stressing their serious reservations about symbol standardization. Nonetheless, NCR asserted that if there was a market for scanning equipment, NCR would be there.

RCA, by contrast, maintained its rather churlish attitude. Its decisions for the future would depend on whether the Committee chose its symbol. RCA did, at least, concede that the symbol-selection process had been fair. Eager to keep RCA as a supplier of equipment, and aware of the impending disappointment, the Ad Hoc effusively praised RCA for its pioneering efforts in the development of a symbol.[20]

In their time, both Pitney-Bowes-Alpex and Singer assured the Committee that they too intended to be in the

---

[20] The Committee's blandishments did not succeed. True to its word, RCA left the field shortly after the symbol decision was announced.

market,[21] whatever the ultimate symbol was. As IBM's presentation unfolded, Eric Waldbaum turned to me and whispered, "My God, they have an entire system developed, and we didn't know anything about it." At one point, the IBM spokesman reached into his back pocket and pulled out a silicone wafer about the size of a silver dollar. This wafer, he said, contains all the computing power necessary to run a checkout system. The IBM explication was a tour de force and did much to buttress the Ad Hoc for the decision it was about to make.

And now it was decision time. There were no more stops on the road that had started in August 1970 at the O'Hare Inn. After nearly three years of effort, the Ad Hoc Committee adopted a resolution formally endorsing the recommendation of the Symbol Selection Subcommittee, thanking them for their effort, and discharging them.

The Committee held a press conference to announce the decision to the world. Suddenly there was a U.P.C. symbol. A new era had begun.

---

[21] Pitney Bowes at least was true to its word, although it did not stay in the marketplace long. On the wall in my office is a plaque bearing a U.P.C. symbol used in the first public demonstration of a U.P.C. scanner, made by Pitney Bowes. The demonstration was at the SMI convention in Dallas on May 8, 1973.

3
UGPIC

The Ad Hoc Committee picked the Uniform Grocery Product Identification Code (UGPIC), but it was not structured to deal with the code's ongoing administration. Accordingly, the Ad Hoc formed a Code Management Subcommittee composed of four of the technical assistants to Ad Hoc Committee members to make a recommendation.

On March 31, 1971, the Subcommittee met for the first time. Since other coding systems had a central coding authority, the committee assumed that one would also be required for the U.P.C. The initial concern was that the cost of administering an industrywide code would be so high that it would prevent the implementation of the Ad Hoc's recommended code.

The first decision by the group made all the subsequent developments possible. Bob Stringer (General Foods), Jack Strubbe (Kroger), Bob Koenig (Super Valu), and Carroll Satterfield (Fairmont Foods) concluded that a central code registry would not be required. A central body to assign the manufacturer's prefix was all that would be needed. In their estimation, this could eliminate 90 percent of the cost of administration.

At that March 31 meeting, the Code Management Committee envisaged the following as the functions of a central code authority: (1) to develop policies for the assignment of manufacturers' prefixes and to assign them; (2) to set general rules for code assignment; and possibly (3) to publish a directory of manufacturers' prefixes. By limiting activities to those associated with the prefix, security problems associated with new items, inherent in central code management, could be avoided. At that first meeting, the group assumed that the prefix could be sold at $10 to $100 plus an annual assessment.

The Committee concluded that to handle these functions, a governing board and an operating service bureau under contract would be needed. In June, they asked potential service bureaus to submit proposals. Four groups expressed an interest, Dun & Bradstreet, Standard & Poors, Distribution Number Bank (DNB), and a group headed by Dave Hackman and Wally Flint, whose master's thesis had been a precursor of the U.P.C. As September began, the group gathered at the McKinsey offices in New York City to receive the bidders' presentations.

Even as they listened to proposals, the Committee remained concerned over how to finance the ongoing effort. It was obvious as they listened to three proposals (due to a scheduling mishap, Standard & Poors never appeared) that only Flint and Hackman were interested in the project for code management alone. The others saw U.P.C. administration as a means of entry into a new market for their other services.

The Committee was troubled by two aspects of the submissions: none was complete, all would have to be supplemented; and the projected annual cost ranged widely among the bidders — from DNB's low six-figure bid to Dun & Bradstreet's stupefying bid of $6 million per year to administer the U.P.C. None of the proposers had any interest in investing their own money in the operation, and the cost estimates were particularly difficult to pin down because of the requirement of maintaining an inquiry service.

O'Hare Airport was the site of the Code Management Committee's decision-making meeting on October 27, 1971. There were three agenda items: (1) a recommendation of a company to handle the code management function; (2) development of a corporate structure to contract with and supervise the winning company; and (3) a discussion of how to fund the on-going project.

Stringer, Strubbe and company discussed each bidder in turn. Distribution Number Bank quickly became the leading contender, not so much because of the inherent strength of its proposal, but because all of the other bidders had more powerful negatives. Standard & Poor's unresponsiveness did them in, while Dun & Bradstreet's costs were totally unacceptable. Wally Flint and Dave Hackman, while knowledgeable, simply lacked the management and resources to do the job.

As noted, the Committee had concluded that costs could be dramatically curbed by limiting the management function to the administration of the manufacturer prefix only. This left DNB. Although concerned over the depth of DNB's financing as a creation of the National Association of Wholesale Distributors, on balance, they believed DNB could be recommended to the Ad Hoc Committee with a clear conscience.

Turning then to the structure of the governing board, the committee refined its earlier suggestion of a fifteen-member board of directors composed of six grocery manufacturers, six grocery distributors, a "consumer," an academic, and a Canadian. Ralph Nader and the consumer movement were at the height of their powers at this time, and Jack Strubbe — of Kroger — was more familiar with consumerism than he really wanted to be. Strubbe was determined that Nader would never get control of this organization. Accordingly, he proposed a membership corporation with a twenty-one-member board composed of users, not trade association executives.

GMA would designate six board members, NAFC two, SMI two, and NARGUS, NAWGA, and CFDA one each. Three more grocery manufacturers and two distributors would be elected by the members at large. In addition, the board would elect a representative from the computer equipment industry, an academic, and an international representative. The position of chairman would alternate between a grocery manufacturer and a grocery retailer. With minor modifications, this was the structure ultimately adopted. Strubbe had one other contribution to the structure. He believed it sounded better to have a Board of Governors than a board of directors, and so it was.

The subject of funding, however, confounded them. No one could imagine how to generate an adequate ongoing revenue stream. All agreed that it should cost something to become part of the system, but the number of potential users seemed limited, and the need for service would go on indefinitely. It was unclear how much could be charged a participant or if there were any money-making services that could be provided to ease the financial burden.

The Code Management Committee realized, however, that it could not walk away from the task. The initial Board of Governors, for the sake of continuity, would have to be comprised of the Committee members.

The Code Management group's recommendations were accepted by the Ad Hoc Committee two days before Thanksgiving, 1971. The functions of the unnamed ongoing organization would be to assign numbers, coordinate with other agencies, provide an inquiry service, offer a self-financing directory of numbers, and, perhaps, advise companies on how to use the U.P.C.

At this meeting, the Ad Hoc accepted an offer from *Progressive Grocer* magazine to prepare a prospectus on fundraising to keep the Ad Hoc effort going. If there was to be anything for the Code Committee to manage, acceptance of the U.P.C. had to broaden. The McKinsey mavens, Wilson and Russell, implored the members of the Ad Hoc to make more speeches and appearances to their brethren on behalf of the U.P.C.

"About the Universal Product Code," a brochure explaining and promoting the U.P.C. was also produced by McKinsey for the Ad Hoc Committee. It quoted McKinsey's economic studies showing that checkout automation could provide retailers with a saving of 1.0 to 1.5 percent of pretax sales. These savings were essentially based on the hard quantifiable productivity savings. The brochure also tantalized retailers with suggestions of other, less quantifiable, but no less real, soft savings: data, "shrink" identification, labor scheduling, control over direct delivered items, space allocations, and the ability to make instant price changes.[1]

The importance of source-marking was highlighted. The cost of source-marking was estimated at 33 cents per thousand, while in-store labeling would cost $5.00 per thousand. The Ad Hoc's efforts paid off; by the end of 1975, 80 percent of all grocery packages were source-symbol marked.

Once the Ad Hoc approved the Code Committee's proposal on an ongoing organization, structured as suggested by Jack Strubbe, I was instructed to make it happen. As the necessary papers were being drafted, an associate who was doing the actual work asked me, "What is the name of the organization supposed to be?" Notwithstanding all the planning and all the work that had gone into this project, no one had ever asked this question before. I did not want to admit, either to the client or the associate, that I had forgotten to ask a question. The committees had often referred to a "uniform grocery product identification code" or "UGPIC," so I im-

---

[1] Twenty years later, the studies have been vindicated. Retailers are taking advantage of each of these benefits.

mediately responded, "Why, the 'Uniform Grocery Product Code Council,' of course." And so it was.[2]

By mid-December 1971, we had created a Delaware non-stock membership corporation. There had been brief discussions about seeking tax-exempt status, but the thought had been quickly dismissed. The tax specialists at my firm were emphatic that UGPIC would not qualify for tax-exempt status. Besides, everyone was convinced that there would be no surplus income to be taxed. Indeed, the real trick was going to be finding sufficient income to keep the project going. No one thought the trade associations would subsidize it indefinitely. It was conceivable, however, that at some point in the future, UGPIC's tasks would become so routine that the organization could be folded into one of the grocery industry associations and numbers assigned and maintained by a secretary.

The first meeting of the UGPIC Board of Governors on January 19, 1972, was momentous only because it was first. An airport conference room at O'Hare was the scene. Only the Code Management Committee[3] who comprised the initial Board of Governors, and McKinsey and Distribution Number Bank representatives were in attendance. Thwarted in his attempt to create a company to administer the U.P.C., Wally Flint had joined DNB, and was present at this first meeting.

Perhaps the most significant action taken was the ratification of a three-month contract with DNB for $134,610. The catch was that the contract was ratified to become effective "at such time as the Board of Governors has the cash or promises of cash." The Board duly observed that the costs of symbol administration (should there be a U.P.C. symbol)

[2] Tom Wilson always called the U.P.C. the Universal Product Code, and that stuck. Thus, the Uniform Grocery Product Code Council administered the Universal Product Code.

[3] The minutes of the first two Board meetings are captioned, "Minutes of the Meeting of the Code Management Subcommittee and Board of Governors."

would almost certainly fall to UGPIC. It was also noted that the administrative guidelines for the use of the U.P.C. were still being reviewed by a task force of company people put together by McKinsey, but UGPIC would have to give them ultimate approval.

Store tests using the new code were liable to be neither a total success nor a complete failure. This ambiguity could slow the timetable for U.P.C. adoption as well as for memberships in UGPIC. To speed up matters, Larry Russell was asked to develop and publicize an analysis of the savings obtainable from the adoption of a code alone.

Two months later, in March, the Board heard from its contract administrator how it planned to issue numbers. For a project born to take advantage of the high tech computer age, it was a surprisingly old-fashioned, simple system. There would be a set of 100,000 tear-off numbers. When a manufacturer ID number was issued, DNB would remove the appropriate number from the set and affix it to the membership certificate, a copy of which would be retained for the Council's records. The assignment would be effective upon the mailing of the membership certificate.

There was a minor problem. DNB wanted to solicit all members of the grocery industry trade associations to become UGPIC members. The trade associations adamantly refused to make their lists available to UGPIC or any third-party organization. Because of their intimate involvement and support of the project, however, they did offer to mail UGPIC materials to their members.

This was completed on April 17, 1972. Numbers would start being assigned on May 15. In addition, Kroger, Jack Strubbe's company, wrote to all of its suppliers urging adoption of the U.P.C. and membership in UGPIC.

These initial Board meetings were full of discussions about "rules of the road," which UGPIC had to establish for DNB to follow. One such decision was to offer three-year memberships for the period January 1, 1972, to December 31, 1974, rather than a sliding three-year period based upon the date of joining. At this time, all assumed that members would be required to rejoin at the end of the period. There was considerable fear, however, that once a company had its U.P.C. number, it would have neither incentive nor need to remain a member and "re-up."

By early December 1972, things had gone well enough that Larry Russell could report to the Ad Hoc Committee that the code had in effect been implemented in the grocery industry. Over one hundred manufacturers and eighty-four retailers had joined UGPIC (which now viewed itself as the ultimate successor to the Ad Hoc Committee). Half of the members of the GMA Administrative Systems Committee, representing 70 percent of the product movement, indicated they would have the U.P.C. in use by the middle of 1973.

As soon as the Ad Hoc Committee made its decision on a U.P.C. symbol, the UGPIC Board of Governors was informed, and began plans for the implementation of symbol adminis- tration. At that April 1973 meeting the Board contemplated a three-phase implementation plan: an initial intense phase, expected to last about three months, with a period of heavy activity to follow for the remainder of the year. Around the beginning of 1974, the routine ongoing administration would begin.

DNB was directed to distribute the Ad Hoc press release to all UGPIC members. The Board also ordered the symbol specifications and symbol location guidelines completed by April 20. Presentations would be made at no cost to the sponsoring trade associations. The Board deferred a decision on whether an individual company would have to pay for a presentation.

While UGPIC was beginning its work of administering the U.P.C. code and symbol, its Board members and their ad- visers were simultaneously relating to a wide variety of other organizations. Thus, for example, there was ongoing dialogue with the Federal Trade Commission, where the good will built up by the Ad Hoc Committee was nurtured by the Board of Governors. At the same time, Larry Russell was reporting that the National Retail Merchants Association, engaged in a parallel project for the department stores, had taken its effort to the National Bureau of Standards (NBS), where it sat — unmoving — on dead center. He further reported that NBS wanted to make the grocery industry a part of the effort. (The Ad Hoc Committee and the Board of Governors agreed that this was a terrible idea.) In addition, a Nixon Administration creation, the Commission on Productivity, was reported to be recommending that the Department of Agriculture provide funds for field tests of the U.P.C.

McKinsey had identified potential conflict with three other codes. By working with the Food and Drug Administration and the drug industry, the U.P.C. was able to subsume the National Drug Code (NDC) and the National Health Related Items Code (NHRIC). This was done by assigning the drug industry one of the U.P.C.'s ten-number systems, number system 3. By using the "3" as a prefix, both the NDC and the NHRIC became compatible with the U.P.C.

Nonetheless, the early days of the Code Council were marked by lengthy discussions with drug industry representatives who required considerable stroking to ameliorate feelings that the grocery industry was treating them as second-class citizens. The involvement of Gavin MacBain, CEO, and Fred Butler, Vice President of Bristol Myers, as members of the Ad Hoc Committee proved invaluable. Butler, in particular, served as a liaison between the UGPCC and the drug industry.

The NRMA, as noted above, was also going down a different path. So too was the distilled spirits industry. NRMA also insisted upon a wandable symbol. Unfortunately, there did not appear to be any quick-fix solution to the lack of compatibility with these industries.

General merchandise firms were caught between the UGPCC and the NRMA. Many were applying for membership and obtaining U.P.C. numbers. The Council concluded that it should be pursuing all companies who marketed through outlets with high-velocity checkstands, whether they were food or general merchandise companies. In 1973, the Executive Committee instructed Distribution Number Bank to begin "missionary work" with other industries to persuade them to adopt the U.P.C. or at least coding systems that were compatible.

By May 1974, DNB reported that the Distilled Spirits Institute had developed a compatible code. At the same meeting, Guideline 18, establishing compatibility with the National Drug Code and the National Health Related Items Code was adopted, and Jack Strubbe reported that he had met with the NRMA.

One year after the U.P.C. symbol was selected, the first store scanning product bearing U.P.C. symbols opened on June 26, 1974. It was a Marsh's Supermarket in Troy, Ohio, utilizing NCR scanners. Obviously, NCR, having lost its attempt to persuade the Committee that a symbol was premature, had moved aggressively to protect its interests in grocery store checkouts.

The opening of the Marsh Store is very important from a historical perspective. By no means, however, did it signify the success of the U.P.C. Several years would pass before it became obvious that scanning would become widespread. In the interim, a number of doubters publicly proclaimed the failure of the U.P.C.

In part, this skepticism arose from the perceived slow growth of the Code Council. However, no one had a good idea of what that growth should be. After six months, there were one hundred members, a year later there were five hundred. By January 31, 1974, there were one thousand members and at the end of five years there were six thousand companies on the membership rolls.

After twenty-five years, the UCC had almost 200,000 members, a phenomenal success by any standard. It wasn't so clear in 1974 and 1975, however.

Notwithstanding the extension in 1974 of the U.P.C. to nongrocery companies selling product through high-volume checkstands such as drug and discount stores, Tom Wilson and McKinsey, based on careful research and analysis, continued to insist that the *maximum* possible universe of Code Council members was in the five to six thousand range. In July 1975, Don Martin of DCI told the Board of Governors that the rate of membership applications had peaked. A year later, after noting that all the major distillers had joined, Wilson again warned the Board that we were pressing the upper limits of membership.[4]

Notwithstanding moments of doubt and a skeptical press, the Board of Governors pressed on with efforts to structure a permanent organization to sustain the U.P.C. Among the issues the Board saw as critical was enlarging the Board to its full membership. The Board also had to establish guidelines for DCI to follow in the administration of the code. Even though there was no symbol, preparation for symbol administration had to begin.

Chairman Bob Stringer agreed to approach the sponsoring trade associations for additional members of the Board. In March 1972, the Board expanded from four to eight with the addition of Bob Lee from Johnson & Johnson and Marv Eberts from Stokely, both representing GMA, Wilbur Stump from NARGUS, and Fritz Biermeier of Red Owl representing NAFC. Alan Haberman, Don Lloyd, Art Juceam, Bill Oddy,

---

[4] This erroneous estimate became one of the standing jokes of the UCC, and a caution on the difficulty of accurate predictions.

and Bill Hollis joined the Board in early 1973, bringing the Board to thirteen, a size at which it would stay for some time.

In those early months, it was necessary to develop the rules to govern the issuance of U.P.C. numbers by Distribution Number Bank. Some of the questions could be anticipated; others simply emerged. It was apparent, for example, that numbers with trailing zeros were quite advantageous. These numbers would more efficiently conserve label space than others. After alerting the Federal Trade Commission of its intention, UGPCC adopted a "modified" velocity coding scheme. this meant that numbers with three and four trailing zeros were reserved for the eighty companies with the largest sales volumes; the next nine hundred companies would be assigned a number with two zeros.[5] DNB was instructed to make sure that no one company received more than one number containing three zeros.

A request from a trade association to become a member of UGPIC was turned down but the association was offered the opportunity (for fifty dollars) to be placed on a mailing list to receive information from the Board of Governors.

An early, and ongoing, confrontation between the Board and applicants was over the number of numbers to be assigned. The Board entered each of these fights stating that only one number would be assigned and only grudgingly agreed to more. A formal policy was adopted that no more than ten numbers could be assigned to a single company. However, to receive even a second number a company was required to justify the need. Mere inconvenience would not qualify as a justification. Larry Russell visited many of these companies and helped them to solve their problems while minimizing the need for additional manufacturer numbers.

Others also provided input to the U.P.C. Guidelines. The GMA Administrative Systems Committee suggested revisions,

[5] Later, it was recognized that label size, rather than sales volume, should govern the assignment of "zero-suppression" numbers.

and other trade associations were given the opportunity to make recommendations. The Board cautioned that wholesale changes should be avoided unless absolutely necessary.

Not everything went smoothly. The first version of print specifications mailed turned out to be out of tolerance and had to be destroyed and remailed. Problems with the coding of magazines were referred to the Supermarket Institute.

The Board sought to broaden the input it was receiving by amending the bylaws to provide for representation on the UGPIC Board from the printing and equipment industries, and by inviting a representative of the drug industry to attend Board meetings. UGPCC agreed to support the work of the Symbol Selection Committee by underwriting the $40,000 laboratory tests of candidate symbols conducted by Battelle Institute.

The Board wrestled for some time over whether it should hire an Executive Secretary[6] to oversee the Council's activities. Fritz Biermeier suggested that McKinsey & Co. be named the Executive Secretary. Chairman Bob Stringer, sensing a controversial issue, decided to defer the issue until his successor, Jack Strubbe, took office. Obtaining a consensus from the founding trade associations proved difficult. Some believed that this proposal was too broad.

Nonetheless, and in spite of the objections of Mike O'Connor, the proposal to make McKinsey Executive Secretary was approved by the Board of Governors in March 1974. Nothing really changed, however. Wilson and Russell had always served as staff for the Board, and this continued. I dutifully identified McKinsey as Executive Secretary in the Board minutes for the next three years. It then finally dawned on me that no one — including Tom Wilson — viewed McKinsey

[6] Curt Kornblau, an SMI staff Vice President was handling the ministerial responsibilities of Secretary and Treasurer.

in that light. Accordingly, Wilson subsequently was identified simply as an invited guest.[7]

As UGPIC matured, some members of the Board became concerned that the Executive Committee was arrogating too much power to itself. This was a theme that would recur for several years. Non-Executive-Committee members complained they were brought to Board meetings only to rubber-stamp decisions that had already been made. Even Executive Committee members recognized that key decisions were first debated by the Committee and not taken to the Board until the Executive Committee had reached a consensus.

Nonetheless, the Council's leaders consistently tried to broaden Board involvement in UGPIC activities. In the early years, this took the form of opening Executive Committee meetings to any Board member. In practice, however, few took advantage of the opportunity.

Another concern in the early years was ensuring continuity. In mid 1974, the bylaws were amended to stagger the terms of the Governors. To reduce the cost of service, the Board also determined to pay the expenses incurred by individuals as members of the Board of Governors.[8]

By the beginning of 1975, the founding members of the Code Council began to leave the Board. First to leave was Tom Nelson, the General Mills financial executive who had done so much to get the organization set up on a sound financial footing. This was quickly followed by the resignation of SMI's Curt Kornblau as Secretary-Treasurer.

---

[7] Another assertion quickly forgotten was Wilson's statement to the Ad Hoc Committee in December 1972 that McKinsey should remove itself from the project as soon as possible because McKinsey is a problem solver, not an administrator. Nonetheless, Wilson stayed with the UCC until late 1990, often acting as a de facto Executive Director. His leaving was not totally voluntary.

[8] Fifteen years later, this policy would be reversed, on the ground that service on the UCC Board was analogous to service on a trade association board, and the member's employer should bear the cost.

Described by Jack Strubbe as "one of the pilgrim fathers of the U.P.C. movement," Curt had been responsible for keeping the books and records of the corporation.[9]

Membership in the Council continued to climb to the point where the quorum requirement for the annual meeting was reduced to one-tenth of the membership in order to ensure that a legal meeting could take place. Later, the bylaws were changed to limit voting rights in the membership to those companies represented on the Board of Governors, thus eliminating the quorum problem.

The Council proved resistible to some. The Grocery Products Manufacturers of Canada saw no need to establish a relationship with UGPIC. As a reaction to antitrust troubles in the paper industry, the Fort Howard Paper Co. refused to join UGPIC (or any trade association) but still needed a U.P.C. number. For the first (and only) time in its history, Fort Howard was given access to the Council's services upon payment of a fee equivalent to the cost of membership.

Initial experience with U.P.C. symbol-marking was surprisingly error-free. Nonetheless, the UGPIC Board, led by its retailer members, urged the retail community to be tolerant and understanding of errors. The fear was that a too-tough attitude would render it less likely that manufacturers would place the symbol on products. However, the early productivity results were not good. The time required for the cashier to search for the symbol slowed the process.[10]

By mid-1975, there was noticeable progress in Europe toward the development of a system parallel to the U.P.C. McKinsey and Tom Wilson parlayed their US experience into

[9] I replaced him as Secretary. While a Board member was named Treasurer, the books were placed in the hands of Dick Foote, an independent bookkeeper recommended by Arthur Andersen.

[10] Nonetheless, customers at Giant Food (one of the early scanning stores) believed they were being checked out faster. In installing scanners, Giant had lengthened the checkout counter. Consumers perceived they had checked out when they placed their groceries on the counter.

a contract to assist the European project being led by Albert Heijn of the Dutch company Ahold A.V. UGPIC determined it would stay informed about developments in Europe, but saw no need to take a more active role. It was felt that Wilson would adequately protect any US interests.

In the US, the Executive Committee held its first discussions on the possibility of changing the organization's name. Apparently, the word "grocery" troubled a number of people. It helped create an "us against them" attitude that many found counterproductive. Thus, in September 1974 the organization became the "Uniform Product Code Council."

After two years as Board Chairman, Bob Stringer retired at the November 15, 1973, meeting. (He was given a pocket calculator as a parting gift.) Jack Strubbe, Kroger Vice President, was elected to a one-year term as his successor. However, a year later, there was no manufacturer ready to take his place, so the bylaws were waived, and Strubbe agreed to serve for an additional year. This started a tradition of two-year terms for the chairman, which was later codified in the bylaws.

At the annual meeting in November 1974, Chairman Strubbe summed up the state of the project: "We are beginning to get it all together and we are seeing very significant progress in making a great concept work." Membership in the Council had gone from seven hundred members representing $55.7 billion of sales to 2250 members having $70.7 billion in sales. Effective January 1, 1975, membership was extended to the drug and mass merchandise industries.

Although the Council had originally planned to charge recurring dues, the Board decided to continue with a one-time charge.[11] Strubbe said that the Council planned eventually to adjust its costs for services to equalize the expenses of

[11] To some extent, the decision was forced upon them. No one could figure out how the Board could realistically pull a number back from a nonpaying member without jeopardizing the system.

providing those services. Income from membership fees was expected to diminish over the next few years.

To further help companies implement the system, the Board decided to create a Technical Information, Education, and Update Service (TIEUP) on January 1, 1975. At this time, eight supermarket chains were operating test stores, with twenty to thirty more expected in the next six months. Source-symbol marking was estimated to be as high as 62 percent, higher than earlier projections.

Discretion being the better part of valor, and recognizing the need to broaden the use of the U.P.C. symbol, the UGPIC Board agreed in September 1974 that it would not take a position on in-store printed symbols, nor would it attempt to develop quantifiable rejection criteria for symbol evaluation. This was calculated to ease the minds of printers who still feared that the printing of symbols would require greater precision than they were capable of. The Board also continued to urge retailers not to press claims against product manufacturers for faulty symbols.

By mid-1975, the Council could claim over 3000 members and 688 TIEUP subscribers. Of even more significance, two key leaders were elected to the Board — Burt Gookin, CEO of H. J. Heinz and Chairman of the Ad Hoc Committee, and Bob Schaeberle, CEO of Nabisco Brands. Both would subsequently become Chairman of the UPCC Board.

At the 1975 meeting, Jack Strubbe made his farewell to the Board, announcing that 67 percent of items were now source-symbol marked. His ability, strong personality, and position with the Kroger Co. had been indispensable assets in obtaining implementation of the U.P.C.

At this same meeting, GMA named two members to the Board who would make enormous contributions. Barry Franz of Procter & Gamble had been a member of the Symbol Selection Committee and even now was working with Don Lloyd's committee trying to solve the problem of coupons.

He would be instrumental in developing a technique for utilizing the U.P.C. symbol on coupons. He would also play a major role as the Board's monitor of DCI and later the Council staff. Doctor William Taubert, Hunt-Wesson Vice President of Logistics, and his co-worker Bill Maginnis, would do yeoman work on shipping-container marking. Taubert would make many other contributions, large and small, during his years on the Board.

Under Burt Gookin's leadership, the Council found it was able to reduce the frequency of Board meetings. The Board also directed that the sponsoring trade associations receive a regular report on UPCC activities. Some members of the Board, especially those representing the Food Marketing Institute, were more faithful about this than others. GMA, for example, received reports only on a sporadic basis. The Board was both concerned and disappointed that not enough people were taking advantage of the TIEUP service, which was characterized as an important communications channel.

At the end of 1976, the alcoholic beverage industry obtained representation when David Chernow of Schenley was elected to the Board of Governors. By now the Council had 4720 members. In addition, 106 stores were scanning, and 77 percent of the products in grocery stores were source-symbol marked; 95 percent of the members were manufacturers. Even with these numbers, McKinsey's research insisted that the maximum membership the Council could attain would be 6000.

In January 1977, Bill Oddy of Jewel, the Board member serving as Treasurer, reported that while subscriptions to the TIEUP service were being received at a rate only half of that anticipated, new members were joining at almost double the anticipated rate.

During these years, the Board of Governors met in a

variety of locations, often in a city where a store had just begun scanning. In those early days, a store visit was an important part of the meeting. Each installation was different. The September 1977 Board meeting was one of the most interesting field trips. That meeting was held in Topeka, Kansas, at the headquarters of the Fleming Companies, one of the nation's largest wholesalers. Bill Brous, a Fleming executive, and a NAWGA representative on the Board extended the invitation, which Burt Gookin accepted.

The majority of the Board traveled to the meeting on either the Nabisco or Heinz corporate jet, guests of Schaeberle and Gookin. The meeting went very well, but most Board members were not accustomed to the life style of a small city in America's heartland.

At this meeting, for the first time the Uniform Product Code Council adopted a Mission Statement. The Mission Statement comprised four paragraphs, identifying the mission of the UPCC Board to direct the provision of administrative support for the U.P.C. system, to maintain the standard U.P.C. code and U.P.C. symbol by providing interpretive rulings. In addition, the Board should seek to remove obstacles to broad-scale implementation of the U.P.C. code and symbol, which are of an industrywide nature and outside the domain of equipment suppliers, and represent the U.P.C. system in dealings with associations, standards boards, and code agencies in other countries.

Barry Franz had been developing a long-range plan for UPCC that involved releasing DCI and hiring someone to handle the administration as an employee of the Code Council. In November 1977, he reported that Board member Dick Mindlin, a NCR Vice President, had agreed to take early retirement from NCR and open an office for the UPCC in Dayton, Ohio where he lived. Beginning January 1, 1978, all technical inquiries would be referred to Mindlin, and by January 31, all administration would be transferred to

Dayton. Franz projected the cost of the Dayton operation to be $125,000 per year.

The arrangement negotiated with Mindlin was an unusual one and reflected the Council's strong belief that the need for administration would diminish steadily over time. Mindlin was signed to a five-year contract, which provided that he would work full-time the first year, but every year thereafter his work time and compensation were to diminish 20 percent each year. Mindlin was allowed to bring his administrative assistant with him. At the end of five years, the Council anticipated that U.P.C. administration could be turned over to a secretary in one of the grocery industry trade associations. The contract also allowed Mindlin to engage in non-U.P.C. consulting.[12] The work load never diminished, but increased rapidly. Dick Mindlin remained a full-time executive, and by the end of his contract, he presided over a staff of eight.

During the first years of U.P.C. administration, the Board had to deal with a number of implementation issues. Some were more difficult than others, but all were tricky because there was no precedent to rely on. The UPCC was writing on a clean slate.

Whenever the Code Council could step aside and let trading partners resolve issues, it would do so. Thus, for example, it insisted the respective liabilities of the packaging supplier and the product manufacturer be resolved between the parties without the involvement of the Code Council.

Usually, however, decisions could not be avoided. The Board concluded that a buying group should be treated as a manufacturer.[13] It also began to wrestle with the question of

[12] This arrangement would work no better than the similar provision with DCI. It was a constant irritant between Mindlin and the Board.

[13] In retrospect, the term "manufacturer number" is a misnomer. The first half of a U.P.C. number really identifies the company that controls the label.

how to handle the symbol marking of variable-weight products. While a random weight guideline finally emerged, the issue would not go away, and the coding of variable-weight product remains a problem twenty years later.

During the development of the U.P.C., there was a generally accepted belief that product manufacturers would have to bear the costs of source-symbol marking, while retailers would reap the benefits of scanning. There was also recognition that scanning would generate a great deal of detailed information on product sales and movement. Many manufacturers assumed that this data would be made available to them at no cost, to "repay" them for the costs they were incurring. Retailers agreed that scanning data would be very important to both buyers and sellers. They did not, however, share the assumption that it would be provided to suppliers at no charge.

As manufacturers came to realize that they would have to pay to obtain item movement data regarding their own products, many became convinced they had been duped by the Ad Hoc. This caused a growing resentment. This led to increased and continuing pressure to develop a mechanism for scanning coupons at point of sale, a perceived benefit for product manufacturers. Finding a solution proved to be very difficult (see Chapter 10). Some would say that no solution has yet been found.

Another problem that proved intractable was the coding of variable-weight product.[14] To figure out how to handle such product, a committee was formed that ultimately developed a solution that worked — sort of. This same committee also took on the issue of how to code magazines. In August 1974, Guideline 21, which represented an unusual accommodation with the Council for Periodical Distributors, was adopted.

[14] Fresh meats, cheeses, fresh produce, etc. — any product sold by weight in non-uniform packages.

The good news was that after a year and a half of real-world scanning experience, there were very few problems reported with the scanning equipment. And scanning was expanding, even if slowly. A year after the first scanning store opened, 50 percent (by volume) of the items in a super-market were source-marked with U.P.C. symbols, and thirty stores were actually scanning at the checkout counter.

Some problems surfaced that no one anticipated. In September 1975, I reported that a committee of the US Trademark Association was studying the abbreviation of trademarks appearing on cash register tapes in scanning systems. The Board took no action, which apparently was wise, since no more was ever heard of this issue.

The register tape with full product description was perceived as one of the real consumer benefits of the U.P.C. During early discussions, committee members and symbol submitters suggested it could be used as a shopping list, as a place to print recipes or promotional material, and as a purveyor of meaningful price information. No one has ever asked consumers if they share these rosy views. Nonetheless, producers of trademarked goods now know that consumers are receiving another impression of the product's mark, even if in abbreviated form.

As 1976 began, the Gallo wineries joined the Code Council. This was considered significant because Gallo was viewed as the bellwether of the vintners. By September, the Board was told that the domestic wine industry had adopted the U.P.C. The distilled spirits industry came along much slower. In large part, this was because in eighteen states, hard liquor was sold through state stores, and each state had its own numbering system. Producers were concerned at the possibility of multiple numbering systems and pushed for the U.P.C.

A company, founded by Tommy Greer, former President of Texize and one time UGPIC Board member, applied for membership in the organization. UP$ had no products. It was a promotional company that used U.P.C. product symbols as proofs of purchase. Because Greer was a good friend of many Board members (and Tom Wilson), it was with great reluctance that the membership application was turned down. There was considerable discussion of the need to amend the bylaws to allow any organization that used the U.P.C. to become a member.[15]

At the September 1976 Board meeting it appeared that expenses were about to go down significantly. No future expenditures for public policy issues (see Chapter 4) were anticipated. UGPIC's future tasks seemed limited to list maintenance and membership processing. Don Martin reported that ten additional stores were scheduled to begin scanning in September, the largest number in a single month.

On the other hand, increasingly, grocery manufacturers were expressing concern over the slow pace of scanning installations. This concern was not alleviated by the widespread misunderstanding of the 1973 economic projections by McKinsey. McKinsey had said that *if* there were five thousand scanning stores in 1975, *then* the savings attributable to scanning would be significant enough to justify the investment. This was widely interpreted to mean that McKinsey had predicted there *would be* five thousand scanning stores by 1975, over 4900 more than were in place. The Board recognized there was a considerable job to be done with respect to the management of expectations.

Notwithstanding the perceived slow pace in the grocery industry, other industries were beginning to express interest in the U.P.C. In November 1976, the Board agreed to appoint a committee to work with the National Retail Merchants

---

[15] The discussion would subside. It soon became an article of faith (but not the bylaws) that companies without products were not entitled to membership.

Association (NRMA) on the overlap of items in the super-market and general merchandise industries, although for the foreseeable future, products likely to go into either channel would have to bear both U.P.C. and OCR-A. A representative was also sent to a meeting of the record industry to discuss the feasibility of U.P.C. marking for records and tapes. As 1977 began, Don Martin reported that a retail drug chain was preparing to implement U.P.C. scanning.

Moreover, fame — or notoriety — was coming to the U.P.C. A tee shirt designer asked for permission (which was really not needed) to make a U.P.C. symbol the design for a shirt, and the April 1978 cover of MAD magazine featured a U.P.C. symbol.

The startup phase of code and symbol implementation was over: 92 percent of dry grocery product was source symbol marked, and 65 to 80 percent of the overall product mix had symbols applied at the source. Some retailers were actually getting a return on investment. The soft savings were rapidly developing. Much of 1977 was devoted to a look at the appropriate future role of the Code Council. Equipment companies told the Board that the industry needed to do much more to publicize the successes of the U.P.C. The Board concluded it needed to stay in existence to set U.P.C. policy.

At the Topeka meeting in September 1977, the Board decided there was no need to continue with a newsletter. To operate in the future, three potential structures were offered for consideration: continue as is, turn the program over to the trade associations for execution, or hire an executive to run the program as a UPCC employee. DCI was informed of the conclusions and encouraged to submit a bid on the business.

At this meeting a new Mission Statement for the Code Council was adopted. It had four parts. The Code Council was to (1) provide administrative support for the U.P.C.

system including the issuance of manufacturer identification numbers, the provision of manuals on code use and symbol printing, and the maintenance of membership records; (2) maintain the code and symbol by providing interpretive rulings, discouraging unauthorized use, and modifying the specifications and guidelines as required; (3) remove obstacles to the broadscale implementation of code and symbol when those obstacles are industrywide and beyond the normal domain of equipment companies; and (4) represent the U.P.C. system with industry associations, standards boards, and code agencies in other countries.

By the end of 1978, estimates were that the number of scanning stores would triple — to six hundred. The Board hoped this would put an end to the negative publicity about the "scanner that failed" and reassure both product and equipment manufacturers.

Within six months of the selection of the U.P.C. symbol, some distributors were requesting the development of a shipping container symbol. The Board of Governors referred the issue to McKinsey. Three years later, both GMA and NAFC made the same request. Once again, the issue was referred to McKinsey. A considerable amount of time was spent investigating the costs of printing symbols on shipping containers. While the preliminary results were promising, in November 1977, the Board learned there was a serious problem with obtaining satisfactory print contrast. Moreover, they were told, there appeared to be no ground swell of support for a distribution symbol.

A recurring concern of the Board during the early years was how to fund the Council's activities. One of the earliest ideas, quickly dismissed, was to fund code administration by an override on the annual dues paid by companies to the sponsoring trade associations. This and other schemes were debated by the Code Management Committee in its search for a means to fund the U.P.C. in perpetuity. At this time (in

1971) no one believed there was any need to pursue tax-exempt status.

In order to obtain the money to fund the symbol selection work, Bob Wegman undertook a fund-raising drive among grocery retailers. Almost a million dollars was raised in this fashion.[16] Retailers who participated were given three-year memberships in UGPIC.

The Ad Hoc Committee recommended a dues schedule based on the member's annual domestic sales. The dues would range between $200 and $10,000.[17] It was assumed that the dues would be for a fixed period, initially set at three years and that members would be expected to renew their memberships. Two things happened to change this. As the three years raced by, Board members realized they could not take away a U.P.C. manufacturer's number from a dues delinquent member without running the risk of seriously disrupting the newly installed systems at scanning stores. Moreover, even though the Board was not comfortable with its financial position, enough new members were joining so that the organization could continue to function without asking members for another dues payment.

The Ad Hoc Committee tried to put the operation on a businesslike basis. In November 1971, it ordered that all money spending groups develop budgets for the years 1972, 1973, 1974, and appointed a Finance Committee of Tom Nelson, Alan Haberman, Bob Stringer, and Curt Kornblau to review the submissions. About a year later, the Ad Hoc complied with all the necessary formalities, so that it could qualify for tax-exempt status.

One of the first actions taken by the Board of Governors was to hire Arthur Andersen to audit and prepare tax returns

[16] A side benefit to the fund-raising effort was that its success had a major impact on equipment companies who became more inclined to take the whole effort seriously.

[17] Today, twenty-five years later, the dues range from $300 to $10,000.

for both UGPIC and the Ad Hoc Committee. The work was to be done at a cost of $2500.

In September 1972, the Board was told the Council needed to receive $130,000 over a four-month period if it was to meet its budget. At the same meeting, a very conservative investment policy was adopted. Short-term investments in treasury bills, certificates of deposit, and prime commercial paper were the only approved investments, and no investment could be for a period longer than ninety days without Board approval.[18]

On October 31, the bank balance was $153,000, reflecting income to date of $495,000. Nonetheless, the Board was greatly concerned over whether there would be funds to operate in 1973. These concerns persisted for several years. Total expenditures over the five-year period 1970–1975 were projected to be over $2.5 million. Board members visualized a continuing hand-to-mouth existence.

As memberships continued to come in at a much faster pace than anyone predicted, the attitude began to change. Thus, Jack Strubbe suggested to the Executive Committee in mid-1974 that the Council should change its policies so that the organization's income would be adjusted to result in a break-even financial condition. He also said that it was time for the Council to think of its obligations to those who put up the seed money.

The sponsoring trade associations expressed themselves well pleased with the UPCC's stewardship of the project. Strubbe urged, "Today, not only do the trade associations need the money, but the return by the Code Council would set a valuable precedent for other projects requiring seed money."[19] The Board of Governors agreed and voted to set

[18] This policy was reaffirmed in March 1974.

[19] Minutes, Board of Governors, July 17, 1974, p. 2.

aside the appropriate amount of money to return to the trade associations. By the end of the year, the Board was secure enough to vote that existing members would not be asked for additional dues — at least through 1977.

Arthur Andersen advised the Code Council that it faced a projected tax liability of $60,000 for 1974 and $200,000 for 1975. Losses were projected for subsequent years. This presented the Board with a delicate issue. The industry would not be happy to learn that taxes were due, and even though losses were required to get the tax payments back, it must be presented very carefully to avoid a perception that the Council was going under.

The Board asked me to have the tax lawyers reexamine the issue of a tax exemption for the UPCC. In January 1975, the Ad Hoc Committee, using funds advanced by the U.P.C., repaid all of the seed money that had been put forward by the trade associations. I reported back that the organization probably would not qualify for tax-exempt status, but there was nothing to lose by filing. Accordingly, a decision was made to file the application.

In May 1975, the Treasurer, Marv Eberts, reported a significant excess of income over expenditures. He urged all legitimate requests for funds be submitted for approval before the end of the month. He also observed (as other Board members would over the years) that the UPCC needed either to spend more or earn less. Six months later, the Council was in a negative cash flow with membership revenue tending downward. By March 1976, everything seemed to be in balance. The number of new members was down, but the fee per member was up.

Another six months, and it appeared that revenues were way below expectations, while expenses were right on target. The Executive Committee concluded that the UPCC would run out of money about the time that its projects evaporated.

Financial solvency seemed dependent upon receiving a tax refund, which would happen only if the tax-exemption application was granted.

As the lawyers predicted, the IRS rejected the request for tax exempt status. However, the Council filed a protest, and much to the lawyers' consternation — but delight — the protest was granted, and the UPCC became a tax exempt business league. This led to a refund of all taxes paid by the Council and established the solvency of the organization.

Finances would soon cease to be a concern of the UPCC.

4
Public Policy

One criterion for the selection of a symbol was that the symbol must benefit the consumer. Throughout the gestation period for the code and symbol there was often rhetoric at committee meetings concerning the potential benefits to the consumer of the U.P.C. system. While much of this discussion was programmed — the automatic response of an industry executive asked to justify a new development — some of it was real.

Several Symbol Selection meetings were enlivened by excited discussions of the potentials implicit in the marriage of scanner, computer, and expanded register tape. In these discussions, the checkout counter was envisioned as a chatty, wise, grandmotherly figure dispensing gratuitous advice:

> "You have just bought a ham, would you like to purchase sweet potatoes to go with it?"; or

> "You have just bought a ham, here are five recipes that call for ham"; or

> "You have just bought a ham; here is a coupon for pineapple," and so forth.

Yet, such discussions were infrequent. The U.P.C. was perceived, discussed, and implemented as a means to improve the efficiency and productivity of the checkout process.

If consumer benefit was seriously considered, it was in a context that any improvement of system efficiencies would of course benefit the consumer. As one retail member of the Ad Hoc Committee put it, "Obviously, consumers will benefit from the U.P.C. The industry has never been smart enough to hold on to efficiency savings in the past. They always get passed through to the consumer. Why should this project be any different?"

Still, the committees focussed on improving business efficiencies, with any consumer benefit a fortuitous byproduct. As related earlier, the Ad Hoc worried about potential problems from the FTC and worked hard to demonstrate that the U.P.C. would not disadvantage small business. But not even the Trade Commission raised concerns over the U.P.C.'s impact on consumers.

The U.P.C., however, was developed in the early 1970s, at the peak of the consumer activist movement. Consumer groups tended to be aligned with labor unions. The U.P.C. was threatening to the Food and Commercial Workers Union, which feared the introduction of high technology to the checkout would mean the loss of union jobs. Indeed, any innovation proposed by an industry consortium was certain to be viewed with a healthy skepticism by the activist community.

The Board's first formal recognition of a world beyond the industry was to designate a seat on the board for first an academic governor and later a public governor.[1] No attempt, however, was made to fill the position until 1981 when Alan Haberman left First National and therefore was no longer eligible to serve as a Food Marketing Institute representative on the Board. The board did not want to lose his expertise, and so he became the first public representative.

A decade later, in 1990, Haberman was involved with two manufacturing enterprises, and Byron Felter, a GMA Board member, was retiring from Quaker Oats. Felter became the

[1] In 1993, the post of public governor was eliminated.

public governor and Haberman a manufacturer-at-large governor. Thus, never in the history of the organization was there a true "public" governor, let alone a consumer activist.

That is not to say the public was unrepresented. Both men took their responsibilities seriously and regularly raised issues on behalf of their "constituency." If a major issue had arisen, however, their credibility would have been extraordinarily difficult to establish.

At the outset, however, there was not even nominal consumer representation on the project and very little focus on even the identification of consumer issues. Board of Governors and Ad Hoc members were therefore totally unprepared for the furor consumer groups were to raise over the prospect of the removal of prices from products with the advent of scanning. In virtually every jurisdiction in the early years, the announcement of a new scanning installation would be followed by a call for legislation banning item-price removal. These demands were usually instigated by organized consumer groups, aided by the Retail Clerks union.

The Board of Governors received its first report on consumer issues in November 1973. As Board Chairman Jack Strubbe noted, however, the Board was made up of information and technical specialists and not general management. Political issues fell outside their normal realm of experience. Not to worry, said Strubbe, the Ad Hoc Committee had not been disbanded; it was still there as a resource. The Ad Hoc, by contrast, was composed of senior managers, mostly CEOs — men more accustomed to politics and the corridors of power.

In mid-1974 Burt Gookin met with the industry trade associations to discuss the public policy issues facing scanning. They decided to reactivate the Ad Hoc Committee to work with the trade associations to combat demands for mandatory item pricing. Removal of item pricing was estimated to represent up to 20 percent of the potential savings attributable to scanning. Ad Hoc concluded it should be neutral on whether items should bear prices, but vigorously oppose legislation to mandate item pricing.

Gookin and the associations also agreed that the Ad Hoc's efforts would be subordinate to those of the trade associations. A small public policy committee under the leadership of Bob Wegman was created to work this issue, and about a quarter of a million dollars was requested from UGPIC to fund the effort. The committee's charge was to deal with legislation, consumer education, responses to consumers, labor, and government.

In reality, while the Public Policy Committee met several times, funded some research, and dabbled in lobbying, NAFC and GMA were the dominant groups opposing state and federal item-pricing legislation. The U.P.C. effort focussed on the need for scanning accuracy. Tom Wilson's greatest fear was the "golden chicken," a low-priced item that, when scanned, showed a price over $90. This in the hands of a consumerist, union member, or publicity-seeking legislator could be the spark that precipitated legislation. Fortunately, no one ever found a golden chicken.

Most, if not all, stores engaged in considerable consumer education when scanning was introduced to a new area. This usually included tours of a scanning store for elected officials. As representatives of the developers of the U.P.C., we participated in several of these tours. Most legislators were favorably impressed and accepted as true our assurances regarding pricing accuracy. If a consumer was charged incorrectly however, most stores adopted a policy that would penalize the store to assure the consumer she was not being cheated.

Scanners have proved remarkably accurate. Mistakes in the system are almost always traced to human error. Failure to change the price in the computer or on the shelf are the most common sources of incorrect prices being charged.

Familiarity breeds contempt, and the passage of time has led all too often to the relaxation of the discipline in shelf marking and data entry that was commonplace in 1974. In the early 1990s, muckraking journalists and broadcasters became fond of locating pricing errors in scanning stores.

In light of the furor over item pricing, the UGPIC Board decided to postpone indefinitely the addition of a consumer representative to the Board. If truth be told, no serious effort had been made to fill the slot. Most Board members were privately relieved to have a reason to avoid this subject.

The Public Policy Committee was composed principally of Ad Hoc Committee members, augmented by lobbyists for the sponsoring trade associations. In addition, the Committee reached out to Wayne Horwitz of the Joint Labor Management Government Tripartite Committee, and Jim Turner, a self-styled consumer advocate who had settled on food for his niche.

The Committee met regularly but walked a delicate line and struggled to find its role. Defense of U.P.C. scanning against the threat of mandatory item-pricing legislation was the Committee's primary reason for existence. Pricing decisions, however, were the sole responsibility of the retailers. Also, the established trade associations had the necessary expertise to deal with legislators. With considerable misgivings, because it did not know what the result would be, the Committee sponsored a study on consumer price awareness by Michigan State University (the study turned out to be innocuous, neither helpful nor hurtful).

The Public Policy Committee also provided technical support to the lobbyists for the trade associations. Tom Wilson and I would accompany NAFC lobbyist Tom Zaucha[2] on his visits to legislators, patiently attempting to demystify checkout scanning, and persuade the skeptics that it was not a way

[2] Zaucha later became president of the National Grocers Association, created by the merger of NARGUS and CFDA.

to raise prices to consumers. In fact, we argued, scanning ensured greater pricing accuracy than reliance on item marking by low-paid, low-motivated store personnel. It was a tough sell.

The approach to the consumer groups was even tougher. In the first place, they brought to the table an instinctive and deeply held mistrust of business. From their perspective, of course industry wanted to remove prices from items: using computer technology would enable prices to be manipulated without fear of detection!

We responded that the new, more detailed cash register receipt would in fact facilitate price comparisons. Also, prices would be marked on the shelf, and some stores offered grease pencils to customers who wanted to mark products with prices. Most stores even offered to *give* the consumer the product if the wrong price was charged. Consumer leaders argued that none of these measures took the place of a price marked on the item.

Consumer groups, in concert with labor leaders, also expressed a legitimate concern over the impact scanning would have on store labor. A significant portion of the savings from scanning arose out of labor savings at the checkout.

The head of the Consumer Federation of America, Carol Tucker Foreman, was married to an official of the retail clerks union. She was a formidable adversary. The U.P.C. cause was not helped when Alan Haberman asked her what "you girls" really wanted at a Public Policy Committee meeting. In many ways, that exchange illustrated the vast lack of understanding between the industry leaders who truly believed the U.P.C. was a modern miracle, universally beneficent, and labor and consumer leaders wary of one more deception by big business.

Although the Public Policy Committee was officially neutral on the removal of prices from items, but vigorously opposed to legislation that would mandate the retention of item prices, that distinction was not always clear, especially since all the Committee's pronouncements were about the productivity gains made possible by item-price removal and assurances of the many ways other than item-price marking that consumers would be able to retain price awareness.

The Committee, however, became intrigued with the political game and began to play it seriously. Committee members offered testimony in several state legislatures. In early 1975, there was an official meeting with consumer leaders, and a deal was floated. The consumers would back off price-marking legislation for twelve months, while the supermarket industry would commit that no more than one store per chain would test the U.P.C. without prices. Nothing ever came of this proposal.

The desire to be political operatives infected us all. Dealing with legislative aides is a heady experience. Nonetheless, for those involved with the U.P.C., lobbying was not our primary expertise. The Board of Governors recognized this. After excusing Tom Wilson, there was a lengthy discussion in May 1975 of how to handle legislative issues. The Board expressed concern over the active role being taken by McKinsey because "McKinsey is not strong on legislation." This is why the grocery trade associations had the lead. Nonetheless, the "amateurs" made a significant contribution.

Was the effort successful? No federal item-pricing legislation has ever received serious consideration, and relatively few states and localities have adopted such laws. Nonetheless, it is a subject that will not go away and is always strengthened by sensational news reports of overcharges at the checkout.

The U.P.C. was vindicated by a 1996 FTC study on Price Scanning. This study concluded that scanners reduced pricing errors from 16% to less than 5%. Not only that, but a majority of errors *favored* the consumer. The FTC found that errors came from failure to program computers, not from the computer itself.[3]

Yet the greatest deterrent to item-price regulation was not the Ad Hoc Committee, Board of Governors, Public Policy Committee, nor the industry trade associations. The rise in popularity of no frills warehouse stores turned the absence of item prices into a marketing advantage. Consumer activists who had attacked conventional supermarkets for removing item prices cheered the no frills stores. Item-pricing legislation lost much of its appeal to politicians.

By early 1977, the Public Policy Committee had ceased to exist. The Board of Governors seldom ventured into the field again. During the chairmanship of Michael Wright, CEO of Super Valu, in November 1984 the Board met with Jesse Madison, head of the Department of Consumer Services of the city of Chicago. Madison's major issue was the fear of scanning expressed by his elderly constituents. There was no followup, by either side, to this meeting.

The Board of Governors made one more bow to the consumer movement. Very slight. In 1991, new public governor Byron Felter (a retired Quaker Oats executive) demanded a staff study on the organization's promises and benefits to consumers. The study came up with little data. Everyone continues to assume consumers have benefitted from U.P.C. scanning. Precious little hard data exists to support that assumption, even though it is well known that scanning has significantly reduced costs. Cost reductions in the grocery industry are typically reflected in savings passed on to consumers.

Felter had to fight to get time and attention from both Board and staff. In mid-1993, following a major consulting study on the future of the U.P.C. and the organization, the Board finally bit the bullet. The bylaws were amended to eliminate the consumer position.

[3] "Price Check: A Report on the Accuracy of Checkout Scanners" FTC Staff Report, Oct. 22, 1996.

5

Distribution Codes, Inc.

The first five years of U.P.C. scanning (1973–1978) were entrusted to Distribution Number Bank (DNB),[1] a subsidiary of the National Association of Wholesalers. Although DNB had a limited track record, no one ever challenged its competence as U.P.C. administrator. Whatever other complaints were laid at DNB's door, its record as steward of the U.P.C. system was spotless, and DNB's bid was several-fold lower than its nearest competitor. Yet a significant portion of the Code Council's relationship with DNB concerned the cost of DNB's services.

Year by year, the Board was concerned about the amount of the contract and its escalating costs. The Executive Committee repeatedly (and unsuccessfully) tried to identify which DCI costs could be lowered. In the latter years of the relationship, DCI was paid through a formula tied to the number of new members serviced. The DCI contract was both half-full and half-empty. The approximately $300,000 cost of DNB's services in 1973 was roughly one-twentieth of the other bids for the contract. Nonetheless, the Board of Governors suspected the job could cost much less. Years later, an economic analysis by McKinsey demonstrated that the cost per member application was much lower when handled in-house than under DCI.

[1] In January 1974, Distribution Number Bank became Distribution Codes, Inc. (DCI). The terms are used interchangeably.

In attempting to control costs, the Board placed dollar limits on DCI, and imposed a profit cap of 12.5 percent. As the number of new members grew, DCI's income rose. So did the Board's concern. By September 1976, the Executive Committee concluded the current growth rate of three hundred to four hundred new members per year was insufficient to justify the DCI overhead. The UPCC appeared to have few issues left to address (except, perhaps, couponing).

Although DNB was a wholly owned subsidiary of the National Association of Wholesaler Distributors, the UGPIC board had next to no contact with NAWD personnel. For us, DNB was a free-standing and simple organization with a small staff.

Don Martin, president of the organization, was a retired Air Force quartermaster officer with a middle-American openness. Leo Beinhorn, responsible for the newsletter, also had an Air Force background. To handle technical issues, DNB recruited a bright young computer expert named John Langan.

At the outset, DNB included two U.P.C. pioneers on its staff. Wally Flint, retired from NAFC, was regarded by many as the father of the automated checkout based upon his master's thesis in the 1930s. He brought credibility and a channel of communication with the grocery industry. Burt Gookin's technical assistant on the Ad Hoc Committee, John Hayes, also joined DNB for two years. This was a major asset for DNB.

The U.P.C. was in the forefront of technology. DNB, as administrator for the project, was effective, but decidedly low tech. DNB purchased two sets of 100,000 numbered, gummed labels. When a U.P.C. manufacturer number was assigned by DNB, a numbered label was affixed to the membership certificate, and its counterpart to the file copy. It was simple, but it worked. DNB never made an error in assigning numbers.

About a third of DNB's time was spent in symbol administration, over another third in membership administration and general activities. The remaining third was divided between code administration and communication. The contract with UGPIC, however, represented 80 to 90 percent of DNB's total activity. Some members of the UGPIC Board suggested we should insist upon a seat on the DNB Board of Directors, considering the importance of the contract to DNB. In the end, UGPIC decided it was better to remain at arm's length.

Distribution Codes published a newsletter to promote U.P.C. scanning and to respond to technical questions. The newsletter was fun to read, but had no visible impact on its intended audience. The Board of Governors was reluctant to give its contractor unfettered editorial freedom and would often discuss the need to review the editorial content before an issue was published.

The contract specifically authorized DNB to engage in other profit-making activities — provided the UGPIC Board gave its approval. The problem was that *every single project* DNB proposed was viewed by the Board as a conflict of interest with DNB's responsibilities to the U.P.C. For example, DNB wanted to publish a catalog of U.P.C. numbers. The Board disapproved, fearing the public would believe it was an UGPIC product. As Secretary, I was designated to work with DNB to make sure that DNB's publications did not resemble UGPIC publications.

The trademark issue was a classic example of the conflict between UGPIC and DNB. According to Don Martin, in an effort to protect the U.P.C., DNB filed an application to trademark the letters "UPC," but did not tell UGPIC. Distribution Number Bank appeared as the owner of the "UPC" on the application.

Immediately, an angry Board insisted DNB assign the application to the UGPIC and quickly retained trademark counsel. He reported that the application had been mishandled, and the chances of a mark issuing were slight. The trademark office denied the application on the ground that "UPC" was merely descriptive of "universal product code."[2]

DCI decided the combination of its experience with the distribution code, its role as a subsidiary of the National Association of Wholesalers, and its work with the U.P.C. gave it a special expertise to develop a symbol for use on shipping containers in a warehouse setting. In 1974, it persuaded another NAW affiliate, the Distribution Research and Education Foundation (DREF) to create a Shipping Container Symbology Study Group with DCI as secretariat.

UPCC Board members Bob Koenig and Bob Stringer agreed to become a part of the Study Group. In addition, DCI asked the Symbol Technical Advisory Committee to review the Study Group's recommendation to be sure it would not adversely affect the U.P.C. DCI clearly believed it had protected itself against any concern the Code Council might have, but DCI was wrong once again. In 1976, the UPCC Executive Committee learned that DCI had applied for patent protection for the distribution symbol. This immediately raised red flags. From this point on, the Code Council became much more interested in the distribution symbol. On one level, it was concerned that outsiders would perceive the distribution symbol as a UPCC project when in fact it was not. This argued for a clear and public "hands off." On another level, it wanted to be sure that any distribution symbol was practical for and met the needs of the grocery industry. This required deep involvement. Above all, the Board was adamant that any distribution symbol be in the public domain and freely available without license. This was important not only legally, but also politically. If the symbol's availability was limited in any way, the UPCC was convinced it would never achieve major acceptance.

[2] Obtaining a trademark might have been possible. See Chapter 12.

Distribution Codes insisted, however, it was important to obtain a patent in order to protect and control the distribution symbol. It refused to withdraw the application. The UPCC Board remained distressed and became increasingly concerned that the rest of the world could not separate DCI's independent activities from its responsibilities on behalf of the Code Council. Moreover, the free availability of symbology was an article of faith for the Code Council. Persuading the members of the grocery industry to adopt the U.P.C. was the major task of the Code Council. In the mid-1970s, it was a difficult task. If the industry concluded there was a potential of having to pay a royalty to use a symbology, the assignment would be virtually impossible.

The patent issue exacerbated the latent tensions between the UPCC and DCI. As the months passed, Board members became more concerned with the workings of the Shipping Container Symbology Study Group and the leadership of DCI. In June 1976, the UPCC Board asked McKinsey & Co. to do an economic study of the proposed shipping-container symbol.

As 1976 ended, the UPCC assumed it faced a dilemma. It was not sure that a shipping-container symbol was desirable, but unless the Code Council took charge of the effort, it was doomed to fail. In this fashion, the UPCC took on a new — and major — assignment. At first, the efforts went on in parallel, but gradually the SCSSG meetings waned. In January 1977, DCI threw in the towel in the face of the UPCCs unrelenting pressure, and agreed to abandon its patent application.

The UPCC, after years of effort, finally adopted a fourteen-digit interleaved two of five symbol for shipping containers. The major problem that lengthened the development process was assuring printability and adequate contrast for readability. Even after the symbol was selected, however, companies were extremely slow to put it into use.

Sometimes it seemed as if everything Distribution Codes

did was calculated to offend the Code Council. To call the UPCC leaders of the mid-1970s frugal is an understatement. Their mission as they perceived it allowed for no frills. Imagine their reaction when DCI took an entire floor of a new office building in Alexandria, Virginia, and furnished it nicely. The UPCC could not even allow DCI to negotiate its own lease. An independent real estate agent and I as counsel reviewed the proposed lease at the UPCC's request. We were not satisfied and proceeded to negotiate better terms for them.

To the Code Council, the new offices represented Middle Eastern opulence and further weakened its confidence in DCI's judgment. DCI, by contrast, was proud of its new digs. It encouraged the Board to meet in Alexandria, where the new offices were a real but unspoken issue between the two.

This discomfort was especially manifest at contract renewal time as the Board annually wrestled with its evaluation of DCI and its services. Early on, the Board acknowledged it was very difficult to evaluate DCI's performance and that the real or imagined problems with DCI would be present with *any* outside agency. Evaluation was further complicated by DCI's refusal to break out its costs for Code Council review.

In 1975, the Executive Committee conducted a detailed review of the arrangement. On the plus side, DCI provided a bridge to other industries with coding schemes. However, it could also create controversies and embarrassment for the Code Council. Three years into the relationship, it also appeared that DCI was simply not able or willing to reduce its costs.

DCI obviously wanted to use its administration of the U.P.C. as a base for expansion. All such attempts, however, were perceived as trading on the relationship with the UPCC and adverse to the Code Council's best interests. Thus, for example, DCI published a newsletter and update service for the UPCC. However, it simultaneously offered a parallel service at a lower price. Similarly, one of the mantras of the early U.P.C. days was that there were no quantifiable rejection criteria for symbols. A printer should print to specification. That would be adequate and insulate him from liability. DCI, however, offered to evaluate symbols for a fee. But with all of the problems with DCI, the UPCC Executive Committee admitted to itself that any other third-party agency would create its own set of problems. The discussion, while perhaps cathartic, led to no action. Officially, DCI was acknowledged for a "creditable" job.

A year later, the UPCC Board decided it should exercise greater management over DCI's stewardship of the U.P.C. The Board asked Barry Franz to be its watchdog with DCI and to prepare a long-range plan for the administration of the U.P.C. To maximize its options, the Code Council negotiated a one-year contract with DCI. DCI would receive a fixed price of $286,000. The contract also placed a ceiling on the amount of profit DCI could earn. A comparable provision that had protected DCI against losses was removed from the contract. Nonetheless, the Board cautioned that this contract would put the UPCC in a deficit position. The contract price was greater than the revenues projected for 1977.

The quest for alternatives to DCI continued. In April 1977, the choices appeared to be to retain the status quo, turn the job over to one or more of the sponsoring trade associations, or have the UPCC assume some DCI tasks. Barry Franz told the Executive Committee in September that a transition to an in-house staff might be feasible. Dick Mindlin, the NCR representative on the UPCC Board faced mandatory retirement from NCR in June 1979. He expressed willingness to take early retirement, and along with an Administrative Assistant, administer the U.P.C. Both Franz and Mindlin saw the job as a purely transitional one.[3]

DCI's lease would end in March 1978. The UPCC was a

[3] See Chapter 7.

guarantor of that lease, so that became a landmark for making a change if one was to be made. By the end of November 1977, an employment contract with Mindlin had been negotiated, and work had begun on the transition from DCI. The UPCC created a fund of up to $50,000 to go to DCI for satisfactory performance plus cooperation in the transition to Mindlin. An article announcing the switch to paid staff was prepared for placement in Supermarket News.

DCI fully cooperated. Its professional staff worked diligently to make sure that the UPCC office was prepared to open on January 1, 1978. Leo Beinhorn and John Langan provided consulting services to the new operation for several months. On January 31, 1978, the Board received DCI status report number 75 and the keys to the DCI office.

A few months later, UPCC received an auditor's report showing a $52,000 loss to DCI in the last year of the contract. It also formally concluded that the transition had gone well. Accordingly, the Board voted the entire $50,000 bonus to DCI.

After May 1978, DCI disappears from the Code Council's records except for a notation in 1982 that DCI and the European Article Numbering organization were in conflict. The Board concluded it had neither the obligation nor the need to intervene to resolve it.

6

Symbol Technical Advisory Committee (STAC)

Once the U.P.C. symbol was selected, the Ad Hoc Committee gave the Symbol Selection Committee its heartfelt thanks and disbanded the group. Ongoing administration was placed with the Uniform Grocery Product Council Board of Governors. This group (née the Code Management Committee) lacked technical expertise about symbologies.

Larry Russell of McKinsey suggested that UGPIC create a committee of technical experts to provide advice and resolution of the technical questions about the U.P.C. symbol that would inevitably arise. To give added clout to this group, the Board decided to add a printer or converter and an equipment company representative to its numbers. These two would in turn serve as co-chairs of a Symbol Technical Advisory Committee (inevitably shortened to "STAC"). Jim Porter of Chase Bag was elected the converter governor, and Dick Mindlin of NCR the equipment governor.

In a joint meeting with the Symbol Selection Committee on May 17, 1973, the Board of Governors identified the mission of the new technical committee to be (1) refining the symbol specification, (2) working with other code groups, (3) advising UGPIC about potential conflicts, and (4) providing some of the "missionary" work needed to encourage adoption of the code and symbol. The Symbol Committee particularly emphasized the need for a group that would sustain the project's momentum.

To involve the maximum number of technical experts, STAC was composed of six specialized subcommittees. The chairman of each subcommittee would represent the subcommittee on the full technical committee. Another strength of this arrangement was that it gave the U.P.C. the benefit of the best technical expertise.

The original STAC subcommittees consisted of the following: Printability gage and film master production;[1] Converter, printing processes, and quality control; Scanning, computer and related equipment; In-store equipment other than computer; Problem substrates, and color, ink and measurement; and Graphics and symbol location.

A blueprint for the new committee was prepared by Jim Porter, Vice President of Chase Bag, a "converter" in U.P.C.-speak. At its July 1973 meeting, the Board of Governors reviewed and approved the plan, named Porter and Dick Mindlin of NCR co-chairmen of STAC, and elected them to the Board. The plan called for the STAC subcommittees to be created by August 1 and for each subcommittee to meet before September 15.

The excitement and challenge of this new application of technology spurred the new committee to action. The subcommittees were organized, met, and began action. The actual STAC committee (the co-chairs plus the chairs of each subcommittee) also met and processed the initial recommendations of the subcommittees.

At the November Board of Governors meeting, the agenda called for STAC's technical interpretations. It agreed with STAC's insistence that there be no relaxation of film

---

[1] The U.P.C. symbol was created by use of a film master (like a photographic negative). The symbol quality could be tested by means of a "printability gage" (a template). The gage was provided with the Symbol Specification manual.

master tolerances. Similarly, STAC recommended the development of a film master buying checklist to be included, along with the metric dimensions of the U.P.C. symbol, in the Symbol Specification, and Guidelines manuals.

Even in its inception, STAC became embroiled in an issue that would continue to plague the Code Council — symbol validation. There were pressures for UGPIC to offer a symbol verification service, but the Board was concerned over the potential liability exposure. Other groups had the capability to verify symbols, so STAC subcommittee 1 was directed to screen and list organizations offering a symbol verification service.

Typical of the problems assigned to STAC in those early days were questions of symbol placement on multipack items. STAC suggested to Cracker Jack that it cover the symbols on an individual package with a band bearing the symbol for a three-pack when the product was sold that way. The familiar "hi-cone"[2] six-pack presented similar problems.

With STAC providing a forum through subcommittee 2 (Converter, printing processes, and quality control), the Board of Governors received continuing concerns from the converting industry. Printers and converters saw the U.P.C. as a threat, not an opportunity. They were very wary about the scannability of symbols. From the printers' perspective, the $250 subscription fee for the U.P.C. TIEUP service was only adding insult to injury. Though the Board recognized the need to present the U.P.C. to printers and converters more positively, it is not clear that the efforts were notably successful.[3]

By mid-1975, STAC's workload had diminished significantly, and it became difficult to keep the subcommittees

[2] The plastic ring used to hold bottles and cans together in a multipack is called a "hi-cone."

[3] Notwithstanding the printers' fears, there have been no major problems with printing the U.P.C. symbol.

together. The STAC Committee, composed of the subcommittee chairs, continued to meet and began to develop a life of its own, independent of the subcommittees. Subcommittee 3, Scanning, computer and related equipment, turned out to have the longest-lived agenda. It remained as a working group long after the other subcommittees had become little more than lists of names.

The magazine industry approached the Code Council seeking a supplemental symbol for use in processing returns. The Board decided it would not get in the business of developing add-on symbols. It would, however, allow STAC to provide the Council for Periodical Distributors with informal advice and to ensure that any add-on symbol would not have an adverse impact upon the U.P.C. symbol.

Ultimately, the industry came forward with a five-digit add-on symbol, developed with the advice and acquiescence of STAC. More importantly, STAC established the principle that the U.P.C. symbol must have adequate clear space. Beyond that, one would be able to essentially do anything without needing approval of the Board of Governors.

In the early days, there were but a handful of stores scanning the U.P.C. symbol. This enabled McKinsey & Co. to monitor them closely and prepare a regular "problem symbol report." This report described packages and symbols that did not scan well. STAC took the report and analyzed the problems. This led to interpretations and guidance from the technical experts.

From the outset, the number of problems reported was astonishingly small. Many on STAC, especially the printer and converter representatives, instinctively assumed the report grossly understated the actual number of problems. Despite this widespread belief, all available data indicates that from the very beginning the U.P.C. symbol scanned with an extraordinary paucity of problems.

In November 1975, STAC reported to the Board of Governors that the printability gage, distributed with every set of symbol specifications, was not useful as a determinant of symbol quality. Fearing that people would interpret this, incorrectly, as meaning the print gage had no use at all, the Board decided not to publicize the STAC conclusion. STAC, especially subcommittee 2, was not satisfied. It continued to press for an official statement from the Board that the printability gage was for pressroom guidance only, and should never be used as a quality determinant.

The Board asked Tom Wilson to draft an appropriate statement, which, when issued, quieted the printing community for a time. A STAC-sponsored U.P.C. symbol seminar was a great success, particularly in alleviating the concerns of the printers. This issue, however, like others would not go away. Many printers continue to believe that users of the U.P.C. hold printers to unreasonable standards of print quality.

Similarly, the U.P.C. system works so well that at any given moment, there are groups who are convinced that information on problems is being withheld from them. In 1976, STAC voiced this complaint. It simply did not seem reasonable that a new technology in a new application could work as well as it did.

This does not mean that the system was static. STAC recommended revisions to the U.P.C. symbol specification from time to time. These were routinely approved by the Board of Governors. For example, STAC 6 decided in 1976 that the Symbol Location Guidelines manual could use an update. In January 1977, it was almost ready to issue the revision.

On January 1, 1978, the Board of Governors terminated its relationship with Distribution Codes and opened its own offices in Dayton, Ohio. Heading the two-person office was Board member and co-chair of STAC Richard Mindlin. Dick Mindlin took early retirement from his position at NCR and agreed to become Executive Vice President of the Uniform

Product Code Council. While this ended his service as a Board member,[4] he decided to continue to co-chair STAC.

In light of Mindlin's background, he made a special effort to preserve and enhance the role of STAC. At least once a year, STAC members were invited to attend a Board of Governors meeting. STAC-type issues were featured at these meetings, and the Board was effusive in expressing its gratitude for the volunteer efforts of the STAC members.

Nonetheless, STAC began to wither away, although it never disappeared entirely. Subcommittees met infrequently, if at all, and some lost all members except the subcommittee chairman. As noted above, after the initial burst of activity, the workload of the subcommittees diminished rapidly. Mindlin's appointment as UPCC staff head inadvertently accelerated this development. With his technical background and expertise, many problems that would have been handed over to STAC were instead handled internally.

STAC remained a staunch bastion against those who sought to degrade the U.P.C. symbol by "minor" variances from the specification. This was particularly true when it came to symbol truncation.

Many producers of products desired to reduce the size of the symbol. An easy way to do this was to truncate the symbol, that is, lop off the top part of the symbol. The result was still scannable, but the truncation caused the symbol to lose omnidirectionality. In order for it to be scanned properly, it had to be presented to the scanner in a particular orientation with a resulting loss of productivity. Over and over again, STAC proclaimed the importance of avoiding truncation, limiting its use to those packages whose small size (such as chewing gum) required a smaller symbol.

On Dick Mindlin's retirement from the UPCC in 1983, his successor, Hal Juckett, didn't quite know what to do about STAC. It still existed, but no longer met. Indeed many STAC

[4] Fran Beck of Sperry Rand succeeded him as equipment governor.

members were unaware they were on the committee or if they were had no idea of what they were supposed to do.

STAC, however, was the only standing committee of the UPCC. There were issues that either did not rise to the level of Board issues, or on which input was needed prior to Board meetings, which were scheduled less frequently now. Hal turned to his existing resource, the STAC subcommittee chairmen. Since the subcommittees had de facto gone out of existence, they were allowed to rest in peace.

In addition to the five subcommittee chairs,[5] Juckett asked the Automatic Identification Manufacturers (AIM) to designate the chair of the AIM scanning committee to STAC. A few U.P.C. users were also named to the committee.[6] Hal Juckett named himself to chair the reinvigorated STAC.

This committee met on an as-needed basis, as determined by the chair. Meetings were infrequent, but served a useful purpose, both as a technical group and as a sounding board for proposals for UPCC activity. These came more often as the organization increasingly was recognized for the success of its standards and its enviable cash position. While the committee never grew to an unwieldy, or even a particularly large, size, as time passed individuals were added to STAC (especially new chairs of the AIM committee), but no one left.

As chronicled elsewhere,[7] in the late 1980s, under the leadership of Byron Allumbaugh, there was a distinct change in the governance of the Code Council. One aspect of the change was the creation of a number of Board committees to take a more active role in the development of policy. This had

[5] Subcommittees 3 and 4, both dealing with equipment, had been combined.

[6] This distressed Tom Wilson who believed it subverted the purpose of a *technical* advisory committee.

[7] See Chapter 13.

a significant impact on STAC, which remained a standing committee.

In the first place, STAC's recently acquired role of policy adviser was removed, and the committee was restored to its original role as a technical adviser. This, however, was becoming an increasingly important function. STAC had few problems with the U.P.C. symbol to deal with, but the Code Council was now addressing new and more complicated issues, such as the extension of UCC standards to more and more industries. At first, the extensions were into other retail industries, but the strength of the standards, the competence of their administration, and the blending of channels of distribution, led the UCC inexorably to the industrial commercial sector.

There were demands for standards to handle not just fixed data about a product as the U.P.C. had always done, but for variable data — batch, lot, shipment, and so forth — as well. STAC has been instrumental in developing standards to meet these needs.

The need for encoding variable data was handled by the adoption of UCC-EAN Code 128. This whole process was facilitated enormously by the presence on STAC of Ted Williams, the inventor of Code 128, and David Allais, the inventor of several other widely used bar codes, including Code 39.

STAC also, after twenty years, faced up to the question of symbol verification, developing a standard for measuring the quality of a printed symbol and a set of calibration standards traceable to the National Institute for Standards and Technology (NIST). These calibration standards make it possible for symbol verifiers to produce reliable and consistent results.

With the encouragement of the UCC and at the request of the joint grocery industry coupon committee, STAC came up with a recommendation for a Code 128 add-on to the U.P.C. coupon symbol. Thus, after twenty years, manufacturers were provided the capability to scan coupons and obtain marketing data. Manufacturers believed this had been promised them when the symbol was adopted. Until 1994, however, the Code Council did not know how to deliver on its promise.

As STAC's resurgence continued, Hal Juckett encouraged a reorganization that would maintain the vitality of STAC, but give it a structure. This would put STAC on an equal footing with other UCC committees.

By the mid-1990s, STAC meetings once again resembled the original meetings. The air was charged, discussions intense (and often abstruse), and the resulting synergy awesome to behold. Once about to die from inactivity, STAC today represents an unparalleled capability in bar code technology, recognized for its leadership the world over.

7
UPCC—On Its Own

The year 1978 marked a significant change for the Code
Council. After five years of contracting U.P.C. administration,
the Board of Governors decided it was more economical to
transfer code administration to a hired staff. No one expected it to be a difficult or demanding task. The Board did
not conduct a formal or extensive search. They quickly found
their candidate among their own. Dick Mindlin, Vice President at NCR, Board member, and co-chair of STAC, agreed to
take early retirement from NCR to become Executive Vice
President and Chief Administrative Officer of the UPCC.

The title reflected the Board's determination to keep for
itself all executive authority. Yet the title was also quite expan-
sive. In reality, Mindlin's staff was limited to Sharon Focht, his
secretary at NCR, who followed him in this new endeavor.

Mindlin and the UPCC struck a unique five-year contract.
The Board believed that by the end of the contract the duties
would be purely clerical, the staff would be disbanded, and
the job turned over to a secretary in one of the grocery trade
associations. And so the employment contract provided that
each year the compensation and the duties would be reduced
by 20 percent. By year five, Mindlin would be working 20
percent of the time for 20 percent of the first year's salary.

Dick Mindlin never worked less than full time during the
five years. Nevertheless, the Board of Governors held to the

dream. At the end of each year, a formal resolution was passed, acknowledging that for at least one more year the UPCC needed a full time staff. Grudgingly, the Board acknowledged that the job was growing, not contracting, by granting pay raises.

The UPCC had hired its own staff to reduce costs. The arrangement worked. A McKinsey analysis showed that the cost to the organization of processing a new member was approximately one-third that paid to DCI.[1] It soon became obvious that, while the economy would not be rejected, it may not have been necessary. At the end of the first month of its own operation (January 1978), Treasurer Bill Oddy advised the Board that revenues were $125,000 ahead of expenses, instead of the predicted $80,000 loss. Looking ahead to the end of the fiscal year in May, Oddy expected a close to break-even financial report, in spite of the expenses of start-up, payment of rent on DCI's offices, and a full bonus to DCI.

The UPCC's offices were located just outside Dayton, Ohio. The location was part of the negotiations with Mindlin. He had spent his career with NCR in Dayton, and had no desire to move. There was no strong resistance, and costs were much lower in Dayton than in cities like Washington or New York.[2]

DCI employees Leo Beinhorn, a marketing specialist, and John Langan, a technician, were hired as consultants to ease the transition. Although they were to be on call, available as needed by Dick Mindlin, he found few occasions to use them.

The switch from DCI caused some to believe the UPCC had gone out of business. Board members agreed to work to counter this impression and to have more formal communication with the membership.

[1] According to Treasurer Bill Oddy, the cost of processing a member was $82, compared with over $300 by DCI.

[2] Later, when the UCC became a significant enterprise, the relative isolation of Dayton caused some problems.

Early 1978 brought some difficult decisions on Board membership. Alan Haberman, chair of the Symbol Selection Committee, a member of the Ad Hoc Committee, and an FMI representative to the Board of Governors, left the grocery industry. This meant he needed to resign as a governor. The other members did not want to lose his services and scrambled to figure out a way to keep him.

The solution was to select him as the first "public" governor of the UPCC. This position was intended for a representative of a public interest group. To some, the Haberman nomination made a mockery of this intent. However, Alan took his responsibilities seriously and diligently sought to express the consumer viewpoint.

There was another problem. Procter & Gamble took exception to some of the Grocery Manufacturers of America's policies (unrelated to the UPCC) and withdrew from GMA for a time. Barry Franz of P&G was a GMA governor, so he too had to resign. He was reelected as a grocery manufacturer at large, however, then returned as a GMA governor when Procter rejoined GMA.

By 1978, some scanning retailers had discovered that there was a market for the product-movement data generated as goods passed over the slot scanner. While the Ad Hoc Committee recognized the availability of data might be interesting to some, they did not see it as a significant value. Data was not listed as a U.P.C. benefit. The Ad Hoc had assumed retailers would make the information available to manufacturers at no charge.

Retailers, however, found out there was a market for it, and it eventually became a significant source of income. Many product-makers were not amused, and it created a problem for the Code Council. From the manufacturers' perspective, U.P.C. meant extra cost with no corresponding savings. They believed the Ad Hoc had held out the promise of movement data and more efficient, lower cost coupon handling.[3] They were now having to purchase the data created from the symbols they placed on the product.[4]

After four months, Mindlin reported he was receiving an average of twenty calls per day. Three hundred of the three hundred fifty membership applications in this period were $250 minimum-fee memberships. At this point, for the first and only time, the minimum membership fee was increased from $250 to $300.

In addition, the bylaws were amended to limit voting rights to "voting members," defined as members of the Board of Governors. Since most members did not realize they had joined an organization, there was no resistance to this move. It enabled the UPCC to avoid the problem of attaining a quorum at an annual meeting. It also virtually eliminated the mailing cost of an annual meeting notice.

Contrary to its normal passive posture, the UPCC arranged for a presentation on the advantages of U.P.C. scanning to officials from liquor control states, where alcohol was sold only through state-owned facilities. Some of these states were investigating other marking systems, and the UPCC effort helped forestall those investigations. This was welcome news to the liquor industry, which was facing the prospect of selling identical product requiring multiple labels.

Nonetheless, at the seventh annual meeting, the chair reiterated that the Code Council's aim was to have trade associations provide more of the basic U.P.C. services. In the UPCC's opinion, this was being accomplished. Now there were 461 scanning stores with thirty to forty more being added each month. Several chains had announced their commitment to reach full scanning. Not surprisingly, the Board

[3] See Chapter 10.

[4] In Europe, part of the process for adopting a variant of the U.P.C. was an agreement that manufacturers could receive their own data at no charge.

decided that Dick Mindlin would remain a full-time employee through 1979.[5]

As the fear of insolvency faded, hopes turned to the possibility of endowment. The need for endowed status was premised on the assumption there was a finite number of potential members. At some point, expenses would dramatically outstrip revenues because revenues were heavily tilted toward membership income, and the fee was a one-time fee. It was further assumed that, although the membership fee was only collected once, the UPCC had committed to provide services in perpetuity. An endowment was the answer.

The organization has always assumed it could not collect periodic or annual dues, and identified no other source of revenue large enough to support itself. In addition, though many have tried, no one has been able to predict what the upper limit on membership will be. McKinsey, in the early years, made several serious attempts and concluded there would never be more than 6000 members of the Code Council. This modest number later became a standing joke at board meetings.[6]

The initial impetus toward endowment came in May 1979, when the treasurer reported he needed only $120,000 to balance the budget, Yet, since January 1, receipts totalled over $520,000. The endowment has continued to grow. In the early nineties, an aggressive investment strategy was adopted. Endowment is within reach as this is being written.

Though the UPCC had its office in Ohio, Dick Foote, an independent accountant in Vienna, Virginia, continued to be the organization's bookkeeper. An independent CPA in Foote's community, Tom Collins, was named outside auditor.

A need for a major communications and education effort

[5] A similar decision was made before each new year of his contract.

[6] As the use of UCC standards crosses more and more industries, today there is an assumption that strong member growth will continue indefinitely. In 1996, there were more than 180,000 UCC members.

on problem numbers came from a recurring failure by manufacturers to let retailers know about U.P.C. number changes. The U.P.C. is worth nothing if the retailer's scanner cannot recognize an item as it passes over the scanner. Communication is a primary function of the UCC education program.

In the first year of its independent operation, the UPCC also began to deal with two new issues that would ultimately be satisfactorily resolved. The Poultry and Egg Institute presented an unworkable proposal for U.P.C. coding of variable weight products. The Board, correctly, worried that this proposal could never attain consensus of interested parties.

The issue of coding of variable-weight products (meats, cheeses, and so forth) had to be addressed. The UPCC felt a responsibility to exert leadership, and it did. The result was a use of number system 2 for random-weight coding. The solution worked, but not perfectly. It also consumed one-tenth of the total U.P.C. capacity. Fifteen years later, the UCC began to worry about capacity.

Ultimately, the Code Council parceled out blocks of numbers to industry groups representing variable-weight products. When they began to run out of numbers before all product variations had been covered, the problem became acute. To date, it has been patched, but not really solved.

Governor Taubert also told the Board that the UPCC needed to take on the responsibility of developing a shipping container symbol. DCI and the Distribution Research and Education Foundation (DREF) were continuing their project, but it appeared to be grinding to a halt. DCI had identified the need and sparked interest, but proved unable to resolve the problems and reach a solution. Again, the UPCC ultimately succeeded, but the solution was lengthy and difficult. Taubert, and his Hunt-Wesson colleague Bill Maginnis, took the lead.

At the end of the 1970s, Burt Gookin turned the chair over to retailer Bob Wegman, CEO of Wegman's Super

Markets. Wegman had also led the effort for the Ad Hoc Committee that raised money from retailers to keep the effort going, and had chaired the Ad Hoc's Public Affairs Committee in the mid-1970s.

Education and what to do about it were the first issues addressed by the Wegman-led Board. Here, too, the UPCC adhered to its fundamental, non-activist posture. The Board concluded U.P.C. education should be the responsibility of the grocery industry trade associations.

The Board did agree that the UPCC should provide a scanning information exchange. Using the UPCC as an intermediary, retailers could report problem symbols, and manufacturers could take remedial action. Interestingly, this was considered an appropriate activity even though the Food Marketing Institute[7] was offering a similar service.

Its utility proved difficult to measure. Those who participated found it extremely useful. Not many retailers, however, submitted bad symbols. After six months of operation, only 54 retailers had reported to the exchange. Some wanted a list of nonscannable symbols published. This was rejected on legal grounds. It would have been considered a "blacklist," which creates very serious antitrust issues.

Barry Franz was elected UPCC Treasurer in 1980. He would hold this position for over fifteen years. As one of his first acts, he was able to predict that revenues would exceed expenses for at least the next five years and he proposed the first formal, written investment policy for the organization.

After years of discussion, a symbology for use on shipping containers was finally adopted in 1981. Designed with the grocery industry in mind, the "interleaved two of five" symbology was well suited for direct printing on corrugated boxes in connection with fixed quantities of like goods. In a

---

[7] FMI was the association of supermarket chains. It was created through a merger of the Supermarket Institute and the National Association of Food Chains.

few years, the Code Council would need to develop a more flexible standard for other kinds of shipments.

The UPCC was pleased to recommend something finally. Concerns over the symbol's printability led to multiple tests and seemingly endless discussions. Where implemented, the new symbology worked well. Yet very few companies actually tried to scan cases in the warehouse, so the efficacy of the symbol remained unmeasured for many years.

Wegman's term ended in the fall of 1981. Following the bylaw-prescribed cycle of alternating retailers and manufacturers in the chair, he was succeeded by another Board chairman of GMA, Robert Schaeberle, CEO of Nabisco Brands. The credibility such executives brought to the UPCC was incalculable.

During these years, when growth was steady but not overwhelming, the Board each meeting approved the remarkably small list of companies who sought relief from the fee schedule.[8] Growth eventually put a stop to this practice (although hardship memberships at low or no fees are still available if approved by the UCC president).

As the end of Dick Mindlin's five-year contract approached, the Board began to think of a successor. It was obvious to all by now that the post was a full-time one. There were now three or four support staff working in the Code Council offices processing applications for membership and assigning U.P.C. manufacturer identification numbers.

The Executive Committee concluded that Mindlin's successor should be an educator and a motivator. In the spring of 1983, the Board retained the executive search firm of Spencer Stuart to find such a candidate.

Memberships continued to grow, predominantly influenced by mass merchants such as KMart and Wal-Mart, who had made the commitment to U.P.C. scanning. This had a

---

[8] The Board also insisted on reviewing the list of new members to decide which new member had the most amusing name.

profound influence. Grocery retailers have hundreds of suppliers, each of whom was a candidate for Code Council membership. Mass merchants purchase from thousands, even tens of thousands of suppliers. The growth potential for the UPCC was enormous.

The Board decided it would be appropriate to include a mass merchant as a distributor-at-large member. Jim Tuttle, a KMart lawyer, was selected to join the Board in 1983.

The year 1982 was noted by the appearance of two issues, one which disappeared, the other which appeared, quieted, but would recur several times over many years.

The November Board of Governors meeting was enlivened by a presentation from VISA. The credit card company suggested using a variation of the U.P.C. on its debit cards to identify individuals. The Board was somewhat bemused by the presentation, since it was so far removed from the identification of items in the grocery store. In addition, they were a little concerned at the potential public relations problems inherent in the "Big Brother" aspects of a code identifying each individual. Accordingly, their response to the presentation while not unfriendly, was muted. Therefore, when nothing more was heard from VISA, the UPCC suffered no remorse.

On the other hand, appropriate U.P.C. marking of magazines when the cover price is changed proved a more substantive and long-lasting problem. Working with the Council for Periodical Distributors (CPDA), a solution was proposed, and the problem seemed to go away. Nine years later, however, the identical issue arose. This time, CPDA retained a consultant and developed a detailed proposal. Different types of magazine retailers, however, had different needs. Moreover, the UCC was unable to determine whether the industry as a whole viewed the issue as serious. Accordingly, the UCC has so far declined to take further action.

In the fall of 1983, the executive recruiter presented his

candidates to the Executive Committee. The winner was Harold Juckett, a career Xerox executive with a significant background in customer education and training. He matched almost perfectly the profile for a successor to Mindlin. Juckett made his first appearance at the November Board meeting, a month before he became an employee.

It suddenly became very important to Dick Mindlin to receive a formal pronouncement from the Board that he would remain in charge through calendar year 1984. The Board was quick to oblige, but the year of overlap was difficult for both men. Both were decent, hard workers, and in later years, their relationship greatly mellowed; 1984, however, demonstrated the adage that any organization suffers when there is more than one person in charge. The Executive Committee watched the conflict, for the most part sympathizing with the new kid in town. Trying to ameliorate the situation, the Executive Committee directed Juckett to focus his attention on the administration of the Uniform Communications Standard (UCS),[9] the newly acquired activity.

Both men were given high marks for their performance. Juckett provided proposals to meet U.P.C. education needs. He also emphasized the need to establish and maintain quality control over the system. Mindlin retired at year's end. One of his important legacies was the promotion of his former secretary, Sharon Focht, to the position of Manager, Operations. Sharon remains the voice of calm competence for the administration of U.P.C. numbers.

As the organization spread beyond the grocery industry, there were at least glimmerings of a need to focus on the needs of general merchandise and industrial users. Even Tom Wilson, who firmly believed that the UCC's primary job was to serve the needs of the grocery industry, admitted that the organization needed to reexamine its mission.

The expanded role delayed the attainment of endowed

[9] See Chapter 8.

status. It also prompted an announcement to scanner manufacturers that equipment needed to be able to read all U.P.C. number systems, because there would be a need to start assigning numbers in them in the foreseeable future.

By now, the organization was well into its teens, and the pioneers of the system were leaving the Board of Governors. The May 1984 Executive Committee minutes reflect a discussion of McKinsey's role. It made no sense to the newcomers. A consultant did not normally hang around after the project was up and running, nor did a consultant retain such an influential role. And certainly a consultant was never so cavalier about billing as was Tom Wilson. The UPCC had to beg him to submit bills. When they were submitted, they were at bargain basement rates.

Wilson probably would have worked for free. Involvement with the UPCC gave him unparalleled access to grocery industry executives, many of whom needed consulting help. It all came at a cost, however. While Wilson's influence continued strong, opposition built up which would in time break the relationship.[10]

Governor Marsh Blackburn had been the leader in bringing UCS, a form of electronic data interchange, to the Code Council. In his view, the organization's name no longer accurately reflected its mission and constituencies. He proposed to drop the word "product" from the name. The Uniform Code Council, Inc. then directed Hal Juckett to develop a new logo.

As the Council adopted a new name to match its broader responsibilities, the Board also expressed concern that the organization would outgrow its capacity. To minimize that concern, I was asked to develop a proposal for recalling U.P.C. manufacturer IDs which had been issued, then abandoned by the member. Although never implemented, recall

[10] See Chapter 13.

remains a concern, and someday the plan will have to be put into effect. Capacity for the foreseeable future remains adequate.[11]

The Food Marketing Institute had published a monthly list of new scanning stores. It was the best way to measure scanning's growth. However, it was limited to supermarkets. As scanning in general merchandise increased, the value of the FMI report diminished, and soon it was stopped.

Not until 1985 did the Code Council purchase a computer for its internal use. Although the organization was a leader in new technology, the office remained "low tech" and well behind in its use of the most advanced technology. At the same time, the number of complaints about bad symbols trebled.

Both the purchase of an office computer and the increase in the number of complaints reflected a maturing of the U.P.C. It was no longer adequate to assign numbers by picking one from a roll of 100,000 numbers. Similarly, the increase in complaints meant that the tolerance of retailers for bad symbols was ending. The system was no longer an experiment. For it to work effectively, high quality was required from suppliers.

Less than six months after taking the reins from Dick Mindlin, Hal Juckett was on the road 60 percent of the time. There was a clear need for a second executive to serve as Juckett's backstop. Spencer Stuart was again asked to conduct a search. The office was growing too. There was a need for larger space.

McKinsey prepared a final study for the UCC, an analysis of the "final system architecture" for the U.P.C. This report concluded that the organization needed to announce its intention of using all the number systems available in version A of the U.P.C. symbol. This was an especially important message for the scanner manufacturers. It put them on

[11] This conclusion was reenforced by a 1996 study for the UCC and EAN by AT&T Solutions.

notice that equipment needed to be capable of reading all ten U.P.C. number systems. In the early days, some companies, in a rush to get to market, sold machines that could read only number system 0.

The McKinsey report also emphasized the need to maintain compatibility with the EAN code. This was surprising, since Tom Wilson continually pointed out that few European grocery products came into this country, and those that did had to be relabeled to comply with FDA requirements. This meant a U.P.C. symbol could easily be added in the place of EAN coding.[12]

The U.P.C. symbol came in three varieties: Version A, Version D, and Version E.[13] Versions A and E were in widespread use, but version D, an up to thirty-digit version of the U.P.C. was not. No specification for its use had ever been developed. Periodically, someone would propose Version D to solve a coding problem or for a new application. After considerable pressure, version D was authorized for use by meat producers for random-weight product. No one ever used it. Accordingly, in the 1985 final system architecture report, McKinsey said that the costs associated with version D far outweighed any benefits. If it was to be considered at all, it should only be for future uses. Under no circumstances should companies be expected to retrofit scanners in place to read Version D.

The McKinsey Final System Architecture Report launched a discussion on the future of the UCC. The Board's first decision was to keep the document internal. It was not made public, nor was it even released to the founding associations.

Issues facing the UCC included whether it should continue to focus on retail applications or broaden its scope. By

[12] The growing global marketplace has almost completely eliminated this argument.

[13] Symbol versions B and C were never developed.

this time, all agreed that use of the U.P.C. would expand. Should the UCC take a proactive or reactive approach to that growth?

Tom Wilson proposed a revision to the mission statement, which was ultimately adopted in 1988. The tone of the statement was essentially reactive. The mission explicitly warned readers they must

> recognize that the U.P.C. was developed by the grocery industry and other applications must not endanger the system in the grocery industry. The burden of proof should be on those who propose a change in our principles. It must be recognized that the UCC in the past has made accommodations for the grocery industry which it cannot make for other industries.[14]

While the tone was not a welcoming one, it did make a valid point. Some early U.P.C. decisions, such as allocating a complete number system[15] to random-weight products, clearly could not be duplicated for other industries. There simply wasn't enough capacity. Still the reluctance to welcome expansion remained. This was to be its last gasp, however. The times were about to change.

In 1986, a charity requested a U.P.C. number so that consumers could make donations directly at the checkout. After a lengthy discussion, the UCC turned the request down. U.P.C. numbers were associated with products, not services or intangibles. The charity was directed to work out a solution with the retailers involved. Ten years later, this policy was still in place, but under examination. As the use of the U.P.C. broadened, it is more difficult to argue that U.P.C. numbers are only associated with products.

The Produce Marketing Association requested a U.P.C.

---

[14] Minutes, Executive Committee, Uniform Code Council, May 4, 1987, p. 1.

[15] Each number system (there were ten) allowed for 999,999 U.P.C. manufacturer ID numbers.

number to be used with generic codes for produce. Food retailers supported the request. The Board was reluctant to grant it. Generic or commodity codes raised legal problems and undercut the ability of a producer to establish brand identity for his product. After an impassioned plea from the FMI governors and a legal opinion from the PMAA's counsel assuring that any supplier who wished to have a separate manufacturer ID number could do so, the Board took its first recorded vote. David Carlson of KMart insisted his opposition to the proposal be recorded. With that noted, the request was granted with a formal statement that the action was unique and should not be viewed as a precedent.[16]

Hal Juckett was becoming more comfortable in his job. He advocated a more expansionist vision of the UCC than that reflected in the Mission Statement. Those who preferred to keep a low profile dubbed him "the glacier." Like a glacier, they said, you never saw him move, but every time you looked he was occupying more space, with more staff, performing a larger task.

In an effort to slow the growth and to maintain his own influence over the UCC, Tom Wilson convinced the Executive Committee to create an Operating Committee, composed of Wilson, Barry Franz, and me. This committee was supposed to serve as an oversight group. Wilson saw it as a mechanism to rein in Juckett. Juckett resented the implicit criticism. The stage was set for a major confrontation. It took two years. Juckett emerged victorious.[17]

---

[16] Within three years, the floral industry requested the same thing, citing produce as a precedent. The Board rejected the request, sending the applicant to the Produce Association to obtain commodity codes if it wished.

[17] See Chapter 13.

8

Electronic Data Interchange (EDI)

With the selection of the U.P.C. symbol, the grocery industry celebrated the success of the Ad Hoc Committee. Hopes were high that other productivity projects could use this model. Bill Reidy of Kraft Foods, and chairman of the GMA Administrative Systems Committee, was especially hopeful. This committee's efforts to develop a universal product code[1] had been frustrated for years. The Ad Hoc's success shone most clearly to them.

Reidy hoped to use the Ad Hoc Committee model to establish industrywide standards for computer-to-computer ordering and invoicing. It was a good time for such an overture. There was an aura of good feeling in the industry and hope that the U.P.C. success marked an end to bitter divisions between buyers and sellers. The Administrative Systems Committee met with its NAFC counterpart to begin the exploration in the spring of 1974.

The retailer community seemed to feel that a computer-to-computer ordering project would benefit manufacturers much more and viewed computer-to-computer as a payback to grocery manufacturers who had incurred the costs of U.P.C. source marking.[2] Before the retailers would commit,

[1] See Prologue.

163

however, they insisted the scope of the project must exclude any consideration of electronic funds transfer (EFT). Most retailers had developed sophisticated techniques for managing float, using remote disbursing banks to pay bills. This gave them an extra one or two days' control of their money.

Excluding EFT from consideration was not a deal-breaker for manufacturers,[3] and a joint group was created. There was, however, a fundamental difference between this group and the Ad Hoc Committee. The computer-to-computer group consisted of information systems vice presidents, not CEOs.

There was also no precipitating event (such as the FDA's nutritional labeling regulations) to impel adoption of the system. Without direct CEO involvement, it was difficult to persuade either manufacturers or retailers to spend the money required to implement computer-to-computer. Failure to implement made it difficult to document results. Failure to have results further slowed implementation.

The joint committee first selected a consultant and adopted an approach to the subject. When the usual consultants vied for the project, the early smart money was on Larry Russell and McKinsey. The McKinsey proposal envisioned computer-to-computer transmissions via a "black box" in the middle of the transaction that would translate each computer's output so it could be read by the other computer. This was the conventional wisdom.

The committee was more intrigued by another approach to the subject. Arthur D. Little, Inc., a Cambridge Massachusetts consulting firm, suggested creating a common for-

[2] History has shown that both sides of the transaction receive benefits from computer-to-computer ordering.

[3] In 1993, when grocery manufacturers and distributors initiated the Efficient Consumer Response (ECR) program designed to take billions of dollars in costs out of grocery distribution, EFT was one of the subjects targeted as a source of cost reduction for both sides.

mat for computer-to-computer messages so that the same information always appeared at the same point in the message. If feasible, this would cost far less.

The committee cast its lot with Arthur D. Little. The project was under the direction of David Boodman, assisted by Dick Norris. For whatever reason, the chemistry between Boodman and the industry committee was bad. Rather quickly, Norris became the de facto leader of the project. Very quietly, Boodman's role was reduced, until it finally disappeared completely.

The Arthur D. Little approach took a long time to develop, because the top management commitment to the project was not as strong as it had been for the U.P.C. It also lacked a strong retailer push. To many companies this was just another MIS project, competing for limited capital with dozens of other information systems projects, to say nothing of other company needs.

Arthur D. Little's report was finally completed in 1980. It proposed the creation of a new, uniform communications standard (UCS) which would make possible industrywide computer-to-computer ordering and invoicing. The industry associations endorsed the Little study, and began to encourage companies to adopt and use the UCS. Paul Kelly, GMA's Marketing Vice President, became the de facto administrator of UCS. The Arthur D. Little study concluded that if 50 percent of the message volume was transmitted via UCS, the industry could save $324 million. UCS was the subject of pilot tests in 1981, and in 1982 the UCS standards were published.

UCS was constantly measured against U.P.C. It was not a success on that scale. No matter how it was promoted, usage remained limited. The Code Council Board designated Governor Bill Taubert of Hunt-Wesson and very active GMA member, as official liaison to UCS as a way to stay in touch.

UCS lacked some critical attributes of U.P.C. that had contributed mightily to the adoption of U.P.C. To continue to do business with a scanning retailer, a supplier really had no choice but to adopt the U.P.C. Moreover, FDA's nutritional labeling regulations meant that most food labels had to be changed at approximately the same time that source-symbol marking was needed, so the incremental cost of adding the U.P.C. was minimal. UCS had neither of these "advantages."

Nonetheless, those in the grocery industry who had developed the UCS continued to believe it held the potential for major savings for the industry. A dedicated cadre continued to test the system. Industry forums were urged to use electronic communication. As month followed month with no significant increase in usage, the industry committee began to think about finding a permanent home for the project that could offer strong marketing help.

In late 1982, the UPCC Executive Committee approved participation on a joint study team under the leadership of food broker Marsh Blackburn, a major supporter of UCS. The team's mission was to investigate the feasibility of merging administration of the UCS with that of the U.P.C.

Within six months, Dick Mindlin and Paul Kelly were directed to prepare a transition plan to guide the integration of UCS into the Uniform Product Code Council. The merger was approved in concept, and the UPCC's bylaws were changed to accommodate the projected arrangement. The positions of printer and equipment governor were eliminated, and the National Food Brokers Association (a financial contributor to UCS) was given the right to name two governors. Those with interest and experience with computer-to-computer ordering would be sought as candidates for governor.

In May 1983, the Board of Governors decided that U.P.C. and UCS were to be maintained as separate divisions with separate budgets. Although the technical issues were different from U.P.C., the users were the same.

Tom Wilson particularly tried to dispel the notion that UCS was simply the "son of U.P.C." and its development, implementation, and success could simply mimic U.P.C. U.P.C. was a relatively static system, adopted by a company once and requiring little maintenance. UCS, on the other hand, lacked the U.P.C. imperative for adoption. It never received the top management push U.P.C. did. It was also very dynamic, requiring extensive management.

For the Code Council, this meant that UCS cost more to manage, while it generated considerably smaller revenues. Some on the Board saw this as irrelevant. If the UPCC takes on a responsibility rightfully belonging to it, it should fulfill that responsibility whatever the cost. The majority of the Board, however, felt the new division must set a goal of breaking even (despite the fact that the U.P.C. was generating enough cash to build a significant endowment). Years went by before this happened. Yet strong leadership, gradual but growing implementation, and innovative financing programs led to a break-even balance sheet by the early 1990s.

The first NFBA governors, Marsh Blackburn and Dick McReady were elected in November 1983. At the same time, Jim Tuttle of KMart and Dick Keener of Kraft[4] were also named to the board. Both men came with a background in computer-to-computer ordering and invoicing.

This was also the first board meeting attended by Hal Juckett, who was joining the Code Council to take Dick Mindlin's place on his retirement at the end of 1984. Juckett's initial assignment was to take charge of the newly acquired UCS program.

A major part of the Board's responsibility was to determine how much the UCS program would cost and how much revenue it would generate. UCS brought a dowry of about

---

[4] Dick Keener had been under Bill Reidy at Kraft. When Reidy left the company, Keener had taken over his position.

$30,000 to the Code Council, but the estimated program costs were sheer guesswork.

The first UCS orientation session sponsored by the Code Council attracted ninety individuals from thirty-nine companies. An advisory committee and a standards maintenance committee were created to give the program a structure within the organization. After one year under the UPCC, forty-five companies had joined the Code Council specifically because of UCS. Spurred on by Governor Blackburn, the name of the organization was changed to the Uniform Code Council, since UCS did not deal with products.

The UCC differentiated between members who joined to obtain a U.P.C. number and those who participated in the UCS program. Companies who chose to do both ended up with two memberships.[5] Growth of UCS continued to lag far behind that of U.P.C. At the end of 1985, there were only 115 UCS members.

UCS was not the only application of computer-to-computer communication developing.[6] As electronic data interchange (EDI), spread throughout various industries, efforts were made to develop nationally recognized protocols. An accredited standards committee under the American National Standards Institute, ANSI X12, was created for this purpose.

The UCC had a historic antipathy toward ANSI. The Ad Hoc Committee had consciously rejected the ANSI standardization process, fearing it would take so long that momentum would be killed. They had seen the problems the NRMA had in obtaining a parallel product-identification standard through ANSI. This confirmed their view.

[5] Each fee was a one-time fee until 1994, when EDI (UCS) went to an annual fee schedule.

[6] The transportation industry had actually pioneered in the field. UCS relied on the Transportation Data Coordinating Committee (TDCC) to edit and publish the UCS standards.

Nonetheless, the UCS leaders became convinced that X12 was where the action was going to be in the future. They had serious misgivings, but in late 1985 began an exploration of how to make the UCS standards compatible with those of X12. As the study progressed, it appeared that the technical problems of standards accommodation could be addressed. But the political issues of moving UCS into X12 were much more formidable. The UCS team moved very cautiously, concerned the X12 bureaucracy might take over UCS.

Ralph R. Roll, from the accounting firm of Ernst and Young, joined the UCC as Vice President in the spring of 1986. He was given responsibility for UCS. Roll became the staff liaison to the negotiations with X12.

To add to Roll's load, Governor Bill Taubert reported that several manufacturer logistics professionals were reporting technical problems with UCS. Investigation proved the problems were with the understanding of the system, not with UCS.

Thus, UCC required a significant education program and political skills for dealing with ANSI. In addition, Tom Wilson's prediction that UCS would require great effort to keep it up to date was proving accurate. The UCS mavens and the grocery industry associations launched a major project to extend UCS to direct store-delivered product. This led Juckett to advise the Board that more staff was needed.

The demands on the UCC increased further. McKinsey and Tom Wilson were working with the textile industry's "Crafted with Pride in the USA" group seeking to improve the fortunes of domestic textile manufacturers. Computer-to-computer communication was one obvious technique. The Voluntary Interindustry Communications Standards Committee (VICS) was created to pursue this. VICS soon settled on ANSI X12 EDI standards and asked the UCC to administer them.

In a parallel effort, the UCC had created the General

Merchandise and Apparel Implementation Committee (GMAIC) to see if the U.P.C. could be made applicable to the general merchandise world. Soft goods companies had finally given up on the NRMA-sponsored OCR-A product identification standard.

The Board's initial reaction to the VICS request was negative. Administering X12 standards could be construed as undercutting UCS protocols. But some argued that the long-term future of UCS required it to move closer to X12. In late 1987, the UCC agreed to take on the VICS and WINS (public warehouse) standards in the same manner and to the same level as for UCS.

VICS EDI and U.P.C. in general merchandise prospered more quickly than in the grocery industry for two primary reasons. First, these industries were not pioneers; they were following in the path laid down by the grocery industry. This enabled them to learn from the grocers' mistakes. Even more significant, VICS and GMAIC were led by large retailers who were not shy about informing suppliers of their expectations.

This meant that thousands of new members needed U.P.C. numbers. While a grocer might have hundreds of suppliers, a KMart or Wal-Mart would have thousands — each of whom needed a U.P.C. number. Under the divided UCC structure, the membership fees thus brought in were attributed to U.P.C., not EDI.

Consistent with the Board's attitude of nervousness toward any activity by the Council that could be construed as pushing the UCC into new areas, the Board decided in 1987 that the UCC was not to develop an implementation strategy for the apparel industry. Implementation plans were to be the responsibility of the apparel industry associations.

The VICS Steering Committee aggressively assumed this responsibility with a program called Quick Response. Marked by an annual conference, QR was soon initiated. It was a promotional, educational program on the advantages of integration and implementation of bar coding and electronic data interchange. Quick Response has been so successful that other industries have adopted programs modeled on QR.

One of the tenets of the UCC is that a manufacturer should be content with a single U.P.C. ID number. The entry of the apparel industry with multiple sizes, colors, and styles forced a modification. Multiple U.P.C. numbers could be assigned, but only if an applicant proved the need due to its numbers of SKUs.[7]

In the late 1980s, the grocery industry sought UCC funds for a study on invoice deductions in the hope that the study would force increased usage of UCS. About the same time, the UCC agreed to help fund a study by VICS of the costs and benefits of bar coding in the retailing industries. The word was getting out that the UCC was building a considerable financial reserve, which could be tapped by an industry with the right proposal.

Within the UCC, the leaders of the EDI Advisory Committee were reluctantly concluding that the EDI standards administered by the UCC would somehow have to be made compatible with the broader EDI standards of the American National Standards Institute (ANSI). ANSI X12 is the committee responsible for establishing and maintaining EDI standards. The UCC decided to approach X12.

This was a cultural revolution. Historically, the UCC had rejected the ANSI standards process as too time consuming. In their opinion, events had proven them right. To receive Board approval even to meet with X12 was no mean feat. It was accomplished by assuring the Board that the UCC would insist on the right to govern its own standards.

Discussions with ANSI began in the summer of 1988 and proved every bit as difficult as envisioned. The UCC soon

[7] Stock keeping unit.

realized that personalities and politics were far more important than the merits of the standards.

After eighteen months of intense negotiation, an agreement was reached to bring the UCS standards under the ANSI tent. A new ANSI X12 subcommittee was created with the UCC as secretariat. This Warehousing and Distribution Subcommittee was to be the conduit for the migration of the UCS standards to ANSI standards.

It took almost four years, but all of the UCC-administered EDI standards successfully navigated the path to become American National Standards. The UCC has maintained its control over the Warehousing and Distribution Committee and is a full-fledged player in X12. Although it had to sacrifice some autonomy and control, being part of a single, worldwide EDI standard made this a small price to pay.

Under pressure from the Executive Committee to cover expenses, the EDI Advisory Committee in the early 1990s launched an intensive search for ways to obtain annual revenues to match the cost to the UCC of EDI administration. One vehicle was the semi-annual User Conference that grew more popular each year. In 1993, a radical proposal to charge annual dues, at a low level, was instituted. Initial results have been promising.

After literally a decade of stagnation, UCS membership and usage seems to be growing. The growth is spurred by the grocery industry's massive Efficient Consumer Response project, whose lofty goal is to take $30 billion out of the cost of grocery distribution.[8] ECR recognizes that EDI is essential for efficient distribution, from purchase order to payment.

Like the U.P.C., other industries are approaching the UCC requesting UCC administration of their EDI standards. So far, the organization has been reluctant to expand beyond retail. Reflecting the broader perspective of the contempo-

---

[8] ECR is the brainchild of former UCC chairman David Jenkins, retired CEO of Shaw's Supermarkets.

rary UCC, however, these overtures are no longer dismissed out of hand. Future expansion is not out of the question.

Again like the U.P.C., the UCC's focus on EDI is going global. There is a difference however. UCC's goal is to protect the existing US standards for North American trading partners rather than to force a change to an entirely new global standard. This issue remains unresolved.

EDI objectively has matured within the UCC. The administration of EDI standards is of critical importance to suppliers and distributors in the retail industries. Nonetheless, old attitudes die hard. Some of the EDI leaders active within the UCC continue to see themselves as second-class citizens to the cash cow U.P.C. The fact there is no basis for such feelings does not mean they are not deeply held. Time and the continued blending of U.P.C. and EDI will surely bring new understanding and cooperation.

9
Beyond Retail

The universal product code was created for the grocery industry by the grocery industry. The founders of the system (and their consultants) had a mission to protect the grocery industry from any application that might in any way hinder the U.P.C.'s full implementation in grocery stores. Other industries expressing interest in the code and symbol were given scant comfort by the Board of Governors.

Strict adherence to this policy proved impossible from the outset. Many products sold in supermarkets were also marketed through other channels of trade, some of which, especially drug and discount stores, also used high-volume checkstands. These industries needed to be included under the UCC umbrella, and so they were.

Occasionally, DCI would propose an expansion, and be told emphatically by the Board of Governors that it was inappropriate. The UCC was not only passive in these early years, it was minimalist. But with success came a broader vision and a different understanding of the marketplace. Increasingly, it was recognized that channels of distribution were not rigid and unique, they were intimately intertwined.

Ultimately, the Board would change its policy to see more than grocery, but not quickly — or easily. The first breach was seen as simply a necessary step to protect the integrity of the U.P.C.

DCI also administered the Distribution Code adopted (but not widely used) by the industrial commercial sector, especially electrical. The DC and U.P.C. were compatible, and the Code Council believed its supervision of DCI would prevent any damage to the U.P.C. from the DC. DCI agreed that all DC assignments would begin with 6 or 7, while U.P.C. numbers started with 0 or 3.

Even after the Code Council ended the contract with DCI and opened its own office, there seemed no need for further action. But in the early 1980s DCI began to go out of business, and its management needed to decide how to preserve the Distribution Code.

Ironically, they turned to the UCC. Tom Wilson took primary responsibility for negotiating with DCI. After several months of talks, in May 1983 the Board of Governors agreed to take over the administration of the Distribution Code, now to be known as the Uniform Industrial Code (UIC). Previous holders of Distribution Codes could have those numbers ratified as Industrial Codes for a nominal $100 fee. New companies could acquire UIC numbers for a $300 fee.

In 1990, the Board decided to simplify the pricing for industrial code users. Henceforth, all industrial users, whether new or transferees from the old system, would be charged $300. For the most part, it was an academic action, generating little response in the industrial arena.

According to the deal brokered by Wilson, the UCC would only assign supplier ID numbers and maintain the data base. It specifically disclaimed all other responsibilities. The UCC also agreed to add two representatives of industrial products companies to the Board of Governors. This became the most significant aspect of the deal, since both industrial governors refused simply to be quiet and occupy a space.

The first two industrial governors, Ben Cooper, an electrical distributor, and Allen Messerli of 3M, saw the Board of Governors as a grocery-industry cabal that needed to be pushed to recognize the broader implications of the system it had created. Despite the lack of early success, they remained undaunted.

Although the UCC had a mostly passive role in the administration of the industrial code, it commissioned a guidelines manual. This was written by George Wright, a consultant to the magazine industry, with a few industrial companies participating. In November 1984, Dick Mindlin advised the Board that only 200 of the approximately 15,000 distribution code users had joined the Uniform Industrial Code (UIC).

The relationship with the industrial code worked relatively smoothly. Wilson's deal with DCI, however, was never reduced to writing. Years later, whenever a question about the relationship came up, staff was forced to develop its own interpretation. The absence of a formal contract naturally resulted in some misunderstandings.

Fortunately, none of the problems was major. Also, DCI had gone out of existence. During the first years there were few companies either moving their Distribution Codes to the UIC *or* applying for a new industrial code. The Board continually reminded staff that the UCC was to remain passive and not attempt to evangelize the industrial market.

Though a distinct minority, Cooper and Messerli were frequently pointing the Board to opportunities in the nonretail sector. From their viewpoint, the UCC was derelict in neglecting this marketplace. Led by Tom Wilson, the rest of the Board insisted its primary function was to protect the use of the UCC standards in the grocery industry and not to proselytize new industries. Nonetheless, Messerli and Cooper were like the drops of water that eventually form a stalactite.

After two terms, Ben Cooper was replaced in 1989 by Steve Tecot. An electrical supply distributor, Tecot was every bit as committed as his predecessor and much more emotional. The following year, the quiet battle, both philosophical and personal, between Tom Wilson and Hal Juckett came to a head.[1] Juckett, and his broader vision for the UCC, won out.

In 1990, Chairman Dick Zimmerman of Hershey Foods initiated a long-range planning process, which included a review of the organization's mission. Al Messerli aggressively pushed his agenda, and, with Wilson's voice urging restraint diminishing, made considerable headway. Staff encouraged the organization to see itself as much broader than simply the grocery industry.

The result was a mission statement, which, while still tied to support of the retail transaction, allowed the UCC to look beyond its founding industries. At the end of the year, Juckett convened a meeting of trade associations from a variety of manufacturing and distribution industries. Electrical, computer, machinery, electronics, and industrial distribution were represented.

Their interest generated creation of a formal structure for an industrial commercial committee. Unlike other UCC activities, this group insisted on a formal charter, which took months to develop. The UCC insisted that only users could vote on the committee, although association staff and others (consultants mostly) could attend. The UCC also made it clear that this committee had no independent authority and reported to the U.P.C. Advisory Committee, composed entirely of members of the Board of Governors.

Governors Messerli and Tecot served as co-chairs of the Industrial Commercial Advisory Committee (ICAC). This gave them a stage on which to push a nonretail agenda. It also gave them an automatic spot on the U.P.C. Advisory Committee agenda to move their program to the Board of Governors. They took full advantage of this arrangement. Since there was no organized advocacy group for retail industries, the

[1] See Chapter 13.

industrial community actually ended with an advantage within the UCC.

As ICAC became established, a separate fee schedule for industrial companies was no longer justified. Over some opposition in the IC community, the UCC proceeded to abandon separate treatment for industrial companies. A Uniform Industrial Code was no more; there was only a universal product code.

Although the ICAC charter limited voting to users, association staff members and consultants attended and participated fully in the committee's deliberations. Since ICAC quickly adopted a style that pushed for consensus and eschewed formal votes, consultants attained a disproportionate influence within the committee. Users served on the committee as volunteers, an extracurricular activity, but for consultants ICAC was a valuable source of current information and a place to push their own agendas.

A restructuring of the Board of Governors in 1993 gave the industrial commercial community a 50 percent increase in Board representation (two to three). Doctor Walter Mosher, president of Precision Dynamics, a California-based producer of medical devices, was the first holder of the new seat, an appointment reflecting the growing involvement of the health industry with the UCC.

It also reflected significant attitude changes by both the UCC and the health industry. In the early days of the organization, some in that industry made overtures to the UCC. At that time, the UCC saw its role only in terms of the grocery industry. While it did not oppose the health overtures, it neither encouraged nor assisted them. The result was a withdrawal by the health industry to launch a product-identification scheme of its own.

The Horizon Scan study[2] by Andersen Consulting sug-

2 See Chapter 13.

gested the UCC should have a broader, more proactive focus. Accordingly, staff approached the health industry, whose own system had never been widely adopted. The health industry group HIBCC (Health Industry Business Communications Council) became an active participant in ICAC. Here, ideas were floated. In 1993, HIBCC adopted UCC standards, tailored for their needs. The UCC was a full — and enthusiastic — partner in this activity.

As this is being written, the industrial commercial interests within the UCC are clearly on the cutting edge, providing much of the direction and vitality of the organization. This is due both to the people involved and to the broadening of the UCC's mission. A major reason, however, is that the IC sector is the only group within the UCC that has its own forum, ICAC, to debate issues and develop recommendations.

The rise in importance of nonretail influences is also the major impetus leading to the UCC's second major nonretail initiative — the federal government. The U.P.C.'s first foray into the government occurred, logically, in commissaries and post exchanges that serve the military and their families as supermarkets and department stores serve the civilian population.

Because PXs and commissaries offer self-directed shopping ending at a high-volume checkstand, they are precisely the environment for which the U.P.C. was designed. Moreover, the products sold in the military stores were the same as those marketed in the civilian economy. They already bore U.P.C. symbols.

Thus, DeCA, the Defense Department agency responsible for commissaries and exchanges, could either equip its outlets to handle the U.P.C. or adopt a system of its own. The latter approach not only would force suppliers to relabel to accommodate the commissary, but also require the store to make a capital expenditure for equipment to read the government-imposed code.

Faced with these options, DeCA made the obvious choice and embraced the U.P.C. DeCA representatives even participated in a UCC effort to define code and symbology for shipping containers. Although the government adopted the commercially used system for goods sold through government outlets to individuals for their own use, it developed a separate system for goods purchased for the government's own use.

The government code was called the National Stock Number (NSN). It employed the Code 39 symbology.[3] For years, the UCC showed no interest in trying to gain greater government acceptance for its standards. The grocery industry, which dominated the UCC, was already accommodated, and the prevailing attitude was that the Code Council should not take proactive stances unless absolutely necessary to protect the existing system.

Nongrocery manufacturers, on the other hand, such as office products suppliers, sell many products to the government for its own use. Government requirements forced these companies to take products marked with U.P.C. symbols and relabel them with government codes and symbols, adding significantly to the costs.

As the 1990s began, the UCC attitude began to change. Tom Wilson, the leading protagonist of a restricted mission, was gone, and Al Messerli, the industrial governor from 3M, made government acceptance of UCC standards a priority. But even after the UCC saw an opportunity, the government did not reciprocate. There was little incentive to change a system and the bureaucracy familiar with it. That attitude began to alter as exposé after exposé highlighted government waste in the form of $750 toilet seats and other telegenic excesses.

---

[3] Code 39 is another linear bar code, older than the U.P.C. It is not as sophisticated as the U.P.C., but can be used effectively in a number of environments. One such environment is corrugated boxes.

The Department of Defense is by far the largest purchaser of goods in the federal government. For the UCC's purposes, the key to Defense approval appeared to be the LOGMARS committee, an interservice group responsible for government involvement with automatic identification technology. This group had endorsed Code 39 symbology and had little, if any, contact with the UCC.

In 1993, the LOGMARS chair was Stuart Crouse, a civilian employee of the Army. In late spring, Hal Juckett asked me to arrange a meeting with LOGMARS to show them the advantages of the UCC standards. Thus began a frustrating series of phone calls and letters. Stu was unfailingly polite, but each time he told me how busy the committee was and how unlikely it was they would even consider UCC standards.

Finally, on a Friday afternoon in late August, Hal and I met with Stu and representatives of the other services in a vacant classroom at Fort Belvoir, just south of Washington, D.C. It was not a formal LOGMARS meeting. Crouse simply dragooned three other people to meet with us. It was clear to the UCC representatives that Crouse wanted us to stop bothering him — this was a sop to us, intended to make us go away.

Nonetheless, Juckett put together a highly professional and effective presentation. At the conclusion, Frank Murray, of the Naval Supply Systems Command, said, "I don't know if what you said is true, but I owe it to my customers to explore it further." Crouse was forced to offer us the opportunity to make a formal presentation to a scheduled LOGMARS meeting.

It took six months. The UCC was convinced that Crouse did not want to give us a hearing. A large part of his reluctance seemed to come from his ownership of the existing system. Also, adoption of UCC standards would mean additional work for those responsible for implementation.

On a snowy February morning, Hal Juckett and Al

Messerli traveled to Fort Belvoir to make an official presentation to the full LOGMARS committee. The presentation went very well, and the group's attention was riveted on Al when he showed slides asserting that the Defense Department (DoD) purchases $150 billion worth of goods and services annually. From that, he projected that one-third ($50 billion) represented commercially available products. Messerli then estimated that accepting UCC standards could save the government at least three percent, or $1.5 billion dollars.

The pressures within government to reduce costs made these numbers very significant. After the meeting, the representatives of both the Defense Logistics Agency (DLA) and the General Services Administration (GSA) asked the UCC to make presentations to their agency. Nothing came of the presentation to GSA, but the DLA presentation has led to a test program with the Defense General Supply Center in Richmond Virginia.

Then, in June, Professor Emeritus John Dunlop of Harvard bridged UCC to the head of federal procurement policy in the Office of Management and Budget. Steve Kelman is a full-speed-ahead government official who has made improving federal procurement his crusade. Under his leadership a new procurement law was passed that was intended to enable the government to purchase at commercially competitive prices.

Naturally, he was very receptive to the UCC delegation. After our meeting, he assigned one of his staff to follow through and evaluate whether UCC standards should be accepted governmentwide.

During the development of the U.P.C., someone suggested the U.P.C. would be like computers — developed and used for a defined purpose, but there would arise many uses never contemplated. The Naval Supply Systems Command (NavSup) came up with one. NavSup had a problem tying hazardous materials with the Material Safety Data Sheet associated with a specific product. They have decided to use the U.P.C. number as a link between the two.

Much remains to do in moving UCC standards into the federal government. But the process has begun, and success appears to be inevitable.

10

Coupons—
Quid Pro Quo?

The parties to the Ad Hoc Committee, US grocery manufacturers and grocery distributors, came to the table from opposite directions. Distributors came eagerly, lured by the potential of dramatic productivity and efficiency improvements, which would clearly ultimately translate into an improved bottom line. Product manufacturers entered more reluctantly. Their incentives were of a more defensive nature. First, their customers asked for it. Second, by agreeing to a standard code and symbol, they would not be faced with demands to place multiple codes on labels to satisfy different customers.

Still, the adoption of the U.P.C. meant cost savings to distributors (although it also required a substantial capital investment), and expenditures to manufacturers. Arguments could be made (and were) that some so-called soft savings from the U.P.C. would accrue to manufacturers.[1] Still, many manufacturers sought additional incentives to consider the U.P.C.

These suppliers were susceptible to arguments that the U.P.C. could become a vehicle for automating coupon redemption. This would have two positive effects upon manufacturers. It would lower the cost (paid by couponers) of coupon handling, and control coupon fraud. Both repre-

[1] All agree that today the soft savings greatly exceed the hard savings.

sented large sums of money to product manufacturers. As McKinsey and the Ad Hoc Committee went about their work, however, the focus was on automating the checkout, not coupon redemption.

Nonetheless, as the project progressed, its leaders would occasionally ruminate about the potentials within the U.P.C., including the ability to automate coupon redemption and processing. They were speaking of possibilities. Product manufacturers in their audiences heard promises.

When the Ad Hoc Committee announced the U.P.C. code and symbol, it said nothing about coupons. There was, in fact, nothing to say. None of the McKinsey or Ad Hoc work had dealt with coupons. Some people, such as the president of GMA, believed Tom Wilson misled them on the subject of coupons. The ill feelings and mistrust would last for years.

Cooler heads, however, insisted only that the work was not yet done and that the fledgling UGPCC must take on the coupon agenda. In January 1974, the Board of Governors held a lengthy discussion of coupon validation. The board recognized that coupon validation probably involved major systems problems. On the other hand, all knew the subject was important and deserved full study.

The issue was considered of sufficient importance that it was referred to the Ad Hoc for handling. A coupon committee, chaired by Ad Hoc member Don Lloyd (CEO of Associated Grocers in Salt Lake City), was formed to investigate if, and how, the U.P.C. could be applied to coupons. McKinsey would provide the consulting assistance.

In mid-1974, McKinsey reminded the committee that grocery manufacturers were very sensitive on the subject. The issue of coupon validation, however, was not simple, nor was the answer clear. Three years would pass before the committee would recommend a solution. Even then they were forced to acknowledge the answer was far from perfect.

It was a lonely time for the Coupon Committee. More than once, Don Lloyd protested that though the committee was working, it appeared that no one knew or cared. Progress was extremely slow. At times, it appeared that there was no answer that would meet couponers' needs.

If couponing in the grocery industry had been limited to a coupon good only for a price reduction on one specific product, it would have been easy to automate the coupon process. Grocery manufacturers, however, used coupons in much more complex ways. A coupon might be redeemable for any size of a product, or any flavor. It might require the purchase of multiple or different products. The only limit on the potential variations was the creative imaginations of the manufacturers' marketing departments.

The goal was a system that would assure the manufacturer that the specific requirements of a coupon promotion had been met. Once that was reached, the industry hoped to virtually eliminate the manual handling of paper. Electronic coupon clearing would save labor at the supermarket front end, thus reducing — or at least stabilizing — the allowance manufacturers paid retailers for handling coupons.

Months passed with little progress by the Coupon Committee. Barry Franz of Procter & Gamble, an original member of the Symbol Selection Subcommittee, joined the Coupon Committee. The most promising lines of inquiry employed differing versions of a family and value code. It was Franz who proposed the first workable solutions, after discussing the issue with almost a dozen equipment manufacturers.

He suggested a coupon code that would include the manufacturer identification number, a family code that would identify a number of products grouped as a family, and a value code specifying the amount of the coupon allowance. This was, at best, a partial solution because a consumer could still obtain the price reduction without buying the specific promoted product. It did, however, ensure that the consumer had at least purchased a product of the couponing manufacturer, and one in the family of products assigned by that manufacturer.

In March 1975, the committee announced it had settled on a code containing two digits for family and three for value. It acknowledged this was a compromise that did not fully satisfy any of the parties. The proposed code meant each manufacturer could create 99 family groupings of products. It could offer coupons worth up to $9.99.

In announcing its recommendation, the Coupon Committee said it was seeking the input of the Grocery Manufacturers of America (GMA), Supermarket Institute (SMI), and the Symbol Technical Advisory Committee (STAC) before seeking formal endorsement of the Board of Governors. The initial reaction was mixed. Some complained that the proposed Guideline 22 really did not dramatically automate coupon handling. Others, while acknowledging its limitations, believed its use could cause substantial efficiencies.

The committee decided it had received the support it was seeking. Nonetheless, the approval process was confused. In September 1975, the Board adopted the recommended Guideline 22 for coupons. In November, they approved it again, but subject to the approval of STAC. Three months later, they approved it for manufacturer coupons only, but delayed publication pending the resolution of how to handle "free" and on-pack coupons.

Finally, in March 1976, Guideline 22 on Coupon Code was approved for publication. GMA immediately asked that the guideline be withdrawn and the makeup of the code reconsidered. GMA members had decided they preferred a three-digit family code and a two-digit value code. This increased the number of potential families by each manufacturer ten-fold, while reducing the maximum amount per coupon to $0.99. It was a more accurate measure of the contemporary marketplace, but it did put relatively low limits on future growth.

The Coupon Committee and Board of Governors were in no mood to argue with the product manufacturers. They quickly acquiesced in the GMA request. At long last, on September 21, 1976, Guideline 22 was released.

The manufacturers were pleased, retailers indifferent. The marketplace went for a long time without seeing coupons bearing U.P.C. codes. The mere addition of the symbol, moreover, did not mean there was coupon scanning. Talk was cheap. Changing the software at point of sale came at a cost. The retailer had no incentive to make the necessary changes, especially since there was an almost universal belief that coupon-scanning economies were the reverse of those for products. The costs accrued to the retailer, the benefits to the manufacturer.

An early development after the adoption of the coupon code involved attaching significance to the value code. Originally, the concept had been for the amount of the price reduction to be identical to the value code. Manufacturers soon realized that no one offered a coupon worth, for example, 1¢. In addition, ninety-nine value codes quickly seemed excessively restrictive to manufacturers.

The GMA Coupon Committee, therefore, with the assistance of the Code Council, launched an effort to assign specific amounts to each value code. Value code 11, under this scheme, represents a coupon offer of $1.85, while code 98 means "Buy 2 or more, get $0.65 off." It took a great deal of research and negotiation to arrive at a conversion table.

But promotions change. The job, once done, has to be constantly monitored to make sure the table reflects current practice. On the other hand, a standard is not a standard if it is constantly changing. Thus, the UCC and the GMA Coupon

Committee only change the table once every few years. Unlike most instances when the UCC has varied from the fundamental principle that the U.P.C. is a "dumb" number, the attaching of significance to the coupon code has been mostly satisfactory. The objections, in fact, relate not to the family/value concept, but to the inherent failure of the code — it does not allow for an exact match of coupon and item.

Eight years later, in 1984, only fifteen product manufacturers were marking coupons with the U.P.C. coupon code, and only Wegman's in upstate New York was attempting to scan coupons. This was a scant payback for a significant investment of time and money. It would be almost another decade before coupon scanning became widespread.

The lack of implementation was not for lack of effort by the UCC. Hal Juckett's background was in customer service, education, and training. He took coupon coding as a challenge. The UCC developed an extensive educational program consisting of regional seminars and a video. Unfortunately, attendance at the seminars was not good. The programs were well designed, but the only marketing efforts for the seminars were mailings to lists created and maintained by the UCC.

Staff and Board remained undeterred. A U.P.C. solution for coupon scanning during these years still had great symbolic significance even if hardly any companies were actually using it. In November 1984, the Executive Committee acknowledged that coupon scanning would take considerable maintenance from the UCC, and it would be a long time before there was significant retail coupon scanning. Nonetheless, it is an important advance and eventually will be an excellent application for the consumer.

Although it was hard to point to results, the UCC and GMA continued to support the coupon code. This kept it a topic within the industry. This, with the potential benefits of coupon scanning, kept interest alive. A. C. Nielsen Co., which operated coupon clearing houses, announced it would be a repository for coupon codes.[2]

The GMA Coupon Committee began pressing for a suffix code or the use of U.P.C. symbol Version D 3.[3] They hoped that if couponers were allowed to encode additional information (such as demographic data), they would be encouraged to use the coupon code. If most coupons bore a U.P.C. symbol, they reasoned, retailers would be more likely to adapt their scanners to accept the coupon code.

However, the UCC's attitude toward suffix codes was uninvolvement. Many groups sought to encode additional information. The UCC would allow this, provided the add-on symbol did not encroach on the space required for the U.P.C. symbol. The Code Council, however, would not develop such codes or symbols. As for any use of Version D, the UCC showed no interest. It had approved one application for Version D (random weight). No one adopted that application, and the Code Council's interest in Version D had evaporated.

They were quick to point out the difficulties the use of Version D would raise. These included the fact that no one was using Version D, which meant most scanning installations were not programmed to recognize Version D symbols. If Version D became the symbology for coupons, the scanner could not read it until modified. This meant an added cost to retailers, who already saw little benefit from automating the coupon process. In addition, scanners would not be able to tell whether it was a Version A or a Version D symbol when the symbol was first presented to the scanner. This could wreak havoc on product scanning.

No matter how often they raised the subject — and it came up frequently — the Board of Governors, supported by

[2] Nielsen, aware that technology could eventually destroy its clearing business, sought to adapt to the new world.

[3] Version D 3 is a much longer symbol than Version A, and capable of encoding more data.

STAC, rebuffed all suggestions that Version D be used for coupons. However, couponers would continue to seek ways to encode additional information on the coupon.

Still another potential obstacle to coupon scanning arose as the 1980s ended. The increasing popularity of the U.P.C. system meant that the Code Council would soon have to begin issuing numbers in number systems other than "0." Only U.P.C. numbers in number system 0 are assured of a unique match with a number system 5 coupon.

The problems seemed great enough that Dan Wegman, co-chair of the Joint Industry Coupon Committee[4] reported that coupon scanning was "dead in the water." The UCC, however, remained steadfast. Believing that coupon scanning was technically feasible, the Board said it was up to the industry to decide if it made sense to implement it. Meanwhile, the UCC continued to offer seminars on coupon coding.

Coupon scanning finally became a reality. The prime driver of retailer scanning of coupons was the growing prevalence of double and even triple couponing in the late 1980s. Coupons, being issued by the manufacturer, represented a cost to the couponer and revenue (in the form of a handling allowance) to the retailer. Retailers, however, had to bear the cost of double couponing. This gave them a financial incentive to improve efficiencies by adopting scanning.

The Code Council also brought together a group of experts to work with the Joint Industry Coupon Committee. The industry wanted to find out if it could encode additional information in a different symbology. By 1990, the UCC no longer refused to participate in such discussions. Now it accepted a leadership role to help industries — and especially its founding industry — solve problems related to product identification.

The first task was for the industry to identify the addi-

[4] Co-sponsored by FMI and GMA.

tional information it wanted to encode on the coupon. This was not an easy matter. Marketing executives always wanted more demographic data. The technical experts pointed out that, while practically anything was possible, the size of the symbol required to encompass the data became larger, using more real estate on the coupon, as the amount of data increased.

As with the selection of the U.P.C. symbol, the result was a compromise. They made trade-offs so that they could encode key information, but the size of the symbol remained small enough that it could appear on a coupon in conjunction with a U.P.C. Version A symbol and leave enough room for at least some selling copy. Once the industry (predominantly grocery manufacturers) agreed what the most important supplemental data was, STAC proposed the use of a UCC-EAN 128 symbol.

This was an ingenious approach. The 128 symbol could not be confused with the U.P.C. Version A symbol, so scanning of the product symbol would not be impaired. In addition, no one would have to upgrade his scanners unless he chose to. The scanners would simply ignore the supplemental symbol. This meant retailers would not be pressured to make extensive capital investments. Since most retailers saw little, if any, benefit from the extended coupon code, they were unlikely to make that investment. This gave the coupon clearing house companies a role in the new world of the supplemental coupon code.

As STAC worked on this project in the late 1980s, Version D rose from the dead. At least two interested parties suggested Version D as the basis for a solution to manufacturers' needs. The experts on STAC, however, closer to contemporary technology, unanimously rejected the proposal. Version D finally seems to be abandoned.[5]

[5] There is one use of Version D in Switzerland. The UCC is aware of no others.

In April 1994, a coupon extended code was approved using a UCC-EAN 128 symbol to encode additional data desired by couponers. Almost no one could read the extended code at point of sale, but it did not impair the scanning of the regular coupon symbol.

As noted above, couponers using the extended code were serviced by the clearing houses. Over the long term, however, the coupon-extended code symbol may serve as a vehicle to introduce the scanning of multiple symbols at point of sale.

Coupon scanning seemed critical, but unattainable, to the success of the U.P.C. in the mid-1970s. By the mid-1990s, it was in place and valuable, but essentially a sideshow to the main thrust of product identification.

11

Spreading the Word

The founders of the Uniform Code Council were fond of predicting the organization's future. Those predictions have almost always been wrong. The U.P.C. was developed for use in the US grocery industry or, more broadly, in distribution channels where product moved to consumers through high-velocity checkstands. At most, there would be 5000 to 6000 companies that would need U.P.C. numbers. Accordingly, the Board of Governors set a narrow, conservative course for the organization. The UCC was to be reactive, acting only when an existing trade association chose not to act.

This philosophy governed the first decade of the group's existence. By then, it was becoming clear that U.P.C. usage was destined for much grander totals, though no one could venture a confident guess on exactly how grand. The growth of the endowment fund slowly turned the UCC into a force to be reckoned with. The timid-child attitude became more difficult to maintain.

This can most clearly be seen in the evolution of the Code Council's relationships with its counterpart organization, the European Article Numbering Association[1] (EAN), in the rest of the world, and in the UCC's shift from avoidance to embrace of the American National Standards Institute (ANSI).

---

[1] Now known as the International Article Numbering Association (EAN).

EAN

At the outset, the Board of Governors believed it was important to keep the organization narrowly focussed. Its mission was to facilitate product coding and scanning in the US grocery industry *only*. There was a reasonable comfort level within the Board that this was a defined channel of trade. Problems in the US grocery industry could be attacked with relatively little attention to other industries or regions.

Thus, there was no attempt by the Council to extend the usage of the code and symbol. Inquiries from outside the US received scant attention. A brief notation in the Board of Governors' minutes for November 15, 1973, mentions an inquiry from Scandinavia. The response was that no one had the authority to negotiate for a number system outside the United States.

Nonetheless, others were watching developments in the grocery industry and wondering if the U.P.C. could address their situation. The leading European supermarket organizations regularly participated in the activities of NAFC and SMI. They were thus in position to receive first-hand reports on the progress of the U.P.C.

In addition, McKinsey & Co., the consultant to the Code Council, had created various forums that brought together noncompeting grocery retailers to discuss common problems. One such retailer was Albert Heijn, CEO of Ahold, a Dutch supermarket company. Albert Heijn concluded the American experience could and should be exported to Europe. Under his leadership, a European equivalent of the Ad Hoc Committee was formed. It turned to McKinsey and Tom Wilson for consulting help.

Wilson was careful to keep the Board of Governors informed of his new assignment. No one saw a conflict of interest. The U.P.C. was for the US grocery industry. The US and European grocery industries were separate creatures.

Because of US labeling requirements, a product destined for the American market could easily be distinguished from its European counterpart.

The European initiative was underway soon after the U.P.C. symbol was announced. Wilson's first report to the Board on the project was in January 1974. By November, he was able to report that the European Ad Hoc Committee had met and decided to pursue the project.

Despite the universal conviction that the US and the rest of the world were separate channels of trade that did not intersect, McKinsey was careful to steer the European group into paths that were compatible with the US experience. In part, this was to maximize McKinsey's expertise, honed on its work in the US. As it worked with the European group, it had every reason to emulate its US experience. No serious problems had arisen in the United States. (Commercial scanning, however, did not even begin in the United States until mid-1974. Before that, all data came from experimental, controlled tests.)

Still, it took the better part of two years to choose a European code and symbol. During this time Wilson, and occasionally Albert Heijn, gave regular progress reports to the Board of Governors. Heijn especially recognized that Europe was benefitting greatly from the pioneering work in the United States.

EAN, as the European code and symbol were called, was unveiled in mid-1976. They looked like the U.P.C., and indeed they were designed so that the U.P.C. would fit within EAN as a subset. This meant products marked with U.P.C. symbols would scan in Europe. The converse was not necessarily true, however.

To accommodate coding authorities of other nations, EAN added an extra digit at the beginning of the code. The first two digits[2] were country codes, identifying the country

[2] Later, some three-digit country codes were adopted.

issuing the code. In the United States, the first digit was a number system character. To assure compatibility, EAN implied an additional "0" to the left of the U.P.C. number system character, and assigned country codes "00" to "09" to the United States, thus encompassing all U.P.C. number systems.

There was some early concern that EAN might conflict with the US Distribution Code,[3] also administered by DCI. As the Code Council began to consider creating its own staff and terminating the DCI relationship, the concern grew. The problem was dealt with by cooperative code management, however. An actual conflict was thus avoided.

Establishing an effective multinational organization was a major challenge to the EAN creators. From the outset, EAN was a federation of independent national coding organizations. At the beginning, a dozen nations participated. Albert Heijn frequently expressed his envy of the United States, which did not have to deal with the national pride of many countries.

EAN had a central organization, but it was weak. Located in Brussels, it had no full-time staff. The administrator of the Belgian product code moonlighted as the staff executive for the federation. The concept had obvious power, however, and EAN quickly began seeking additional members for the federation. By the beginning of 1978, EAN announced it was prepared to deal with all countries outside of North America (which it had ceded to the UPCC). At the same time, it called for closer coordination with the UPCC.

Tom Wilson was still consulting with both UPCC and EAN. He received approval from the Board of Governors to attend the next meeting of the EAN Executive Committee as a representative of UPCC. A pattern soon developed of a

---

[3] A product identification code developed by others, principally for the electrical industry.

UPCC representative going to an EAN meeting, and an EAN person attending a Board of Governors meeting once a year.

Although EAN was still a fledgling organization, Albert Heijn was pressing for closer cooperation between the two groups. As EAN began to add additional countries, it sought to move beyond cooperation to enticing the UPCC to become a constituent part of their organization. The Board of Governors had little interest in that. The United States then — and now — exhibited far greater implementation of the standards. It also seemed to possess greater expertise, energy, and resources.

The UCC established a cooperative, but arm's-length relationship, with EAN. Communication, and cooperation, while not always perfect, continued to improve. The UCC's refusal to join EAN was a constant, but minor, blemish on the relationship. A more serious problem was the capability of the initial US scanners to accept EAN symbols.

The EAN was designed to coexist with the U.P.C., but was a digit longer. This created two potential problems. Some early U.P.C. scanners could not physically handle a code longer than the U.P.C. Nothing could be done about this until those scanners were replaced (and they proved to last much longer than anticipated). The other problem was correctable, but at a price. Some software programs in US scanners would not accommodate the EAN code. A relatively uncomplicated software adjustment would allow those scanners to handle EAN symbols. It would not, however, be free.

Virtually all US supermarkets saw no reason to spend any money to accommodate EAN symbols. In the 1970s and 1980s the amount of EAN marked product received in the United States was extremely small. The cost of equipping stores to scan U.P.C. symbols was very high. US retailers opted not to make what appeared to be a purely discretionary choice.

In fact, the inability of US supermarkets to scan EAN

symbols created very few problems in either the US or Europe. The symbolic significance, however, was great. For the Europeans, it became a cause celèbre, representing to EAN a failure of the US to work in harmony.

Actually compounding the problem, the Board of Governors never really understood the EAN position, viewing it a tempest in a teapot. Thus, although the Board adopted formal positions that equipment and software should be capable of scanning both U.P.C. and EAN symbols, very little energy was put behind the effort. Equipment manufacturers were quick to adapt their equipment. Software developers and retailers were much more reluctant to make the change.

By the early 1980s all scanning equipment marketed in the US could scan either U.P.C. or EAN symbols. Industries moving to the U.P.C., such as mass merchandise, clearly saw the value of a database that could handle fourteen digits. It was only the US grocery industry, the founder, that lagged behind.

A decade later, the teachings of the Efficient Consumer Response (ECR) program[4] finally brought progress to the grocery industry. The full database was clearly demanded if the industry was to attain the efficiencies promised by ECR. These efficiencies were necessary for the grocery industry to meet the competition it faced from other industries who offered grocery products to the consumer through new store formats and concepts.

In 1984, EAN approached the UCC seeking control of one of the UCC's unassigned number systems. This was received with little enthusiasm by the UCC and quickly rejected. Circumstances change, however, and ten years later, the Code Council found itself in the delicate position of negotiating with EAN for control of country codes 10–19 (an additional ten number systems), which would double the capacity of the U.P.C.

[4] See Chapter 13.

In 1996, Hal Juckett successfully negotiated the assignment of codes 10–13 to the UCC. This was tied to a program that would encourage all US scanners to handle EAN codes and to enable EAN numbering organizations to participate (and share fees) in the assignment of U.P.C. numbers to applicants from the EAN country.

Foreign companies selling to the United States typically sought a U.P.C. number in addition to or sometimes instead of an EAN number. The EAN numbering organizations resented this. Yet because the goods were being marketed in the US, the foreign producer was entitled to a U.P.C. number.

It was Hal Juckett who devised a solution that made everyone happy. He created the UCC-EAN Alliance. Under this program, a foreign company contacting the UCC was referred to the appropriate EAN numbering organization. If a U.P.C. number was required, the EAN group would handle the paperwork, forwarding it to Dayton. The UCC and EAN would split the fee.

This has proved to be a workable compromise, although it occasionally causes some culture shock. UCC membership, including a U.P.C. number, is available for a one-time fee. All EAN numbering organizations charge annual dues. Under the UCC-EAN Alliance, a company is joining the UCC, albeit through EAN. The UCC, therefore, insisted that only a one-time fee could be charged the applicant. This was a difficult concept for the EAN organization to master. The UCC abandoned this position as part of the negotiations that brought it country flags 10–13.

Following the success of the UCC-EAN Alliance, Hal Juckett continued his shuttle diplomacy between the two organizations. Even with the Alliance, issues dividing the two organizations remained. The UCC saw itself as the creator and by far the most successful of the organizations, with resources and expertise dwarfing those of EAN. In

EAN's eyes, the ugly American was insisting on special treatment even though it was a single nation in the world community.

EAN wanted the UCC as a member. The UCC had no intention of giving up its autonomy. Hal saw this as a gulf that needed bridging. It took several years, but a document embodying principles of cooperation, was created and endorsed by both governing bodies. To a great extent, the principles were nothing more than a statement of the obvious. The thing Juckett recognized was the great value — especially to EAN — of putting them down on paper, formally adopting them, and having a formal signing ceremony.

At dusk on November 1, 1990, at the UCC's annual meeting in Phoenix, Arizona, Jean Collin, President of EAN, and Dick Zimmerman, Chair of the UCC Board of Governors, executed the Principles of Cooperation between the UCC and EAN. EAN continues to point to this document as the foundation of its relationship with the UCC.

The growing use of UCC-EAN standards across industries and borders continues to test the relationship between the two organizations. The days are long gone when EAN could be ignored because all products had to be relabeled. EAN's structure as a federation of independent national numbering authorities has led to some differences in the interpretation and application of the standards.

To help minimize these differences, the UCC and EAN in the early 1990s created the International Data Applications and Standards Committee (IDASC) to harmonize usages and agree on common definitions for application identifiers. The makeup of the committee reflected the differences between the organizations. In keeping with its user orientation, the UCC appointed Jim Harms of Panduit Corp., a member of ICAC,[5] and Dennis Epley, Kraft General Foods and

---

[5] The UCC's Industrial Commercial Advisory Committee.

Co-Chair of SCMLC,[6] as its representatives. EAN's designees were Andrew Osborne, head of the Article Numbering Association (UK), and Robert Schubenel of the Swiss EAN organization. The group worked well, but slowly, together.

EAN also set some different policies in its efforts to obtain operating revenues, a pressure not faced by the UCC. Thus, companies are required to pay annual dues to the national numbering organization. EAN also sells location codes so that companies can identify specific locations. The UCC only agreed to do likewise at the end of 1996.

Just as the UCC has grown far beyond its origins in the US grocery industry, so too has EAN grown. It now represents over eighty countries worldwide.[7] While still known as "EAN," the official name is now the International Article Numbering Organization. There is, however, some criticism that EAN has not overcome its roots as a European organization. To date, all of EAN's Presidents have been European.

EAN as an organization is dominated by professional administrators of national article numbering organizations. Their views tend toward the bureaucratic and theoretical. The practicality and dynamism of the user perspective — so vital to the UCC — are much weaker in EAN.

Nonetheless, for better or worse, the two are bound together. If the future is to be as bright as the present, EAN and UCC must build on their cooperative successes, and find a way to solve their differences. The creation of a Global Policy Committee in the mid-90s composed of the leaders of both organizations is a hopeful first step. Already, it has served to solve misunderstandings and encourage cooperation.

---

[6] The UCC's Shipping Container Marking and Labeling Committee.

[7] One of them, post-Soviet Russia, was given the UCC's old computer equipment, when the US organization upgraded.

American National Standards Institute (ANSI)

One of the first decisions made by the Ad Hoc Committee at the outset of the project was to avoid the ANSI process, with its multiplicity of time-consuming steps. The concern was that the ANSI process would completely smother any chance for the quick adoption of a grocery industry identification code. Over the years, the power of that belief grew until it reached mythic proportions.

Coincident with the work of the Ad Hoc Committee, the National Retail Merchants Association (NRMA) had a similar project for product identification in department stores. This project was going through the ANSI process. From the Ad Hoc's perspective, the delays and problems that beset NRMA's OCR-A[8] symbol were at least in part due to the ANSI involvement.

The belief intensified as time passed and there was little implementation of the NRMA standard. In time, NRMA and the other general merchandise groups migrated to the UCC standards. This migration, however, was the harbinger that would ultimately lead the UCC to reconsider its anti-ANSI posture.

Twenty years after the adoption of the U.P.C., the world — and the UCC — were very different. Created to serve the US grocery industry, the UCC found its standards in use in multiple industries, some with little or no connection to groceries. This was a reflection of channels of trade that were increasingly global and blurred. Almost no one dealt in a single channel of trade (as that term had been defined in 1970).

This increased the pressure on the UCC to obtain formal national and international recognition for its standards. Some major UCC members operated under corporate

---

[8] OCR stands for "optical character recognition."

policies dictating the use of standards recognized by national standards bodies.

Pushed by the VICS[9] (apparel and general merchandise) community, the UCC's first foray into the world of the American National Standards Institute came when it decided to make its UCS and VICS electronic data interchange (EDI) standards ANSI standards. These standards make it possible for retailers and their suppliers to communicate electronically, even if they have different computer systems. Discussion of the possibility of migration began in 1985. It took until 1992 before all preexisting UCS and VICS EDI standards become ANSI standards under ANSI ASC X12.[10]

This process, while successful, did little to alleviate the UCC's concerns with ANSI. The EDI migration had been difficult and time consuming. Most problems had been political, not substantive. The UCC had never paid that much attention to the politics behind its standards. Now it had to learn quickly.

The other incident impelling the UCC toward ANSI occurred in 1991. By that time, the UCC had begun to develop UCC-EAN 128, a bar code allowing the encodation of a wide array of variable data, such as expiration date, batch/lot, etc. This data is encoded in "Application Identifiers" (AI). Another organization, the Federation of Automated Coding Technologies (FACT), using Code 39, developed a similar structure of "Data Identifiers (DI)." AIs contain only numbers. This allows the inclusion of more data in a shorter bar code. DIs contain both letters and numbers. This takes a longer bar code. On the other hand, DIs enable companies to use their existing codes. In practice, AIs have been more widely used for products that are produced en masse, while DIs are more suitable for made-to-order product.

[9] Voluntary Interindustry Communications Standards.

[10] See Chapter 8.

FACT decided to obtain American National Standard status for DIs. The UCC vacillated on whether it should participate in the FACT effort. The result was a standard developed without effective UCC involvement. In addition, those who were pushing the FACT standard understandably were annoyed at the UCC attitude — dropping in and out of their standardization process.

In the end, FACT approved a DI standard and obtained ANSI accreditation for it. The FACT standard as approved did not mention AIs. At the last moment, the UCC (and some others) objected to ANSI approval of the standard without inclusion of application identifiers. The FACT group rejected the objections, and the UCC appealed to ANSI's Board of Standards Review (BSR). In December 1991, the UCC came face to face with the reality of dealing with ANSI.

The crux of the UCC's appeal was that ANSI rules require a consensus to support a standard. The UCC and its supporters represent a significant segment of users of the standard. Therefore, by definition, there could be no consensus supporting the standard. The BSR is concerned only with whether the ANSI rules have been followed. It has no interest in the substance of the dispute. It had little difficulty rejecting the appeal.

The UCC understandably was frustrated and disappointed at the decision.[11] It was also an object lesson, however, in the problems of operating from outside the system. This, coupled with the pressure from the industrial commercial sector to become a part of the ANSI structure, operated to make the UCC reconsider its anti-ANSI posture.

Accordingly, after consulting with an ANSI expert, the UCC in the fall of 1993 joined the American National Standards Institute and became a member of its Information Systems Standards Board (ISSB). The ISSB's mission is to coordinate and harmonize standards developed by ANSI

[11] FACT, on the other hand, saw the UCC appeal as a betrayal of their efforts.

members in the field of information systems. ISSB is dominated by the suppliers of technology equipment and their associations.

It also appears that most individuals who are active in ANSI are standards specialists. These people take process very seriously. UCC culture focuses on problem solving, even if it must be at the expense of process. The ANSI exposure was eye-opening and a harbinger of the UCC's direction as it became a multi-industry organization.

The ISSB chair was Sandy Paul, a consultant to the publishing industry who also advised the UCC. She suggested the UCC pick up a project originally assigned by ISSB to FACT. By this time, FACT had gone out of existence. FACT had promised to monitor automatic identification standards for the ISSB. It never delivered on its promise, however. Ms. Paul suggested the UCC pick up this ball to establish its presence on the ISSB.

The UCC agreed. Since there was no model to follow, it developed its own report format. The report, submitted at every ISSB meeting, has served its purpose of building credibility with the other members of the ISSB. In addition, the report has become a standard reference work widely used by those concerned with ADC standards.

Shortly after becoming an ISSB member, the UCC took the next step in its ANSI involvement. It applied for accreditation as a standards development organization. This was a necessary precondition to seeking ANSI recognition for UCC standards. Here, Sandy Paul's counsel proved invaluable. ANSI has three ways of processing standards: as a committee, as a canvass organization, or as a standards development organization (SDO). The latter allows the organization much more autonomy than the other two. This was the approach pursued by UCC.

On February 28, 1994, ANSI awarded SDO status to the UCC. The ANSI-approved scope was as follows, "The Uniform Code Council develops and administers item numbering and product identification standards. The UCC also develops and administers standards for product information and details of the sales transaction throughout the distribution chain."[12]

A requirement for obtaining accreditation is to have in place a set of procedures ensuring due process for participants in the standards development process. The UCC "Decision Making Procedures," adopted at David Jenkins' request when he became Chair of the U.P.C. Advisory Committee, served the UCC well. ANSI staff, however, requested and received changes in the document to enhance the right of appeal by those disappointed with a standards decision.

Upon receiving accredited status, the UCC submitted four of its standards to become American National Standards. The U.P.C. Specification, appropriately, was given the designation UCC1. The ITF shipping container symbol and the UCC-EAN 128 serial shipping container manual became UCC2 and UCC3.[13] UCC4 is the Code 128 application identifier standard.

Although all four received ANS status at the beginning of 1995, the process taught the UCC that ANSI approval did not come easily. The standards had actually been in use for years. The UCC therefore expected no comments during the required public comment period. They were almost right. The ANSI process, though, is a gold mine for one's enemies, especially those who love slavish adherence to form.

Naturally, there was one individual who submitted dozens of comments on each of the four, most of which were either minor editorial changes or rehashes of arguments often held and resolved. Each comment had to be taken seriously. Just

[12] Application for Accreditation submitted by the UCC, Feb. 18, 1993; Approval Feb. 28, 1994, reported in Standards Action, Apr. 15, 1994, p. 18.

[13] UCC2 and UCC3 have now been consolidated into UCC6 — Application Standard for Shipping Container Codes.

before the Board of Governors meeting that was to give the four standards a final blessing before sending on to ANSI, the UCC satisfactorily resolved the commentor's objections. The ANSI approval was issued in due course.

A subsequent standard underwent similar treatment even though the two principal objectors had actively participated in the standard's development over a two-year period. This time, the commentors succeeded in forcing a second ANSI public review period. The UCC responded with a two-pronged program. The standard was simultaneously released as a UCC standard and resubmitted for ANSI public review.

Notwithstanding the frustrations and difficulties of the ANSI process, the UCC recognizes it must continue to be a part of the national standards body. Its position as a world leader in automatic data capture standards requires no less.

The next step after obtaining American National Standard recognition for its standards is to have them accepted as international standards. Involvement in ANSI is critical for this. ISO (International Organization for Standardization) is the internationally recognized standards-setting organization. Representation on ISO is by country, and ANSI is the US member.

For the UCC, international standardization was a long-range project that was suddenly expedited. While there were many ISO committees and work groups, there was no group where the UCC-type standards could easily fit. In early 1994, a proposal was made to JTC1, a joint venture of ISO and IEC for international standardization in the field of information technology. The proposal was to create a new JTC1 subcommittee for automatic data capture standards.

JTC1's initial reaction was to pass the subject to the ISSB because of a concern that the subject matter might be outside the scope of JTC1 authority. ISSB responded by creating an Ad Hoc committee to review the subject and make its recommendation. The original committee was chaired by John Leary of AT&T, with Sandy Paul, the UCC, AIM USA,[14] and Craig Harmon (the consultant who made the original proposal) as members.

The committee quickly concluded that an international forum was desirable. There were two possible venues — a new JTC1 subcommittee or a new Technical Committee (TC) directly under ISO. Sandy Paul, past ISSB chair and sometime UCC consultant, took a very strong position that a new ISO TC was much to be preferred to a new JTC1 SC.

In her view, JTC1 was saddled with an unwieldy bureaucracy and peopled by individuals from computer companies whose primary interest was in equipment and only secondarily in applications. An ISO TC would start fresh and could be more flexible and quicker.

Her views predominated, and the Ad Hoc group unanimously recommended to ISSB the creation of a new ISO TC. Several ISSB members — also JTC1 members — filed objections to the recommendation. These members, including IBM (JTC1 chair), Digital, and the Department of Defense, claimed the subject matter was within the scope of JTC1, that JTC1 already had a structure while a new ISO TC would have to create one, and besides, standards could be processed faster through JTC1.

As a result of these comments, ISSB reversed the Ad Hoc recommendation and called for the creation of a new JTC1 SC. This required the referral of the subject back to JTC1, where it had originated. US JTC1 leaders were confident the action could be taken quickly.

A key to moving the proposal forward was identifying candidates willing to serve as secretariat of the new SC and as Administrator to the US Technical Advisory Group (TAG) for the SC. Both posts involve a significant commitment of resources and finances. The UCC and AIM USA made the

[14] AIM USA — Automatic Identification Equipment Manufacturers.

commitment, and the US TAG for JTC1 agreed to take the proposal to the JTC1 plenary session.

There, they received an unpleasant surprise. JTC1 refused to approve. Other countries expressed concern that the US was trying to rush the proposal through without adequate information or opportunity for the other national bodies to assess the interest in their countries. Accordingly, the matter was deferred until March 1996, nine months later.

Meanwhile, the same consultant who delayed the adoption of UCC standards as American National Standards launched an effort to find candidates other than the UCC to serve as secretariat. One result of this display of conflict within the US was to create candidates from other countries. In the end, the UCC was awarded the secretariat.

Whatever the outcome, the UCC's future seems tied to being part of national international standards bodies. The UCC hopes to remain true to its history of responsiveness to users and pragmatic standards-development while adhering to ANSI and ISO requirements.

12
Formal Challenges

During its first twenty-five years, the Uniform Code Council has been blessed with an ability to avoid formal legal challenges to its standards. This does not mean there have been no such challenges. Over the quarter century, there have been three such attacks — one each in the 1970s, 1980s, and 1990s. The first was from someone trying to get rich quick, the second from a zealot, and the third from a quasicompetitor. Yet none of the attacks has had a serious impact on the UCC.

1976–1983 — Walter Kaslow

In June 1976, the Code Council learned a patent had been granted to Walter Kaslow for a coupon-validation system using the U.P.C. The Kaslow invention, however, would only validate a coupon tied to a specific product. This would never work in supermarkets because of the great variety of coupon promotions. Very rarely is a coupon issued that is redeemable only on a single color or size of a product.[1]

Nonetheless Kaslow drafted the claims of the patent so broadly that any time a coupon, a U.P.C. symbol, and a scanner were brought together, it would infringe his patent.

[1] See Chapter 10.

U.P.C. Guideline 22[2] using family and value codes for coupon scanning clearly could be construed as an inducement to infringe the patent.

Mr. Kaslow quickly took steps to publicize his invention. He did not, however, attempt to license it to couponers. Instead, he made sure the trade press reported the invention.

There were not a rash of inquiries from grocery manufacturers seeking to take advantage of his technology. Almost exactly the opposite happened, and that may have been the intent. Perhaps Kaslow wanted to attract the Code Council's attention. The Kaslow patent was clearly a barrier to implementation of Guideline 22. Couponers feared lawsuits if they started to code coupons as directed by Guideline 22.

The UPCC had struggled to find a way to symbol-mark coupons to fulfill what was perceived to be a promise to grocery manufacturers.[3] It now faced an external barrier to coupon scanning. Lawyers for grocery manufacturers urged their clients to go slow in placing U.P.C. symbols on coupons until the Kaslow patent issues were resolved. Yet if the Kaslow patent were valid, it would not have enabled coupon scanning because of its requirement of a single, precise match between a product and coupon offer. Couponers would have been forced to pay royalties for a system that did not work. If that had occurred, U.P.C. scanning of coupons would never have happened.

The UCC's first response was to direct me to consult patent counsel and consider a challenge to the Kaslow patent. Bob McMorrow, a specialist used by others in my firm, first conducted a thorough study of the patent and its claims. He concluded the UPCC could proceed to implement Guideline 22 in spite of Kaslow.

The fundamental basis for his conclusion was that he believed the patent was invalid because of the prior art. This

[2] Ibid.

[3] Ibid.

meant that the "invention" had in fact been both discovered and disclosed before Mr. Kaslow filed his application for a patent. There were two bases for the conclusion. A test of an RCA bull's-eye symbol in a Kroger store in Kenwood Ohio, (a suburb of Cincinnati) had also involved bull's-eye symbols on coupons that were scanned at the checkout. This fact was included in a *Saint Louis Post Dispatch* article, which was published before Kaslow filed his application for a patent. In counsel's opinion, the combination of a test of coupon scanning and a published story about it would be enough to establish prior art and invalidate the Kaslow patent.

Counsel also observed that patent litigation was time-consuming and expensive. It could also be capricious, and even the strongest challenge to a patent could fail. Accordingly, McMorrow suggested the Code Council try to avoid a lawsuit by purchasing the patent from Kaslow. The Board of Governors believed strongly it was in the right. The notion of paying Kaslow for what they perceived as extortion offended them.

Nonetheless, they authorized me to attempt to purchase the patent. I could spend up to $10,000 in the effort. I made my approach through a third party. Kaslow rejected the offer. In his view, $10,000 was a pittance compared with the potential windfall he saw in his future.

During this time, the Newspaper Advertising Bureau received a threatening letter from Kaslow, alleging potential infringement of his patent. There was also an article about the invention in *Editor and Publisher*, which increased the pressure blocking the implementation of Guideline 22.

Accordingly, in early 1978, nearly two years after the UPCC learned of Kaslow's invention, it launched a two-pronged attack upon the patent. The first attack was a protest proceeding within the Patent Office. The second was a declaratory judgment action filed in federal district court in New York. The patent office proceeding challenged the

Patent Office's issuing the patent. The federal court proceeding was a preemptive strike, hoping to obtain a ruling of invalidity before Kaslow brought any infringement actions.

The Kaslow patent addressed the use of bar code symbols to match products with coupons. The perceived major beneficiaries of U.P.C. coupon scanning were product manufacturers. The Board of Governors therefore proposed to split the litigation cost with the GMA Coupon Committee. The initial litigation budget was $40,000. Although the Coupon Committee agreed in principle to the UPCC proposal, in the end the Code Council bore the entire cost.

The federal judge quickly rejected a motion to dismiss the declaratory judgment action. He pressured both parties to arrive at a negotiated settlement. The Board reluctantly agreed that a $25,000 payment to Kaslow for the patent was probably reasonable, but $50,000 would be clearly excessive. There remained an unbridgeable gulf between what the UPCC was willing to offer and Kaslow's view of the worth of his invention. The judicial pressure for a settlement was fruitless.

The UPCC Board viewed the litigation more with its emotions than its intellect. The old saw about "millions for defense, not one cent for tribute" was repeated often by Board members. As we shall see, a more businesslike attitude, weighing costs of litigation against the cost of settlement, prevailed in subsequent legal challenges.

In the spring of 1979, the federal court placed the declaratory judgment action on hold, pending the outcome of proceedings in the Patent Office. This proved advantageous to the UPCC, although two more years would pass before there were results in that proceeding, and two more years before the dispute ended.

A patent office examiner found in favor of the UPCC in early 1981. The decision was based upon the prior public use of the invention in the Kenwood test of the bull's-eye symbol.

Kaslow appealed to the Board of Patent Appeals. He lost again and appealed again, this time to the Court of Appeals for the Federal Circuit.

Finally, in late 1983, more than six years after the issue arose, Kaslow lost his last appeal, and the dispute was over. The UPCC won — at least Kaslow received nothing, and his patent was declared invalid. From another viewpoint, only the lawyers won. For over seven years, the threat of the Kaslow patent impeded implementation of U.P.C. coupon scanning. It destroyed whatever momentum might have developed to use Guideline 22.

Retailers had made (and were making) enormous capital investments in scanning equipment. They did not want to spend one cent more than they had to. Any additional expenditure required a clear demonstration of a more than compensating economic benefit. This was especially true of those who already had scanners in place. And Guideline 22, while not costly, was not free to retailers. The uncertainty caused by Kaslow was a ready excuse for them to do nothing.

1985–1988 — Ilhan Bilgutay

During the Kaslow litigation, the UPCC's patent counsel was quite critical of the patent advice given (by another lawyer) to the Symbol Selection Committee. Following that advice, the Ad Hoc Committee and Symbol Selection Committee simply sought assurances from proponents of candidate symbols that their symbol was in the public domain.

Bob McMorrow and Darryl Mexic, who represented the UPCC in the Kaslow matter, said in hindsight the UPCC should have sought patent protection for the U.P.C. symbol. If a patent issued, the organization could dedicate it to the public domain and still use it defensively against those like Kaslow. If a patent was denied and a Kaslow later came forward, the unpatentability ruling could have been used as a defense.

This became more than a theoretical issue two years later. One spring day in 1985, I received a call from a Florida attorney named Ron Smith. He had heard I was involved with the U.P.C. Smith asked if I knew when the U.P.C. symbol was first publicly scanned. Proudly, I told him there was a plaque in my office that proclaimed the "first public demonstration of . . . the Universal Product Code Symbol" at the Super Market Institute convention May 8, 1973. Smith did not say why he wanted the information.

A couple of months later we found out. A gentleman from Tampa, Florida, sued Exxon claiming Exxon's use of the U.P.C. symbol infringed his patent. He claimed damages of more than a billion dollars. The Uniform Code Council immediately recognized this suit threatened the very existence of the U.P.C. The Board authorized the UCC to seek permission to be substituted for Exxon. All parties, including the court, quickly agreed.

Ilhan Bilgutay was the inventor. If Walter Kaslow appeared to the Code Council to be a man with a get rich quick scheme, Bilgutay was a classic eccentric inventor, outraged at the misappropriation of his invention. He wanted the wealth to which he believed he was entitled. Even more important to him, however, were vindication and recognition of his genius.

On its face Bilgutay's claim seemed even more outrageous and frivolous than Kaslow's, but it proved to be a much more serious challenge. Kaslow's patent dealt with coupons, which were important to the UCC, but peripheral to its central mission. Bilgutay's patent, on the other hand, challenged the U.P.C. symbol itself. Bilgutay's zeal (not to mention his eccentricity) meant this would be a real battle.

Again the UCC turned to Bob McMorrow and Darryl Mexic to handle the litigation. After completing a preliminary investigation, they advised the Board that Bilgutay's claims of infringement were so outrageous as to be almost frivolous. Their certainty of victory was nearly complete, but not total. Like all lawyers, they acknowledged that courts and juries could be capricious. There could be no guarantee the UCC would prevail.

The Board of Governors had changed considerably since the initiation of the Kaslow litigation. This Board took a more pragmatic view. If the cost of settlement was less than the cost of defending the suit, the Board wanted to settle. When reminded of their predecessors' philosophy, the Board was bemused by the unbusinesslike attitude that fueled the response to Kaslow.

Bilgutay, however, had no interest in settling. He remained convinced we had stolen his invention from him, and the lawsuit would not only vindicate his name but make him a rich man.

His theory of the case was unique. He had taken his invention to NCR and tried to persuade NCR to buy it. NCR, following its usual procedures, met with Bilgutay, but required him to sign a nonconfidentiality agreement. After listening to him NCR said it had no interest in the invention.

What happened next, according to Bilgutay, was unusual. NCR, having no interest in the invention, decided to pass it on to IBM. The Symbol Selection Committee was the vehicle for conveying the information. IBM, more attuned to the potential of the invention, and able to appropriate it royalty-free, used it to design the U.P.C. symbol.

Bilgutay's theory assumed that NCR, with a virtual monopoly in mechanical cash registers, voluntarily gave a new technology to IBM, a company with enormous resources that was not presently a competitor. Moreover, as retailers moved from mechanical cash registers to electronic registers to scanners, NCR moved from near monopoly to vigorous competition.

The theory is so farfetched as to defy credulity. Still, it provided a basis for Bilgutay to add NCR and IBM as defendants in the law suit. For a time, the lawsuit belonged exclusively to the lawyers. Litigation has its own internal momentum, generating work and paper. It was also an engine generating large legal fees. All parties scheduled days of depositions of witnesses and discovery of documents. We expected the trial in 1986, then 1987, and finally in 1988.

On the UCC's side, all decisions were now being made by a committee containing representatives of all three defendants. As noted above, the UCC approached the Bilgutay suit from a more cautious and conservative position than it had had in the Kaslow case. Companies the size of NCR and IBM certainly had no stomach for bold tactics. All of the defendants were also appalled at the costs they were incurring.

The matter never went to trial. The defendants finally came up with a sum Bilgutay decided to accept. At the request of the equipment companies, the court sealed the settlement, preventing the disclosure of the terms of the settlement. The UCC's counsel remained convinced the UCC would win the lawsuit. However, even he had to admit the potential cost of litigation was much greater than the agreed settlement.

Thus the matter ended — or so the UCC thought. Mr. Bilgutay had other ideas, however. Almost as soon as the court accepted the settlement, he began an effort to reject it and reopen the lawsuit. For several months, he filed motion after motion, seeking to have his counsel declared incompetent. The court rejected every attempt. Although Bilgutay never lost his zeal, he finally ran out of places to appeal, and in late 1988, the lawsuit ended for real.

The UCC's experience in major litigation was neither as costly nor as lengthy as that of many other companies. It was, however, costly and time-consuming enough. The Kaslow and Bilgutay lawsuits have created a culture within the UCC that strenuously seeks to avoid going to court.

1992 — IAPMO

The Ad Hoc Committee identified its creation as the Universal Product Code, or "UPC." There was nothing magic about the acronym or the name. It was viewed from the outset as simply descriptive. Indeed, for many years the terms "Uniform Product Code" and "Universal Product Code" were used interchangeably. Hal Juckett, unilaterally, decided the UPC was the Universal Product Code.

While not a major concern, the Code Council decided to obtain a trademark for the letters UPC. The trademark examiner rejected the application on the grounds the proposed mark was descriptive, not distinctive. We took an appeal within the trademark office. The appeals board, however, agreed with the examiner. Somehow it just did not seem important enough to go to the trouble and expense of taking the matter to the courts.

As scanning became widespread, the letters "UPC" meant only one thing in the consumer products industry — "universal product code." Marketers asked consumers to clip the U.P.C. symbol as a proof of purchase in numerous promotions. In the *American Heritage Dictionary*, "UPC" is defined as the abbreviation for the Universal Product Code.

Thus, it came as quite a shock in January 1992 when the UCC received an inquiry from a lawyer representing the administrators of the Uniform Plumbing Code, the International Association of Plumbing and Mechanical Officials (IAPMO). He wanted to know just what our "UPC" was.

At the moment, he was engaged in litigation seeking to stop infringement of IAPMO's certification mark UPC. The defendant there argued that the letters "UPC" on its pipe did not refer to the Uniform Plumbing Code, but to its Universal Product Code number. The company had tried and failed to get its pipe certified under the plumbing code.

IAPMO's certification mark conveys considerable market

value. Many municipalities make compliance with the IAPMO code a part of their building codes. IAPMO argued that the company was deliberately trying to deceive customers into believing the pipe was certified under the plumbing code.

The UCC willingly cooperated with IAPMO. The UCC provided descriptions of the organization and the product-identification system it administered. UCC staff gave an affidavit for use in the lawsuit. Neither counsel nor IAPMO staff seemed to have any prior knowledge of the Universal Product Code, though presumably, as consumers, they had frequently come in contact with it.

Shortly after this, IAPMO's attorney turned his attention to the UCC. He suggested that the UCC's use of the letters UPC to identify the Universal Product Code infringed the IAPMO certification mark. The Code Council turned to the trademark lawyers within its officers' companies. Dick Zimmerman (Hershey) and Bob Rich (Rich Products) allowed the UCC so seek advice from their legal departments.

Hershey was particularly helpful. They researched the issue, uncovering several other widespread uses of the letters "UPC." They also cautioned, however, that a challenge to the IAPMO mark would be difficult to sustain, since the statutory period for challenging the mark had ended years before, making the mark incontestable. A court would be very unlikely to sustain a challenge at this late date, no matter how strong the evidence was.

The trademark lawyers, looking backward, told the UCC it had made a serious mistake in not appealing to federal court the Board of Patent Appeals decision rejecting the UCC's trademark application for UPC. If the courts had accepted the UCC's arguments, it would have had a trademark for the letters that would have been senior to IAPMO. A loss would have greatly strengthened the position that UPC — whether Universal Product Code or Uniform Plumbing Code — was purely descriptive and not capable of being trademarked.

After listening to the lawyers, Hal Juckett and I decided we needed to open discussions with IAPMO to see if an accommodation could be found. One thing was clear, abandonment of UPC by the Code Council would be a disaster. The acronym had been in widespread use for twenty years. The world the UCC inhabited knew the code and symbol by no other name. Nonetheless, there was concern that the UCC could actually lose a lawsuit if one were brought.

Accordingly, in February 1992, we set a meeting with IAPMO's Los Angeles lawyer. It turned out to be a strange time for a meeting. Although clear on the day of our visit, Southern California was beset with heavy rains and flooding. I arrived with no trouble, but weather in the Midwest delayed Hal's flight. We finally got together, hours late, and left for the lawyer's office. On the freeway, a car passed our cab. The passengers of the car hurled insults and threats at us as they passed. This was particularly upsetting because there had been several recent incidents of shootings on the freeway.

We arrived at the office late, anxious, and without the preparation time we had anticipated. Nonetheless, the meeting went reasonably well. Peter Selvin, the IAPMO attorney, was gracious, but firm. He had little sympathy for our argument that there could be little confusion between a code used for compliance with building codes and one used for product identification. IAPMO, however, had no strong desire for litigation. We agreed we would continue talking in search of a settlement agreeable to both parties.

IAPMO had a strong legal position, but apparently wanted to minimize its legal costs. A lawsuit, at best, would take months and cost hundreds of thousands of dollars. IAPMO's cost-saving strategy went beyond avoiding litigation. Peter Selvin asked me to draft a proposed settlement agreement. I jumped at the chance, believing that working off your own piece of paper is always better in negotiations.

While IAPMO gave the UCC this advantage, it did not retreat from its position. Several drafts went back and forth. For the UCC, I did the drafting, but had my work reviewed by the Hershey and Rich Products lawyers. It took months, but we reached a settlement acceptable to both sides.

The UCC retained the right to use the letters UPC, but agreed to place a period after each letter (U.P.C.). In addition, a footnote would appear the first time the acronym was used explaining that U.P.C. referred to a product identification system, and not to the plumbing code administered and certified by IAPMO. Finally, an article to the same effect would appear in three consecutive issues of the UCC newsletter.

The legacy of the Kaslow and Bilgutay lawsuits was that the UCC took the IAPMO matter very seriously. It fulfilled the settlement to the letter, without hesitation or grousing. The UCC avoided a lawsuit and retained the use of the acronym "U.P.C." Three periods are a small price to pay to maintain your identity. A side benefit to the dispute was the establishment of a collaborative relationship between the UCC and IAPMO.

Aside from these two lawsuits and the IAPMO negotiation, the UCC has avoided the courts. In part, this is due to the personalities of Board members and officers. In larger part, it is sheer luck. The UCC has always recognized that it administers a voluntary standard. The most effective enforcement of a voluntary standard arises out of the relationship between trading partners, not from a standards administrator.

Nonetheless, several times each year, the UCC is faced with a company abusing the U.P.C. system. Taking the culprit to court has always been deemed an inappropriate allocation of resources. Instead, the UCC tries to resolve the issue through conversation and education.

It has been astonishingly successful. Most of the issues involve smaller, less sophisticated companies. Most involve simple misunderstandings, easily corrected. Many arise when the original UCC member sells all or part of its business. The most difficult to resolve are those coming out of a personal battle between partners. The emotional involvement of the parties makes rational decisions difficult.

As the breadth of U.P.C. usage increases, it seems almost inevitable that some of these disputes will end in court. This is not without risk for the UCC. A company does not purchase a U.P.C. manufacturer identification number from the UCC, it joins the organization. One of the perquisites of membership is the assignment of a number if, but only if, it is required.

It is the UCC's position that the number becomes a limited asset of the member. It can be transmitted to a purchaser of the business, but the number reverts to the UCC if the company simply goes out of business. The theory is based on the premise that an organization can define the benefits and obligations of membership (what it giveth, it can also take away). However, no court has ever ruled on the issue.

Those who wish the UCC to take a more aggressive attitude in court may be missing the point. The marketplace will keep the system working as long as it is serving a useful purpose. If the U.P.C. is no longer an effective mechanism for identifying product, victories in the courtroom will not keep it in use.

13
UCC — A Broader
Vision

Gordon McGovern's term as Chairman of the UCC ended on October 29, 1987. On October 28, his tenure as CEO of Campbell Soup came to an end. Nonetheless, he attended the UCC Annual Meeting to complete the "change of command ceremony." His successor at the UCC was Byron Allumbaugh, a former FMI Chair and CEO of Ralph's, a Southern California supermarket chain.

Allumbaugh's accession marked the beginning of a change in direction for the Code Council. Board members, especially officers, had always taken their responsibilities seriously. In the early years, however, Board members acted as if they were administering a trade association project. Allumbaugh lead the UCC as an independent organization and allowed it to stand or fall upon its own merit.

This meant more attention to developing a strong infrastructure within the Code Council. At first, this enhanced the role of the Operating Committee. Tom Wilson proposed a budgeting and project approval process and the Operating Committee told Juckett he was to carry out the system. Wilson and the Committee had made little, if any, effort to make Dayton a part of the development process. Juckett's lack of attention was understandable, however, because of a serious illness in his immediate family at that time. From his perspective, a project approval process just didn't seem that important.

At the beginning of 1988, Hal Juckett presided over a staff of seven. The workload continued to expand. Applications for U.P.C. memberships grew rapidly, fueled by the spread of U.P.C. scanning through general merchandise and department store outlets. Memberships on the EDI side grew more slowly, but there was a great need for education on the EDI standards. In addition, the industrial governors — Al Messerli and Ben Cooper — were constantly agitating for additional staff, earmarked for expanding the UCC presence into the industrial commercial market.

The Board responded with the authorization to add four new staff, including a U.P.C. professional. They also retained Deloitte, Haskins and Sells to do a business review of the Dayton office.

Despite the increased workload, the time required to process a U.P.C. membership application was cut in half. What took two hours in 1980 needed only an hour in 1988, and the UCC maintained its record of never issuing a duplicate number.

David Jenkins, CEO of Shaw's Supermarkets, a regional chain headquartered in New England, joined the Board as an FMI governor. He took one look at the Council's growing surplus, totally invested in a money market fund, and asked why the UCC was not earning more with its investments. He proposed a review of the investment policy. To accomplish this review, the Chief Financial Officers of the companies represented on the Executive Committee — Hershey Foods, KMart, Shaws, and Campbell Soup — were designated a Financial Advisory Committee with Treasurer Barry Franz.

In November 1989, this group recommended that the UCC adopt a much more aggressive investment strategy and hire a professional investment manager to propose a detailed plan of investment. Simultaneously, tax attorneys were studying the Council's structure and activities. They concluded there was no danger to the UCC's tax-exempt status.

Several investment managers were interviewed, and Highland Associates of Birmingham, Alabama, was retained. Highland's Bill Terry presented an investment strategy to the Board in May 1990. The Board gave its blessing, and the result was immediate and spectacular. After only three quarters, the new investment program was producing a return greater than fifteen percent.

Chairman Allumbaugh provided hands-on leadership to the UCC. But he had a business of his own to run, and like most grocery retailers, he did not have a large staff at Ralphs. To assist with his UCC duties, he turned to the Food Marketing Institute (FMI), which had appointed him. He had considerable clout with FMI, since he was a past chair of the organization. FMI assigned one of its staff, Judy Kozacik, to support Allumbaugh's UCC leadership.

As 1989 began, Chairman Allumbaugh expressed satisfaction that the UCC had a workable budgeting process at last. The process enabled the Board to understand the costs of each element of the business. The increases in the 1989 operating expenses were divided roughly equally among salaries, education programs, and printing and travel.

Another Allumbaugh reform was the creation of Board committees. He and David Jenkins were concerned that Board members who were not on the Executive Committee had become irrelevant. By placing each Board member on a working committee, Allumbaugh hoped to give them a stake in the business, and a reason to continue their service.

I prepared the first draft of a proposal. Wilson, Juckett, and the Executive Committee massaged it. In March, five committees were created: Nominating, Personnel/Compensation, Finance, U.P.C. Advisory, and EDI Advisory. The U.P.C. Advisory Committee, comprised solely of Board members, was given responsibility for all issues dealing with

U.P.C. coding. The Symbol Technical Advisory Committee,[1] with its technical expertise, would report to the U.P.C. Advisory Committee.

The EDI Advisory Committee had a different structure. In the first place, it already existed as a committee with representation from VICS, UCS, and the public warehouses. The new arrangement elevated the committee to Board committee status, prescribed that its chair would come from the Board, and increased Board involvement.

The creation of Board committees was a resounding success, and Board involvement increased significantly. On the other hand, Board meetings now consisted essentially of a ratification of actions discussed in committee. The image of a "rubber stamp" was enhanced because the U.P.C. Advisory Committee had approximately half the members of the Board. It held its meetings the day before the Board meeting. There was scant opportunity for additional discussion at the Board.

Allumbaugh led another change in UCC policy. At the outset, participants (including Board members) were truly volunteers, receiving neither pay nor reimbursement of expenses. Once the endowment fund began to accrue, Board and management decided Board members should at least have their Board meeting expenses paid.

Chairman Allumbaugh decided to reverse this policy. He believed UCC standards provided such great benefits to the companies using them that the employers of Board members should be expected to underwrite involvement with the UCC. After a study revealed that no company objected to this (some were unaware the UCC ever paid Board members' expenses), the policy was changed to eliminate this modest perk. Hal Juckett was given discretion to reimburse the expenses of a Board member if it was necessary to retain the

[1] To prevent the appearance of favoring one company over another, Juckett served as STAC chair.

individual's services on the Board. To date this has been done only for public governors, who have no company behind them.

One other administrative change took place during this time. Treasurer Barry Franz, a member of the Operating Committee, was located in Cincinnati and exercised hands-on oversight of the UCC. Barry's views tended to oppose a proactive agenda for the UCC, which meant he was in the minority on the Board and usually opposed to Hal Juckett's plans.

In addition, Patrick Kiernan, the new GMA staff person responsible for liaison with the UCC, decided that Barry was no longer an appropriate person to represent GMA on the UCC Board of Governors. Nonetheless, Franz still had supporters. He also was one of the few remaining points of contact with the organization's origins. No one could challenge his record of contributions nor his dedication to the UCC.

GMA decided to replace Barry Franz as a GMA governor. This was countered by an amendment to the UCC bylaws to make the Treasurer a member of the Board of Governors. While Franz continued his service as Treasurer and Board member, his influence diminished considerably.

From the outset, the UCC stationery listed the grocery industry trade associations as "sponsoring associations." These were, for the most part, the groups that had contributed seed money to the project. In early 1989, however, I received a call from one of those associations, the National Association of Convenience Stores (NACS), asking how they had become a sponsoring association.

There was no ready answer. NACS had not contributed seed money to the Ad Hoc effort, nor had the association leadership ever been actively involved. It was listed simply because it was a major grocery industry association. This explanation did not satisfy NACS. The listing was removed, though the other associations remained on the letterhead. The Executive Committee believed it enhanced the UCC's credibility.

Al Messerli, however, wanted all references to sponsoring associations removed. He believed, contrary to the Executive Committee, that the letterhead raised a barrier to the industrial/commercial sector by highlighting the grocery industry's influence. UCC growth was now being driven by applicants from other industries. As with most of his crusades, he did not achieve immediate success, but he did not give up. Today, the list of "sponsoring associations" is gone from the letterhead.

Chairman Allumbaugh's term brought many structural changes, but substantive issues were not neglected. In 1989, for the first time, the Council began to discuss seriously the issue of the breadth of the U.P.C. This coding system, devised specifically for the grocery industry was proving to be remarkably adaptable. It now appeared suitable for all retail. Some even argued this was too limiting. Indeed, the Dayton office reported it was fielding inquiries about generic U.P.C. marking of plumbing, heating, and air conditioning supplies. Slowly, the Board realized it must take a broader view.

In the spring of 1989, urged on by its nongrocery retail members, the UCC approved a new symbology for use with serialized shipping containers. Code 128 is the invention of Ted Williams, of Symbol Vision, and an active member of STAC. 128 is another linear bar code, placed in the public domain. It is able to handle more data and information contained in both numbers and letters. Code 128 symbols can be strung together, or concatenated, to enable different data elements to be included.

The approval of this third symbology[2] marked the first time the Board had taken an action with respect to codes and symbols where the grocery industry was not the immediate primary beneficiary. At about the same time, staff announced a new project to decide if a recently developed

[2] The other two are the U.P.C. symbol and the Interleaved Two of Five, or U.P.C. Shipping Container symbol.

7 12345 12345 9

Universal Product Code (data structure & symbology)

3 00 12345 67890 6

SCC-14 (data structure)
Interleaved 2-of-5 (symbology)

(01) 3 0012345 67890 6

SCC-14 (data structure)
UCC/EAN-128 (symbology)

(00) 0 0012345 555555555 8

SSCC-18 (data structure)
UCC/EAN-128 (symbology)

ANSI standard on how to measure the quality of printed symbols could be made applicable to the U.P.C. This was significant because of its embracing the work of ANSI, and because it recognized that the use of symbol verifiers would not disappear. It was important that the UCC make sure the results from verifiers were both comparable and meaningful.

Carefully following a standards development process, the UCC, working with a task force, developed a print quality standard for the U.P.C. symbol. The Code Council contracted with Applied Image, Inc., in Rochester N.Y., a specialist in high-resolution targets. They were asked to develop U.P.C. symbols that could be used as the "golden ruler" for verifier manufacturers to test their equipment.

In April 1994, the print-quality specification was formally approved. Most commentors were enthusiastic at the development. The Flexible Packaging Association, however, was concerned that flexible packaging (plastic bags and so forth) required the operator of a verifier to exercise great skill to come up with correct results. The Council agreed to work with FPA on an education program.

Another critic was more difficult to pacify. Ed Martin had been involved with the printing of U.P.C. symbols from the very beginning. By the early 1990s, his family company was marketing a symbol "verifier." His machine was a supermarket scanner. Accordingly, if symbol verifiers became more reliable, his business would be threatened. He also believed the proposed print-quality specification represented a Cadillac solution for a Chevrolet problem. Apparently alone, he felt the new standard would impose unfair burdens on printers. For months, his complaints persisted. Patiently, the UCC responded to every letter. Eventually, the letters stopped coming.

Byron Allumbaugh's successor as chairman was Dick Zimmerman, CEO of Hershey Foods. While Allumbaugh had transformed the Uniform Code Council from a project of the grocery industry trade associations to an independent business, Zimmerman's mission became the development of a strategic plan for the UCC.

The decade of the 1990s began with a formal strategic planning process, led by John Rawley, a retired Hershey executive. The Executive Committee, augmented by other interested Board members, convened at the Dallas Fort Worth airport. As background, I presented the opinion of my law firm's tax department that the tax-exempt status of the UCC was reasonably secure. I also prepared a memorandum documenting the return of the original seed money to the trade associations. Zimmerman was particularly concerned to establish that the UCC had no financial obligation to its founders.

Everyone assumed, however, that the UCC had taken on an obligation to support its members in perpetuity, even though it only collected a one-time fee. The Board's position had the virtue of supporting the need for a very large endowment. Although history and current practice said membership applications were increasing, it remained a bedrock article of faith that the membership potential had a finite limit. Some day that limit would be reached and revenues would cease, while the need for services would continue indefinitely.

The strategic planning process yielded a revised mission statement that represented a major shift for the Code Council. Gone was the emphasis on reaction, and in its place a call to leadership with respect to the point-of-purchase transaction and related distribution channels.[3] The UCC was given the signal to expand its activities. The industrial governors saw this as a go-ahead for staff to proselytize non-retail industry segments.

Another outcome was the development of formal pro-

[3] "The mission of the Uniform Code Council, Inc. is to take a leadership role in supplying product identification and electronic data interchange standards and services which enhance the point of purchase transaction and enable related distribution channels to operate more efficiently and effectively while contributing added value to the consumer." 5/8/90

cedures to guide the UCC's decision making. This was a difficult cultural adjustment for the UCC since it prided itself on its
ability to respond to situations promptly, focussing on the
problem rather than the procedure used to solve the problem.
However, with success and growth came a need not only to do
things correctly, but to appear to do them correctly. Accordingly, David Jenkins, Chair of the U.P.C. Advisory Committee,
asked me to prepare a set of procedures. The "decision-
making procedures" were developed over the summer of
1990. They were drawn primarily from three sources: the process followed by the Ad Hoc and Symbol Selection Committees, an FTC Advisory Opinion to the American National
Standards Institute, and an OMB circular (since withdrawn)
setting forth guidelines for federal government participation
in nongovernment standardization activities. Although the
procedures were not consciously modeled on ANSI's process,
very few changes were required when the UCC subsequently
decided to submit its standards to ANSI.[4]

The procedures guaranteed openness, notice of impending action, the right to comment upon proposed action, and
the right of appeal if one disagreed with a UCC action. They
were specifically made applicable to actions on proposed or
existing standards. They could also apply to other activities as
decided by the Board or U.P.C. Advisory Committee.

The decision-making procedures were adopted by the
Board and U.P.C. Advisory Committee at the annual meeting
in Phoenix in November 1990. This was a momentous meeting on many counts. Recognizing the growing complexity of
the issues facing the UCC, the Board authorized the creation
of the position of U.P.C. Technical Director. Shortly thereafter, Tom Brady, a career NCR employee and STAC member,
was hired to fill the position.

The capability of Code 128 to handle variable data about

---

[4] See Chapter 11.

products began at that meeting as the Board approved a dictionary of so-called application identifiers (AI). These identifiers covered such product attributes such as date, batch, lot, measurements.

At the Phoenix meeting, the Food Marketing Institute expressed its growing concern over the issue of symbol quality. FMI said it was considering the establishment of a certification service for U.P.C. symbols[5] because more symbols were appearing that violated UCC guidelines and specifications. The Board authorized the release of the draft Quality Specification for the U.P.C. Printed Symbol for public review and comment.

With much ceremony, Dick Zimmerman and Jean Collin, Chairman of the European Article Numbering Association, signed a memorandum of understanding, promising a cooperative global approach to issues. The actual signing took place at sunset on the desert patio of the Arizona Biltmore.

All these issues were important, but the most significant event of the November 1990 meeting came as an added starter, surprising all but a very few. At this meeting, as he honored retiring members of the Board, Chairman Zimmerman also honored Tom Wilson for his twenty-plus years of service to the UCC. The only thing was, until he received his gift, Wilson did not know he was leaving.

Wilson's longevity, his failure to submit bills on time, and Hal Juckett's concern that Wilson was angling for the top staff position combined to bring an end to McKinsey's connection with the U.P.C. Tom had always cemented his position by cultivating the chair, but had neglected this with Zimmerman. Also, his relationship with Byron Allumbaugh, Zimmerman's predecessor, was apparently not as solid as it seemed. In the end, however, a remark attributed to Wilson had spurred Juckett to action. Wilson reportedly was eyeing the corner office in the Dayton office.

---

[5] Such a service has not been created, by FMI or anyone else.

Wilson graciously accepted his gift, but conspicuously left it behind. Quietly and quickly, he left the meeting, never to return. Although he annoyed many people, all agree that without him there would have been no U.P.C.

At the next Board meeting, Zimmerman acknowledged the control of the Board by the grocery industry no longer reflected the realities of the organization or its mission. He was not prepared to propose a change, but did make changing the Board composition a UCC priority. Also as the 1990 audit of the UCC's finances by Tom Collins, CPA, was accepted, the Executive Committee vowed that, in the future, the audit would be conducted by the Dayton office of a Big Six accounting firm.

As the number of users of the U.P.C. continued to increase dramatically, some of its supporters urged the creation of a more user-friendly manual for unsophisticated readers, in addition to the technospeak of the specification manuals. In this way, some of the more obvious, innocent symbol-marking errors might be avoided. Willard Bishop Consulting was given this task. The result was a highly readable "Implementation Guide for New Users."

Topics arose that had been addressed before, but would not go away, and others came forth from the broader mission and growing maturity of the organization. Thus, the National Broiler Council, through its attorney, formally notified the Code Council of its concerns with U.P.C. coding of random-weight products. The Broiler Council had been part of a multi-industry group that allocated available random-weight item designations. The problem was that all of the numbers had been assigned, but chicken producers continued to develop new items needing numbers.

According to the Broiler Council, retailers were refusing to accept these new items because they lacked U.P.C. codes. The UCC was skeptical of the claim, since its investigations found few retailers were actually following UCC guidelines for random weight. Nonetheless, the allegations got the UCC's attention because they implied anticompetitive behavior by the Code Council.

After I responded to the lawyer's letter, Tom Brady met with the Broiler Council in Washington. Tom had to press to get the meeting. The discussion was open and friendly, but did not lead to a neat solution of the problems with random-weight identification.[6] The Broiler Council seemed to lose interest, and the UCC continued to muddle on without changing the existing guideline.

From the UCC perspective, a proposal for a generic floral code, like the produce code, had a happier resolution. Although the Board of Governors had explicitly stated its vote to authorize a generic "Produceland" number did not set a precedent, the Produce Marketing Association now wanted a generic "Flowerland" number. After considering the request, the UCC concluded floral products could be handled like produce and referred the request to the Produce Electronic Information Board, which had been created to administer Produceland.

Almost routinely, other trade associations, especially in the grocery industry, approached the UCC seeking contributions for various studies. Each request was given serious consideration, and if it could be justified as consonant with the UCC's mission, financial support was often given.

One such study was proposed by FMI to study the ergonomics of the checkout counter. Many, including especially the union of retail clerks, expressed concern that scanning at the point of sale could lead to repetitive-motion injuries, such as carpal tunnel syndrome. A study of checkout and scanning design to figure out the most worker-friendly configuration was clearly appropriate for UCC involvement.

---

[6] The problem remains as this is being written. A multi-industry group, led by UCC staff, is once again focussing on this issue.

Occasionally, the UCC was forcibly reminded it was an organization of volunteers. This meant there were some issues where consensus was unattainable. U.P.C. marking of paperback books was such an issue. When U.P.C. scanning was in its infancy, only supermarkets were scanning. Supermarkets wanted to offer paperback books to their customers, but had no interest in the particular title being sold. Accordingly, U.P.C. marking of paperback books showed the publisher and price category of the book, not the title.

This satisfied the supermarket, but presented problems for book stores as they began scanning. Information on title was very important to them. To accommodate their needs, a second symbol was placed inside the cover. However, some book stores realized they could improve productivity if the symbol containing title-specific data was on the outside back cover in place of price point information.

The book stores petitioned the UCC to change the guideline for symbol marking of paperback books, but the supermarkets resisted. For over two years, the UCC tried to resolve the issue. No satisfactory solution could be found. The UCC never changed the guideline, but amazingly, the issue simply faded away.

In 1973, symbol source-marking was given a huge boost by FDA's adoption of nutrition labeling regulations that required most food products to be relabeled. In 1991, FDA did it again, imposing significant new labeling requirements. The UCC took it as an opportunity to impress upon all food companies the need for symbol quality and adherence to symbol guidelines. By 1992, virtually every company selling through retail channels recognized the necessity of placing the U.P.C. symbol on its products. The importance of quality, however, needed constant re-enforcement.

At this time, the Board of Governors changed two fundamental policies that had guided the UCC since its founding. One was ministerial, almost trivial. The other was not.

A regular feature of each Board meeting was the election as members of all those who had joined since the previous meeting. The growing popularity of the U.P.C. meant that thousands of new members were elected at each meeting. The computer printout containing the new member list was several inches thick. Obviously, the Board was not giving detailed attention to this subject. Accordingly, the authority to admit applicants to membership was delegated to staff.

The Ad Hoc Committee (predecessor to the UCC) took as one of its proudest achievements the avoidance of the American National Standards Institute standardization process. They believed it would kill momentum. But many companies, especially global companies, had policies calling for the use of ANSI standards. Twenty years after the beginning, the Board directed staff to explore the possibility of having UCC standards become ANSI standards.

As the work load of the Code Council grew, so did its needs for staff and space. By 1992, there were almost twenty UCC staff members, and the Board authorized the acquisition of additional office space.

That year Board Chair David Jenkins, CEO of Shaw's Supermarkets and a former FMI Chairman, established a formal progression for future officers. A potential chair would first serve as Chair of the Finance Committee, move on to head the U.P.C. Advisory Committee, and then serve two years as Board Chair. Hopefully, a retired chair could be persuaded to be available for a year or two to lend his accumulated experience to the successor.

This ladder was very useful to both the Chair and the UCC. It meant that the Chair had a thorough understanding of the organization by the time he took office. On the other hand, the UCC Chairmen were all CEOs of their companies. The six-to-eight-year commitment called for by the ladder proved burdensome for many chief executives. After only two years, the ladder proved a problem in recruiting a CEO to become chair. Accordingly, the ladder was changed to call for only a four-year commitment.[7]

The 1991 audit by the Dayton office of Deloitte and Touche (the first audit by an Ohio firm) recommended the consolidation of all accounting functions in Dayton. Hal Juckett had been pushing for this for years. The Board by this time was fully supportive. Board members could not fathom why a business in Ohio had a bookkeeper in Vienna, Virginia.

Only Barry Franz, UCC Treasurer, resisted the change. He believed that the administration of the Dayton office was not as disciplined and efficient as it should be. He believed that Dick Foote, physically separated from the office in Dayton, provided a useful review of management practices and a check on any possible abuse. The other officers were bewildered by his attitude, particularly since there had never been even a hint of financial scandal in connection with the operation of the UCC.

It showed how far apart the treasurer was from the rest of the Board. Still he remained, for he faithfully filled the treasurer's office, *and* brought valuable technical expertise to the Board. Dick Foote's services were ended with thanks. Barry's fears proved groundless, as future audits continued to come back clean.

To facilitate coordination with EAN, the UCC counterpart in the rest of the world, an International Data Application Standards Committee (IDASC) was created. This committee was composed of two UCC and two EAN representatives, plus the technical director and top staff officer of both organizations. As either organization developed a new AI, it was forwarded to IDASC, which put some discipline into the process.

The present and the future now looked very different from the past for the UCC. Events were moving too rapidly to get a handle on what was ahead simply by attending two

---

[7] Craig Schnuck, CEO of Schnuck Markets was the only UCC Chair to go through the full six-year ladder.

Board meetings a year. A fresh look at today's situation and at what was ahead was needed.

Accordingly, the UCC began a search for a consultant to conduct a Horizon Scan study. All of the usual suspects submitted proposals, and Andersen Consulting won the contract. It was a massive project, ultimately costing almost a half million dollars. Andersen's conclusions were reassuring, challenging, and exciting.

Andersen reported the existing technologies would remain stable and dominant over the next decade, which was as far in the future as they were willing to look. In addition, there was sufficient capacity within the U.P.C. to handle the anticipated surge in demand. This surge would come about as UCC standards began to be applied in industrial-commercial channels, propelled by pressure by customers.

Andersen noted that business issues, not technology, were limiting expansion of both U.P.C., and especially EDI. A corollary to this finding was a recommendation that the UCC abandon its traditional passive role. Andersen strongly urged the UCC to be aggressive in educating potential users to the advantages of UCC standards.

The UCC began to advocate the implementation of its EDI standards more aggressively. When GMA and NFBA[8] approached it for assistance in developing new EDI transaction sets for use with food brokers, the UCC was quick to respond positively in spite of some concern that the task was outside the UCC mission. Project Info, as the effort was called, was highly successful. It enabled food brokers to avoid having separate software connections with each of their manufacturer principals.

The EDI side of the house, having long felt the poor stepsister to the wealthy U.P.C., began searching for ways to pull its own weight financially. The EDI Users Conferences had been very successful, both substantively and financially. In

[8] National Food Brokers Association.

recruitment of new members EDI lagged far behind the U.P.C. The EDI Advisory Committee decided to begin charging nominal annual dues. Although this program is still in its infancy, it has proven to be a financial success. The number of companies agreeing to continue as members has been well above the projections of the Advisory Committee.

An EDI work group had been formed to deal with packaging and labeling issues. It apparently touched a nerve. Its meetings attracted an ever-increasing number of participants, and its agenda broadened to the point that the EDI Advisory Committee concluded it was beyond the scope of the UCC's EDI mission.

An ingenious solution was devised. The work group's size, mission, and scope were redefined to fit under the U.P.C. umbrella, and a new committee under the U.P.C. Advisory Committee was formed, the Shipping Container Marking and Labeling Committee (SCMLC). Membership was limited to twenty, from all UCC constituencies. The U.P.C. Advisory Committee handed SCMLC a formal charter (like that of the Industrial Commercial Advisory Committee), and one of its members developed a detailed set of Operating Procedures to guide the Committee's actions.

Such emphasis on process and form was foreign to the UCC's traditions. It was a reflection of the growing maturity of the organization. It also reflected the personalities of many of the original committee members. Most of all, the formal structure protected committee members from charges that they were arbitrary. Indeed, the Committee decided that all meetings would be open, and nonmembers, while not allowed to vote, would be allowed to participate fully in discussions.

One of the committee co-chairs, Dennis Epley of Kraft General Foods, led the SCMLC to develop a model of UCC standards that provided a logical framework to understand their uses and interplay. This has proved extremely valuable.

The increasing growth and sophistication of the UCC

meant the organization had outgrown its computer system. Reflecting the worldwide scope of UCC-EAN standards by the early 1990s, the UCC donated its old system to the fledgling Russian coding authority.

The UCC was created by the grocery industry, but never received much recognition from that industry. Now, as its mission broadened to cross industry lines, it began to receive acknowledgement from its founders. During his term as Board Chair, two things happened to David Jenkins — he retired as Chairman of Shaw's, and he began to urge the grocery industry to use the UCC teachings and improve efficiency and productivity.

The result was ECR (Efficient Consumer Response). Co-sponsored by eleven associations (including the UCC), it was the largest cooperative industry effort since the Ad Hoc Committee. New competitive forces in the industry certainly focussed the industry's attention. A study by Kurt Salmon Associates concluded the industry could take $30 billion in costs out of the system by improving efficiencies.

This was a sufficiently large carrot to assure a strong response. The UCC took a significant role in the two-year effort. Whether the industry will realize the full amount of potential savings is still open to question. That ECR is a watershed for the industry and has served to enhance the UCC's reputation is clear, however. The initiative has spawned similar programs in other industries and even other countries.

As part of the ECR initiative, the UCC agreed to take on the administration of another standard, called SIL (Standard Interchange Language).[9] This standard was taken on a temporary basis, pending a study by the EDI Advisory Committee as to whether the UCC should accept administration permanently.

[9] SIL enables intraenterprise communications even if, for example, the checkout systems are different.

The UCC's ECR involvement was capped by the first ECR conference in Dallas in January 1995. This conference, under the leadership and administration of the UCC, attracted 1600 attendees to hear the results of the ECR studies. The UCC received appropriate credit for its efforts.

As the grocery industry became more familiar with the strengths of the UCC, the organization began a restructuring to better reflect its broader constituencies. The first step was to simultaneously enlarge the size of the board and reduce the grocery industry representation. It also changed the by-laws to provide that the post of chair would rotate among grocery manufacturers, grocery distributors, and general merchandise manufacturers or distributors. At the same time, in further recognition of the organization's stature, Hal Juckett was awarded the title of President.

In the early days of the UCC, the health care industry had preliminary discussions about the feasibility of the U.P.C. for that industry. The UCC, however, contributed little to the conversation. It did not discourage the use of the U.P.C., but it did not encourage it either. The UCC also made it clear that nothing could be done to adversely affect the use of the U.P.C. in the grocery industry.

The upshot was that the health care industry went in a different direction, developing its own product identification system. Adoption of a coding scheme, and seeing it implemented are two very different things, however. The "labeler identification code" or LIC was not widely used. Moreover, the industry was feeling increasing pressure for more accurate identification.

So in 1992, discussions began again. This time the UCC embraced the opportunity to develop an application for its standards in the health care industry. UCC-EAN 128 also possessed the capability of encoding considerable information in a very small space. Prospects of the actual use of the UCC standards in the health care industry have been greatly strengthened by the decision of the Defense Personnel Supply Center to support the use of UCC standards on medical products it purchases.

The UCC not only worked with the health care industry in adapting the standard, it agreed to put considerable resources behind the effort. The first manifestation was the publication of a brochure designed to "demystify" UCC standards for the industry.

The U.P.C. symbol, interleaved two of five, and UCC-EAN 128 are all linear bar codes. All have proven their utility and versatility. Technology, of course, continues to progress, and the demands for identification and transmission of information continue to increase. The result has been a plethora of new technologies. For some time, the UCC waffled on its proper role with these new technologies. The Horizon Scan report was useful in focussing the Board and staff on a process for evaluating these technologies.

Two-dimensional symbologies are a recent development. They can compress a great deal more data in a smaller space than conventional linear bar codes. These symbologies hold particular promise for small-item marking, although the business case for their use has not yet clearly emerged.

The UCC initially took a cautionary position, urging that 2D symbols should not in any way slow the implementation of EDI. Members of the Industrial/Commercial Advisory Committee, especially the health industry representatives, urged the UCC to become more involved with 2D. Accordingly, the UCC agreed to co-sponsor with VICS,[10] a study of high capacity technologies.

This study, by Kurt Salmon Associates, was completed in the summer of 1995. It concluded that 2D had potential, but it was premature to settle on a standard. This conclusion, unfortunately, placed the UCC in conflict with an ANSI com-

[10] VICS is the organization in the general merchandise industry promoting product identification and EDI.

mittee that was not only ready to adopt a 2D standard, but to specify specific 2D symbologies for specific applications.

Radio frequency product identification (RFID) is another new technology. Its proponents tout it as a future replacement for linear bar codes. It also holds great promise for the identification of animals and as a method of electronic article surveillance. At the moment, however, a number of technical issues need to be resolved before RFID can realize its promise.

Nonetheless, in the winter of 1993–1994, a research institute partially funded by the South African government, received worldwide publicity for their RFID device. The so-called Supertag would render bar codes obsolete. It would check out an entire grocery cart of products simply by pushing the cart through a tunnel.

The publicity, aided by reports from the South African Article Numbering Association, quickly caught the attention of the UCC. The result was a visit to South Africa by Hal Juckett, U.P.C. Technical Director Tom Brady, and me in March (less than a month before the landmark election that brought Nelson Mandela to power). Once we saw the Supertag demonstration in Pretoria, it was clear that Supertag had many technical and economic hurdles to pass before it could hope to make an impact in the marketplace.

The KSA study, while acknowledging the obstacles, points to RFID as having significant potential for future uses. Reflecting the new UCC, the organization has allocated significant resources to exploring these new technologies.

As the UCC looks forward to dealing with new technologies, it is also looking backward as a good steward. Well over 180,000 U.P.C. manufacturer numbers have been issued. Over the years, some of those entities have gone out of business. Under UCC theory, those U.P.C. numbers reverted to the UCC. However, no action has ever been taken to reclaim them.

In 1995, the Board authorized a formal reclamation project. It appeared as if as many as 20,000 numbers could be brought back for reassignment.

As the UCC matures, its horizons are expanding, in terms of industries using its standards, geographic scope of its activities, and technologies employed. In 1994, as a complement to the Horizon Scan study, the Board of Governors met with Harvard Business School faculty to brainstorm about the potentials and pitfalls facing the organization.

Simultaneously, the UCC also began to look at its own structure as its top staff executives neared retirement age, and the time for a general merchandise executive to become Chairman neared. As this is being written, this work is still underway. It may provide an opportunity to examine the division of the office into U.P.C. and EDI. While this structure has served well, it may be more appropriate in the future to bring the two closer together, to mirror what is happening in industry.

What began as a grocery industry project to speed the consumer checkout process is today an independent organization representing a multitude of industries. The UCC now manages a suite of standards, globally accepted. The future is exciting as the UCC works to develop and implement supply chain management standards.

Appendix A
Giants of the Revolution

The U.P.C. and the life of the Uniform Code Council owe an incalculable debt to the (mostly) volunteer efforts of many people. They brought intelligence, energy, and enthusiasm to the task. Their contribution has changed the way we shop and the way industries identify and track items. What follows are my memories of a dozen individuals who stand out as giants of this revolution. There are many others equally as deserving, and some who have made (or are making) major contributions. To them, I express my apologies. You have done, and are doing, work that is reducing costs, eliminating waste, and improving productivity.

Here are one man's dozen giants of the revolution at the checkout.

Byron Allumbaugh

Byron served as chairman of the Board of Governors from 1987 to 1989. He changed the prevailing attitude toward the UCC. Until his chairmanship, the Code Council was universally perceived as a joint project of the grocery industry trade associations. Byron brought a different sensibility to the organization. He viewed the Code Council as an independent business that should stand or fall on its own merits.

This was an incalculable change. It meant that the oversight of McKinsey and the grocery trade associations was

247

reduced, while the UCC staff, especially Hal Juckett, was freed to develop its own plans for the organization. Allumbaugh's leadership was a prerequisite for the UCC's change from a reactive to a proactive stance.

Byron Allumbaugh started his career as a meat cutter. He rose to become CEO of Ralph's Grocery, a major California grocery chain headquartered in Southern California. Immediately before his service as UCC chair, he served as chairman of the Food Marketing Institute.

Byron and his wife Ronnie are attractive, athletic, and incorrigibly friendly. While he was FMI chairman, they insisted on periodically touring the FMI offices to visit the association staff. When the UCC held a board meeting near his home in Southern California, the Allumbaughs hosted a reception in their home. Of all the UCC chairs, he is the only one to extend such personal hospitality.

His term as UCC chair came as the organization began to recognize its relative affluence. At that time, the UCC, while it did not pay its directors for their services, did offer to reimburse them for their expenses in attending Board meetings. The policy was not well publicized, and very few Governors took advantage of it. Byron took a strong position that the Governors' companies were actually benefitting from Board service, and pushed through a resolution revoking this one instance of the UCC's largesse.

Allumbaugh's other major contribution was the development of a system to get greater involvement of Board members in the organization's work. He created a number of Board committees, most notably the U.P.C. Advisory Committee. Before this, most Board members simply came to meetings, listened to reports, ratified the Executive Committee's recommendations, and went home. Chairman Allumbaugh thought this was a waste of talent. With the new committees, Board members were expected to make a contribution to the functioning of the UCC.

Barry Franz

Barry's involvement with the U.P.C. predates the creation of the UCC. This career Procter & Gamble employee served as a member of the Symbol Selection Committee that picked the U.P.C. In 1975, he joined the Board of Governors as a GMA Governor. Barry became Treasurer of the UCC in 1989, serving in that capacity until his retirement at the end of 1995. Even that did not end his association with the UCC. With the enthusiasm of a teenager, in January 1996, he launched the Franz Strategy Group. One of its first clients was the UCC, which retained him for a study of opportunities in the health industry.

Barry brings exuberant enthusiasm to everything he does, whether it is publishing a magazine on tropical fish, searching for the perfect audio-visual system, or creating the U.P.C. symbol. All agree his enthusiasm and effort are prodigious, but not everyone shares the same passions. During his involvement with the UCC, Barry at one time or another antagonized GMA, Hal Juckett, and several of his fellow Governors. It is noteworthy that, by his retirement, all wounds had healed and Barry Franz was deservedly recognized for his major contributions to the UCC's success.

As a member of the Symbol Selection Committee, Franz was one of the "bees," flitting from one symbol proposer to another, stretching their understanding of the problems and possibilities of a U.P.C. symbol. At committee meetings, Barry, Eric Waldbaum, and Larry Russell had a wonderful, electric synergy as ideas would tumble out from them, each sparking the other.

When the Ad Hoc's Coupon Committee was floundering and a solution seemed impossible, Barry joined it. It was largely his work that led to a successful result. The concept of the family code came from him.

Barry Franz served on the Board of Governors from 1975

to 1995. However, his categorization as a Board member varied. Elected as a representative of the Grocery Manufacturers of America, he became an At Large Governor for a year or so when his employer, Procter & Gamble, withdrew from GMA temporarily. Later, the GMA staff person responsible for relations with the UCC decided to replace him. By that time, Barry was serving as the UCC Treasurer, so the bylaws were amended to give the Treasurer a seat on the Board.

Although his career at Procter & Gamble had nothing to do with finances, Barry brought the P & G mentality, and his computer-modeling skills, to the post of Treasurer. As a good fiduciary, he was conservative, resistant to requests for expenditures, and suspicious of staff calls for money to be spent.

As chronicled in the text, Barry was one of the most outspoken advocates of the view that the UCC should avoid proactive initiatives. As a member of the so-called Operating Committee in the mid-1980s, he had a forum to express his views. For years, Barry's strong belief was that the UCC should act only in response to specific requests and defer if there was any other organization that could conceivably do the job in lieu of the UCC. He was continually amazed as the UCC, led by Hal Juckett, slowly expanded its mission and its staff. The result was a touchy, even hostile, relationship with Hal Juckett. It is a tribute to both men that, by the time of Barry's retirement, fences had been mended to the point that the UCC became the first client of the Franz Strategy Group. Remarkably, given his past conservative attitude, the UCC retained him to explore the feasibility of a potential major expansion of UCC activities in the health industry.

As Treasurer, he carried out a very conservative investment policy that limited investments to money market funds. He also developed a model showing projected receipts and expenditures under a variety of scenarios. The model justified the large endowment. No matter how quickly receipts grew, when Barry plugged in his projections of expenditures, the model showed all surplus funds would be expended within a very few years. The premise of building the endowment fund was that receipts would some day dry up, but demand for services would go on indefinitely. Barry's economic model thus reenforced the continual need to enlarge the endowment.

Barry Franz is constitutionally incapable of dullness. He brings enthusiasm to everything he does, he also is extremely conscientious, and not afraid to state his opinion. This causes some to be put off, but usually he wins you back. He will be missed at the UCC.

R. Burt Gookin

Burt was the first nonfamily member to serve as CEO of the H. J. Heinz Co. His CEO peers selected him to serve as chair of the Ad Hoc Committee. He was the captain who led the effort that ended with the selection of the U.P.C. symbol. Two years later, he was recruited to be the chair of the Board of Governors and served two terms. In between, he served as chairman of GMA, and received SMI's most prestigious award. He gave this effort a decade of his life, all in addition to his "regular" job.

Burt was able to achieve a level of cooperation unprecedented in grocery industry activities. The development of the U.P.C. is *the* example for all subsequent and future joint efforts. Few, if any, have succeeded as the U.P.C. has. This is even more surprising since 1970–1973 was a time of price controls on food, extensive government regulation, and the flowering of the consumer movement.

He not only oversaw the development effort, but also spearheaded the sales effort. A major reason for the success of the U.P.C. was the early adoption of symbol source-marking by grocery manufacturers. There were many reasons for this, but one of the most important was the

CEO-to-CEO presentations of the project, led by Burt Gookin.

As Chair of the Board of Governors, Burt kept the project going through the dark days when many believed the U.P.C. would not succeed. It was during this time that the U.P.C. received national attention from Business Week as the "scanner that failed." At the same time, consumer activists and union leaders were challenging scanning on the issue of price removal.

Challenges were familiar to Burt Gookin. Although he looked exactly like what he had been — a bookkeeper, he was a boxer in his youth. Rising through the ranks at H. J. Heinz, he became the first CEO of the company with a name other than Heinz. During the time of the Ad Hoc Committee, Burt and I shared many meals, breakfasts, lunches, and dinners. At some point during every meal, Burt was sure to ask the server if he could have "some of that good Heinz ketchup."

Gookin was an avid golfer. Once, trying to make conversation, I asked him if he could play any golf course in the world, which one would he pick. Quite seriously, he responded, "I can (play any course I want) you know."

As a CEO of a major corporation, Gookin enjoyed the perquisite of a corporate plane at his disposal. As an accountant, he was aware that the cost of a private plane could not be justified economically. However, as he put it, "there is also no way I will give up the plane." I was fortunate to fly on the Heinz plane on a few occasions. Once, I went to Pittsburgh and met Burt at his office. He drove me in his car to the private airport on the other side of town where the Heinz plane was hangered. We were trying to get across a major city during the height of rush hour. Our progress was very slow. The longer it took, the more frustrated Burt became, beating his fists upon the steering wheel and cursing. Then he stopped, calm and composed. The CEO turned to me and said, "They won't leave until I get there."

This combination of passion and reason is a perfect description of R. Burt Gookin.

Alan L. Haberman

In 1971, Alan Haberman joined the Ad Hoc Committee as Chair of the Symbol Selection Committee. In 1996, the Uniform Code Council asked him to serve as Chair of JTC 1 SC 31 on Automatic Data Capture, an international standardization group. In between, he served continuously on the UCC's Board of Governors, first as a grocery distributor, then as the Public Governor, and most recently as an At Large Governor.

When he chaired the Symbol Selection Committee, Alan was CEO of First National Stores, a New England supermarket chain. In the late 1970s, he engineered the sale of the company, leaving the food industry. This meant he was no longer eligible to serve as a Grocery Distributor Governor. The Board of Governors was so anxious to keep him on the Board, they reclassified the vacant position of Academic Governor. Terming it a "Public" Governor, the Board filled the position by electing Alan Haberman.

Many thought it was simply a ploy to keep him on the Board. Much to their surprise, Haberman became a spokesman for consumers. Points of view expounding the public's interests were heard for the first time in Board of Governors meetings. Still later, when the Board's structure was revised, and Haberman had an investment and managerial position with both a snack food manufacturer and a soft goods producer, he became a Manufacturer At Large Governor.

Thus, over time, Haberman has represented the three fundamental constituencies of the UCC — product manufacturers, product distributors, and the general public. In each post, he has focussed his energies on the interests of each constituency. Alan Haberman also has the longest continuous management service in connection with the U.P.C., an unbroken stretch from 1971 to the present.

Alan's contributions to the effort are beyond enumeration. One of his first is little noted, yet may have been one of the most significant. He helped pick the members of the Symbol Selection Committee. This remarkable group pushed technology leaders to develop and refine symbol proposals for a market they were not sure existed. Alan's leadership created an atmosphere where ideas sparked and true synergy existed.

There are a thousand anecdotes from Haberman's leadership of the Symbol Selection Committee. I offer two. Near the end of the Committee's work, when the intensity and tension were at their height, the committee held a three-day meeting in San Francisco. To relieve the tension, Alan arranged for a dinner in a private room above Jack's, a famous, old San Francisco restaurant. The meal was a great success, allowing the group to relax and develop closer personal ties. The bonding continued after dinner, when Alan led the committee to an adult movie theater, where "Deep Throat" was having its premiere engagement. There, at midnight, on the front row, talking back to the screen, was the grocery industry's Symbol Selection Committee.

As the Committee's work moved toward the decision point, there was concern that members might receive improper and ex parte contacts in attempts to influence their decision. For months, Alan promised he would prevent this. A Budweiser distributor in southern Florida had a yacht he would lend us. We would decide in complete privacy, on the warm and sunny Caribbean. In the event, wiser heads prevailed. Fearing a yacht would be perceived as a costly frivolity, we held the meeting in cold and rainy New York City.

At that meeting, Haberman took a pre-vote vote, not on symbol preference, but on how strongly the individual believed in his vote on the symbol. It was a tactic I had never seen, before or since. The result was a vote on a symbol with which the whole committee felt comfortable.

Alan also served as a member of the Ad Hoc Committee's Public Policy group. In that capacity, he entertained all of us the day he debated with noted consumer activist Carol Tucker Foreman. He was holding his own until he referred to Ms. Foreman and her supporters as "girls." This provoked a ferocious response. The debate quickly ended with the schism between industry and consumers widened.

As a long time member of the Board of Governors, Mr. Haberman is most remembered as one never afraid to express an opinion, even if no one else shared it. He insisted the Board remember its mission and recognize its limitations. At the same time, he remained current, always willing to let go of the old to embrace the new. The UCC has tapped him to serve as Chair of JTC 1 SC 31 on Automatic Data Capture, a committee to process international standards. Once again his skills of mediation and consensus creation will be tested.

It is impossible to sum up Alan Haberman in a word, a phrase, a sentence or even a paragraph. He is truly a renaissance man, melding business acumen, technical ability, and human understanding.

David B. Jenkins

FMI named David Jenkins, CEO of Shaw's Supermarkets, to the UCC Board in 1987. Four years later, he became Chair of the Board of Governors. David could be the model for the Boston Brahmin. Erect and stylish in his bow ties, he reflects his schooling at Wesleyan. As Chair, he also reflected New England frugality by eschewing posh resorts, instead holding Board meetings at the corporate headquarters in Dayton — in November.

David Jenkins made three major contributions to the UCC. The first concerned the management of the endowment fund. At virtually his first Board meeting, he inquired about the Council's investment policy. Although the endowment fund was growing two or three million dollars a year, there had been no change in the conservative investment policy. Excess Council funds were held in a Fidelity money market fund.

Jenkins was appalled. He believed the policy was so conservative as to be bad stewardship by the Board. Excess cash should be working much more aggressively. At his instigation, the chair created an investment advisory committee composed of the chief financial officers of companies represented on the Executive Committee. The result was a much more aggressive investment policy and the retention of a professional investment manager. Today, the endowment fund tops $100 million and continues to grow at a rate in the top percentiles of similar funds.

Jenkins' second major contribution was his broader application of UCC standards to the grocery industry. During his term on the Board of Governors, a British firm acquired Shaws. He retired as CEO, but he retained his positions with both the UCC and FMI. With his new free time, he began to focus on how to improve grocery industry productivity, in light of increased competition from alternative store formats, such as Price Clubs, and giant-sized Wal-Marts.

The introduction of U.P.C. scanning had meant a significant improvement in front-end productivity. Once this was achieved, however, the industry slept on its advantage, never exploring the other supply-chain management potentials inherent in UCC standards. The mass merchandisers were not so shy. Jenkins, as UCC Chair, was exposed to the broader possibilities. He took his considerable prestige, and even more considerable energy, to spurring the grocery industry. This led to the initiation of Efficient Consumer Response (ECR), the biggest industrywide project since the development of the U.P.C.

ECR had an especially salutary side effect upon the UCC. The grocery industry had come to take for granted the UCC's error-free administration of the U.P.C., virtually ignoring the broader aspects of the Code Council's work. ECR, and the UCC's role in it, finally established the UCC's credibility in its founding industry.

For years, as both the UCC and EAN expanded, the relationship between the two organizations intensified and increased in importance. The tension between the two also grew. During and after Jenkins' years as UCC Chair, he and Hal Juckett decided to make the system a truly global one. Under his leadership, bonds with the EAN leadership were forged. This formed the basis for the creation of a global policy committee and an announcement that U.P.C. scanners were also expected to read EAN symbols. The globalization is still in its infancy, but the future looks promising — a tribute to Jenkins' leadership.

Harold P. Juckett

When Dick Mindlin prepared to retire as the first staff head of the UCC, the Board decided his successor should be skilled in the development and implementation of education programs. The development of the U.P.C. was complete and the grocery industry was well on its way to full use. The Board considered education the Code Council's primary ongoing function.

The candidate presented by the search consultant had spent his career with Xerox's customer service department. For health reasons, Hal Juckett needed a less stressful environment. The UCC seemed a perfect fit. Juckett has had a strong career, but it has been anything but stress-free. This was obvious almost from the moment he was hired. His first year in Dayton overlapped with Dick Mindlin's last year. That year proved the wisdom of the Biblical adage that a man cannot serve two masters. It was a very long year for Hal Juckett, as Dick Mindlin saw almost every action as a threat or criticism of his leadership.

After Mindlin's retirement, Juckett began to develop his image of what the UCC should be. In his vision, UCC standards should be expanded beyond the grocery industry and across the ocean. But his Board was not prepared to expand. Juckett had to overcome the resistance of the founders. It was a real struggle, but the persistence paid off. He faced similar resistance as he fought to add staff to meet the growing demand for services. At first, he struggled simply to add bodies. Later, he insisted on bringing in ever-stronger professionals. The UCC is a strong organization today. Hal Juckett deserves much of the credit for broadening its vision and strengthening its competence.

Mindlin's retirement did not end Juckett's stress. As his vision of a stronger, broader UCC became clear, it disturbed some Board members who believed the UCC should remain confined to the grocery industry and only react to needs that the industry trade associations could not meet. Juckett's attempt actually to lead the UCC also posed a threat to Tom Wilson's de facto control of the UCC. For about a year, Juckett was saddled with an Operating Committee consisting of Wilson, Barry Franz, and me. While the committee did some good — it was responsible for instituting a formal budgeting process — it was in a position to second-guess the Executive Vice President.

Hal saw the Operating Committee (and Wilson) not only as a pain in the neck, but as a threat to his survival. Wilson is a consummate corporate politician, but Hal Juckett bested him. Byron Allumbaugh, as Chairman, deferred to the man on the scene. Hal worked the issue as if his life depended on it. Before long, the Operating Committee was disbanded, and Wilson was handed a gift and thanked for his years of service.

This is even more surprising because Hal Juckett is not a

prepossessing man. He does have a vision however. He is also probably the most altruistic corporate executive I have ever met. He genuinely believes the UCC supply-chain management standards are good for America and the world. This conviction gives him a great power.

It was Hal Juckett who recognized that the UCC's future lay in global supply-chain management. For many years, he cajoled an apathetic Board into slowly building its ties with the rest of the world. By the late 1990s, the rest of the organization had caught up with him.

When he joined the UCC, it had a staff of seven. Today, there are more than forty, and fifty is not far away. Hal's management style could best be described as "free form." Organization charts and channels of reporting were foreign to him. Every time you look around, however, the UCC has moved to the place Juckett wanted to go.

He was not a forceful man, but there was steel in his spine. If he perceived a threat to himself or his organization, he became a mother bear defending her cubs. No one who was responsible for bringing Harold Juckett to the UCC could have predicted the growth he engendered. In my view, even more important are the qualities of integrity and decency he brought to the Uniform Code Council.

Richard J. Mindlin

When I first met Dick Mindlin, he was in charge of the NCR team whose mission was to persuade the Symbol Selection Committee that selecting a U.P.C. symbol was premature. At the time, he was the prime NCR contact with the Symbol Committee. For two years, NCR worked cooperatively with the committee, but never wavered in its position that no symbol should be selected.

Once a symbol was a reality, however, NCR was the first to make scanners available commercially, and Dick Mindlin was chairing one of the subcommittees of the Symbol Technical Advisory Committee. Five years later, he would take early retirement from NCR and become the UCC's first paid staff member.

Dick Mindlin spent most of his career dealing with automatic identification standards. Before the U.P.C., he was involved with the development of the MICR magnetic-stripe standard used by the banking industry on checks. Today, well into his eighties, he still maintains a business providing film masters for U.P.C. symbols.

Although Mindlin is frailer now, he has changed very little over the past twenty-five years. The adjectives "crusty" and "feisty" were created to describe him. The intention when he opened the Dayton office was that he work himself out of a job. By the time he retired in 1984, however, no one expected that to occur, and he had built a staff of seven, all women. Never one to be concerned with feminism or political correctness, he always called the staff his "girls."

Mindlin's great contribution to the UCC was that he made an independent, free-standing organization a reality. He was given a limited mandate and made no attempt to broaden it. The marketplace for the Code Council, however, refused to shrink as the Board envisioned it would. Instead, the workload continued to expand. Dick handled the growth well. He left a healthy organization for his successor to build upon.

Lawrence Russell

The group that developed the Universal Product Code consisted of some very bright people. Larry Russell was probably the smartest. Trained as an engineer and a lawyer, in 1970 he was the project manager assigned by McKinsey and Company to the Ad Hoc Committee. He came into his own, however, with the Symbol Selection Committee.

There are several individuals who could lay claim to being

the father of the U.P.C. symbol. No one has a better claim to the honor than Larry Russell. It was Larry who led the committee's colloquies with the various interests contributing to the effort and who analyzed and synthesized their submissions. His presentations were models of clarity and organization. He succeeded in allowing the Committee to reach its own conclusions, but you never doubted what his opinion was.

The Symbol Selection Committee avoided accepting information from symbol proposers on a confidential basis. It believed it was vital to be able to thoroughly document to the public the basis for its decision. Nonetheless, there were occasions when receiving data in confidence was necessary. On those occasions, it was Larry who signed the agreement and received the information. He had the rare ability to receive confidential information, assimilate it, and use it without ever revealing the confidence. This ability greatly eased the work of the Committee.

While his principal on the project, Tom Wilson, had little small talk and constantly focussed on business, Larry had a wide range of interests, and was a lively conversationalist. Physically, he looked like an apple-cheeked choir boy. Whenever the Symbol Committee arrived in a new town, Larry would approach the bellman in our hotel and ask what was the second-best restaurant in town. He assumed the bellman was paid to recommend a restaurant as the best, but would be honest about the second-best.

By the time of the Bilgutay lawsuit, Larry was long gone from the UCC. However, the lawyers took his deposition and videotaped it. At the time, he was an executive with First Chicago bank. Years later, I had the opportunity to view his testimony. His ability to recall events more than a decade earlier was phenomenal. Even more astonishing was his demeanor. Interrogated intensively for more than four hours, he never lost his temper, never got excited, and was never confused by counsel.

Larry Russell was a key element in the selection of the U.P.C. code and symbol. He was also enormously popular with the industry volunteers, especially the members of the Symbol Selection Committee. Perhaps in part for this reason, his relationship with Tom Wilson rapidly deteriorated. By the mid 1990s, he had left the project, and shortly after that left McKinsey & Company.

Flushed with the success of the U.P.C. project, the grocery industry launched a study of computer-to-computer ordering (now known as EDI). Larry Russell headed the McKinsey team bidding on the project. McKinsey lost the contract, in part because its approach, a black box translating data in the middle of the transaction, lost to a proposal of standard formats and data elements.

Larry Russell had his moment of fame from 1970 to 1973. It was a magical time, and he made the most of it. His technical triumphs and his personal strengths combined to make an industry breakthrough possible.

John L. Strubbe

Jack Strubbe was a bear of a man who looked like an aging heavyweight. He was also one of the major driving forces behind the Ad Hoc Committee and the creation of the Uniform Grocery Product Council. As a Vice President of the Kroger Company, he was behind Kroger's exploration of scanning in the late 1960s. His chairman, Bob Aders, served as Chairman Pro Tem at the initial meeting of the Ad Hoc Committee.

Each member of the Ad Hoc was allowed to bring a technical expert with him. Jack Strubbe was Bob Aders' expert. He quickly became a power in the Committee's deliberations. Often, he would be the sole Kroger representative at meetings. Though Strubbe made many technical contributions, I remember him most for his contribution to the organization of the UCC. At the time (1971), the grocery industry and retailers were engaged in daily battles with consumer activist groups, who were at the zenith of their activity and influence. Strubbe often said he would make it impossible for consumer groups ever to take over control of the organization responsible for the administration of the U.P.C. The result was the convoluted corporate structure that has distinguished the UCC. As originally established, there was a twenty-one-member Board of Governors. Of these, eighteen were selected by trade associations, and the other three were selected by the Board.

For reasons I have never understood, the trade associations never tried to control the Board of Governors until it was too late to do so. When the approach was made, the Board respected its independence enough to resist. Yet, the trade associations have been instrumental in providing leadership for the organization.

At Kroger, Strubbe was in charge of the scanning test project with RCA, the precursor to the U.P.C. efforts. This made him an invaluable asset to the Ad Hoc Committee. He also had a passion for the project, which helped breathe life into it.

Jack Strubbe served as the second chairman of the Board of Governors during the start-up years, 1973–1975. His position and experience in the industry were important in giving credibility to the effort. His most significant contribution, however, was done quietly and in the background. He recognized that source-symbol marking of products was the key to the success of the U.P.C. and that product manufacturers had little incentive to source-symbol mark. If they were to be subject to fines or delisting for mistakes in putting symbols on products, few manufacturers would step up to the challenge.

As one of them, Jack Strubbe used his influence with food retailers to keep them from making unreasonable demands on manufacturers. For these early years, manufacturers were able to count on tolerance from their customers while symbol printing was becoming routine. Because he was successful, manufacturers were willing to experiment with symbol marking. Printers learned they could print symbols within tolerances. The freedom to make mistakes actually resulted in very few of them. Jack Strubbe made it practical for U.P.C. scanning to grow and flourish.

Robert B. Wegman

Bob Wegman's name is on an outstanding chain of supermarkets in upstate New York. He was also a leader within the trade associations of the supermarket industry. As such, he was tapped in 1971 to head the fund-raising effort, primarily among retailers, to provide the monies required by the symbol selection effort. Quietly, he went about his task. Miraculously, the money was raised, and at no point during the life of the Ad Hoc Committee were activities curtailed for lack of funds.

Wegman was given a seat on the Ad Hoc Committee. It was not a purely honorary post. Within a year of the announcement of the symbol, activist groups and legislators, both federal and state, were taking aim at the U.P.C. Bob Wegman became the Chair of the Ad Hoc's Public Policy Committee. This group was charged with developing and carrying out a strategy to counter the attacks. Wegman's patrician bearing and easy manner made him an effective leader of this committee. Again, however, he did his work without seeking publicity for himself.

Wegman was called to serve a third time. He was Chairman of the Board of Governors of the Code Council from 1979–1981. He left the Board at the end of his term. His company has served as a leader in pioneering applications of the U.P.C.

In my experience, some of the other men chronicled in this Appendix were more involved (and more passionate) with the U.P.C. than Bob Wegman. Without Wegman's involvement, however, the project would have died for lack of funds. Later, he was instrumental in protecting the system against the assaults of legislators. This qualifies him for inclusion with the giants.

Thomas W. Wilson, Jr.

Within the grocery industry, the creation of the U.P.C. was inextricably — and appropriately — connected with Tom Wilson. A partner in the consulting firm of McKinsey and Co., he specialized in the grocery industry, both manufacturers and distributors. In the late 1960s, McKinsey was probably the dominant consultant to the industry.

Tom Wilson managed a project for the National Association of Food Chains looking at the feasibility of automating the supermarket checkout. This gave him and McKinsey a leg up when the Ad Hoc Committee issued a request for proposal in 1970. Not surprisingly, the Committee awarded McKinsey the project.

Tom also used his work with the Ad Hoc Committee as a lever to obtain other assignments. McKinsey worked with European grocers to develop the EAN code and symbol. He also was the consultant to the "Crafted with Pride in America" Committee, which was formed to improve distribution efficiencies in the US textile industry. US textiles were reeling from the competition of foreign goods. The VICS EDI standards were the result.

In both instances, Tom was careful to assure that EAN and VICS were compatible with UCC standards. He was instrumental in leading the VICS group to the UCC to administer their standards. The association with the UCC, in turn, caused the industry to turn to the U.P.C. when it became clear the industry's OCR-A standard would not work.

Wilson did not foresee the globalization of the U.P.C. nor the growing interrelationship with EAN. Although EAN and U.P.C. are compatible, he believed it was essentially irrelevant. In his view, the two codes were grocery codes, and there was very little European product sold in US stores (and vice versa). What foreign product was marketed in the United States would have to be relabeled to comply with US laws. At that time, a U.P.C. number and symbol would be substituted for the EAN number.

Tom also strongly believed the proper role of the UCC was restrictive and reactive. This contributed to his misperception of the interdependence of the U.P.C. and EAN. For him, nongrocery uses of the U.P.C. were acceptable only if the use did not adversely impact on the grocery industry use, and if no Council resources were diverted from its primary mission. The fact that the UCC moved to a broader vision of its mission, and recognized the need to be proactive, contributed to the waning of Wilson's influence in the late 1980s.

By that time, the Board of Governors could not understand why a consultant was still on the scene, nearly twenty years after the project began. This was foreign to their experience of hiring a consultant for a specific project, who comes in, does the work, and leaves. Tom Wilson stayed with the U.P.C. in part because it gave him access and exposure to potential clients. More significantly, Tom was reluctant to leave because he recognized the significance of what he had helped create. All of us knew the U.P.C. was something special. None of us wanted to give it up.

The precipitating event leading to Wilson's departure from the Code Council arose out of his peculiar aversion to charging the UCC for his services. The initial McKinsey work, in 1970–1973, was handled like most consultant engagements. From that point on, however, Wilson continued to provide services to the Code council, but delayed billing for months. When the Treasurer finally forced a bill out of him, the amount was always exceedingly modest.

Perhaps Tom simply had an aversion to the crassness of billing. More likely, he realized the Code Council could not afford his normal rates. He would rather reduce his compensation than lose his involvement. From the Council's standpoint, it was receiving the talents of one of the industry's brightest consultants at bargain basement prices. There was at least a minor downside, however. With those rates came only Wilson's services; they did not include the full resources of McKinsey & Co.

For years, various Board Chairmen and Treasurers put up with Wilson's vagaries. When Dick Zimmerman of Hershey Foods became Chairman in 1989, the UCC had a Chair with no history with Wilson or McKinsey. Dick could understand neither a consultant who was still on the job twenty years later nor one who would only bill when literally forced.

It was Tom Wilson who forced a budgeting and accounting process upon the UCC. That process did him in. Budgeting was extremely difficult when Wilson had not billed for over a year. This became his Achilles heel. While the real issue was a difference of vision between Tom and Hal Juckett, the justification for ending the relationship was budgeting and financial.

A twenty-year relationship, involving a personality as strong as Tom's, is bound to have its bumpy moments. Even those who resented Wilson's leadership on the UCC must admit that, for a very long time, he kept the organization together and obtained the necessary support from industry leaders to keep the project going during the years it took to reach a critical mass of scanning stores. If ever there was a giant of this revolution, it was Tom Wilson.

Richard A. Zimmerman

Dick Zimmerman, CEO of Hershey Foods, served as UCC Chairman after Byron Allumbaugh, from 1989–1991. He is included here for two reasons, one accidental, one purposeful. During his term, an agreement on principles of cooperation was reached between UCC and EAN. Zimmerman's signature is on the document proudly displayed at the Dayton office. Although Hal Juckett was primarily responsible for bringing this about, Zimmerman gave his full support. The signing of this agreement marked a true transformation in the UCC-EAN relationship. Zimmerman was also the one who ended the relationship with Tom Wilson.

His major substantive contribution to the UCC was the introduction of strategic planning. This truly marked the end of the UCC as a project of the grocery industry associations and its emergence as an independent organization. Not only did the UCC as an organization begin to plan, its staff was required to establish personal objectives and report on their progress toward their objectives. Dick Zimmerman personally received Hal Juckett's monthly report.

Zimmerman donated the services of John Rawley, a professional planner for Hershey, to the UCC. In January 1990, a retreat open to all members of the Board of Governors was held in Dallas. Out of this emerged a revised mission statement reflecting a more open and proactive stance for the UCC. It was accompanied by six strategic objectives with action steps for each.

Subsequent Chairs have followed Zimmerman's lead. The UCC is firmly committed to the concept of planning. The model established by Zimmerman and Rawley has remained the basis for the UCC strategic plan. This is Dick Zimmerman's legacy.

Appendix B

The Board of Governors of Uniform Code Council, Inc. 1972 to 1997

Byron Allumbaugh, Chairman 1987–1989
Chairman and CEO, Ralph's Grocery Company
Food Marketing Institute
1985–1991

David Anderson
Executive Vice President, R. J. Reynolds
Grocery Manufacturers of America
1990–1992

Warren Bailey
Executive Vice President/COO, Parisian
General Merchandise Distributor
1994–1996

Steve Barlow
Barlow Foods
National Association of Retail Grocers of the United States
1974–1975

Francis X. Beck, Jr.
Manager of Engineering Development, Sperry-Univac
Equipment Governor
1980–1981

Paul Benchener
Director Retail Electronic Services, Levi Strauss & Co.
Manufacturer at Large Governor
1990–

F. T. Biermeier
Red Owl Stores, Inc. (1972)
Vice President, Information Services, Supermarkets General Corporation
(1973)
National Association of Food Chains
1972–1976

* Denotes Chairman of the Board of Uniform Code Council, Inc.

269

Marsh H. Blackburn
Chairman & CEO, Sales Force Co., Inc.
National Food Brokers Association
1983–1990

John Bloom
Vice President, NAWGA, National American Wholesale
Grocers Association
1987–1988

Ward C. Bourn
Vice President/Controller, Retail Foods Group, Kraft, Inc.
Grocery Manufacturers of America
1976–1982

Frank Bracken
President, Haggar Clothing Co.
General Merchandise Manufacturer
1996–

William Brodbeck
Dick's Supermarkets
National Association of Retail Grocers in the United States
1977–1986

Bill Brous
Director of Retail Electronics Services, Fleming Companies, Inc.
National American Wholesale Grocers Association
1975–1987

John J. Cardwell
Consolidated Foods
Grocery Manufacturers of America
1981–1982

David M. Carlson
Vice President, Electronic Merchandising Systems, KMart Corporation
Distributor-at-Large Governor
1985–1988; 1993–1995

Ralph Chaney
Director, Data Processing Dept., Giant Foods, Inc.
Distributor-at-Large Governor
1983–1987

David Chernow
Senior Executive Vice President, Schenley Industries, Inc.
Manufacturer-at-Large Governor
1976–1977

Robert L. Comer
Director, Management Information Services, Colgate-Palmolive Co.
Grocery Manufacturers of America
1978–1982

William C. Confer
Vice President, Industry and Customer Relations, Roundy's
National Grocer's Association
1988–1994

Bentley J. Cooper
Chairman, Cooper Electric Supply Company
Industrial-Product Governor
1983–1989

John L. Dean
Vice President, Management Information Services, The Great Atlantic &
Pacific Tea Company
Food Marketing Institute
1979–1980

Ralph W. Drayer
Vice President, Product Supply, Customer Business Development,
The Procter & Gamble Company
Grocery Manufacturers of America
1994–

Robert C. Drury
Vice President, Management Information Services, Pet Incorporated
Grocery Manufacturers of America
1992–1995

Thomas Duesler
Vice President, Sales, General Foods Corp.
Manufacturer-at-Large Governor
1983–1986

Donald F. Dufek
KMA Vice President, Kroger Food Stores
Food Marketing Institute
1983–1988

Marvin Eberts
Financial Vice President and Treasurer, Stokely-Van Camp, Inc.
Grocery Manufacturers of America
1972–1976

George Edwards
President, Family Circle Sales Division
Manufacturer-at-Large Governor
1980–1981

David V. Evans
Vice President/Director of Information Systems, J. C. Penney Co.
General Merchandise Distributor
1994–

Charles Feld
Vice President, Information Services, Frito Lay Inc.
Grocery Manufacturers of America
1990–1991

Byron Felter
Vice President, US Grocery Products Sales, The Quaker Oats Company
Manufacturer-at-Large Governor
1989–1990
Public Governor
1990–1993

S. W. Fraser
Executive Vice President, Hudson's Bay Company
General Merchandise Distributor
1993–

Barry E. Franz
Manager, Management Systems, Operations Support Staff,
Procter & Gamble Company
Grocery Manufacturers of America
1975–1989
Treasurer
1989–1995

Thomas Gallagher
Vice President, Administration, Calkins & Company
Senior Vice President Administration, Sales Force Companies, Inc.
National Food Brokers Association
1988–1989
1991–

Susan Gerhardt
Director of Packaging Services, House of Seagram
Manufacturer-at-Large Governor
1982–1996

*R. Burt Gookin, Chairman 1975–1979
Vice Chairman, H. J. Heinz Company
Grocery Manufacturers of America
1975–1980
Honorary Governor
1980–

Thomas Gorey
Vice President, Logistics Operation Integration, Sears Roebuck & Co.
General Merchandise Distributor
1996–

Tommy D. Greer
President, Texize Chemicals Company
Grocery Manufacturers of America
1974–1975

Alan L. Haberman
President & CEO, First National Stores, Inc.
National Association of Food Chains
1973–1981
Public Governor
1981–1990
Manufacturer-at-Large Governor
1990–

Robert J. Herbold
Vice President, Information Systems, The Procter & Gamble Company
Grocery Manufacturers of America
1989–1990

William J. Hollis
Vice President, Logistics Operations & American Consumer Products,
American Can Company
Grocery Manufacturers of America
1973–1975

Earl D. Holton
President, Meijer, Inc.
Food Marketing Institute
1995–

David B. Jenkins, Chairman 1991–1993
President, Shaw's Supermarkets, Inc.
Food Marketing Institute
1987–1996

Les Jenkins
Special Projects Director, Associated Grocers, Inc.
Food Marketing Institute
1980–1983

Darwin A. John
Staff Vice President, Corporate Planning & Information Services,
Scott Paper Co.
Grocery Manufacturers of America
1982–1989

F. Ross Johnson
Chairman, Standard Brands, Inc.
Grocery Manufacturers of America
1980–1983

E. Richard Jones
Executive Vice President, Safeway Stores, Inc.
Food Marketing Institute
1983–1993

Arthur D. Juceam
Vice President, Manufacturing and Distribution,
Lehn & Fink Products Company
Grocery Manufacturers of America
1973–1975

C. Richard Keener
Vice President, Information Services, United Brands Company
Chiquita Brands International
Grocery Manufacturers of America
1983–1994

Robert Koenig
Vice President, Method & Research, Super Valu Stores, Inc.
National American Wholesale Grocers Association
1972–1975

James Kufeldt
President, Winn-Dixie
Food Marketing Institute
1993–

John Landeck
Gromer Supermarkets
National Grocer's Association
1986–1989

Demetrios D. Lappas
Vice President & CIO, Warner Lambert Company
Grocery Manufacturers of America
1994–

William Larsen
Johnson & Johnson
Grocery Manufacturers of America
1993–

Robert F. Lee
Manager of Administration, Johnson & Johnson
Grocery Manufacturers of America
1972–1975

James LeGere
Vice President, Information Systems, The Quaker Oats Co.
Grocery Manufacturers of America
1996–

Thomas LeMay
Continental Can Co.
Printing/Converting
1982–1983

Phillip Lippincott
Vice President/Group Executive, Packaged Foods, Scott Paper Co.
Grocery Manufacturers of America
1978–1983

Donald P. Lloyd
President, Merchants, Inc., Associated Food Stores
Cooperative Food Distributors of America
1973–1978

John B. McClay
President, V. L. McClay & Son, Inc.
National Food Brokers Association
1985–1988

Richard E. McCready
President & CEO, RMI & Associates, Inc.
National Food Brokers Association
1983–1985

Spencer McIlmurray
Vice President, Information Systems Strategy, Kraft, Inc.
Grocery Manufacturers of America
1988–1989

*R. Gordon McGovern, Chairman 1985–1987
President and CEO, Campbell Soup Company
Grocery Manufacturers of America
1983–1989

Wayne McTeer
Senior Vice President-Distribution, Scrivner, Inc.
National American Wholesale Grocers Association
1988–1994

Allen Messerli
Manager, Distribution Planning and Systems, 3M Company
Industrial-Product Governor
1983–

Richard J. Mindlin
Vice President, NCR Equipment Co.
Governor
1973–1977

Walter Mosher
President, Precision Dynamics Corp.
Industrial-Products Governor
1994–

Everett Muterspaugh
Pay Less Supermarkets
National Grocers Association
1990–1992

Garrett R. Nelson
Executive Vice President-Retail Support Services,
The VONS Companies, Inc.
Food Marketing Institute
1989–1995

Thomas P. Nelson
Vice President, General Mills, Inc.
Grocery Manufacturers of America
1972–1974

David R. Nogle
Senior Vice President, Quaker Oats Company
Manufacturer-at-Large Governor
1986–1989

William E. Oddy
Group Vice President of Administration, Jewel Food Stores
Supermarket Institute
1973–1980

James Paulus
President and COO, Crown/BBK, Inc.
National Food Brokers Association
1989–1994

James Porter
Chase Bag
Printing/Converting
1973–1976

*Robert E. Rich, Jr., Chairman 1993–1995
President, Rich Products Corporation
Grocery Manufacturers of America
1989–

Thomas Rittenhouse
Vice President & Controller, Strawbridge & Clothier
General Merchandise Distributor
1993–1997

Ron Rivers
Director of Data Processing, Affiliated Foods
National Grocery Association
1985–1988

Ray Rose
President, King Soopers, Inc.
Supermarket Institute
1975–1976

Robert M. Schaeberle, Chairman 1981–1983
Chairman, Nabisco, Inc.
Grocery Manufacturers of America
1976–1988

Craig D. Schnuck, Chairman 1995–
Chairman and CEO, Schnuck Markets, Inc.
Food Marketing Institute
1991–

Robert Schwartz
Vice President—Administration and Secretary, Roundy's Inc.
Cooperative Food Distributors of America
1979–1980

Peter S. Sealey
Senior Vice President & Director, Global Marketing,
The Coca-Cola Company
Grocery Manufacturers of America
1992–1993

Everett Smith, Jr.
Reynolds Metals
Printing/Converting
1976–1982

H. S. Smith
Senior Vice President, Information Services, Supervalu, Inc.
National American Wholesale Grocers Association
1995–

Timothy P. Smucker
Chairman, J. M. Smucker Co.
Grocery Manufacturers of America
1995–

Vivian M. Stephenson
Senior Vice President & CIO, Dayton Hudson Co.
General Merchandise Distributor
1995–1996

Michael Stolarz
Vice President, Twin County Grocers Inc.
National American Wholesale Grocers Association
1995–1996

*Robert A. Stringer, Chairman 1972–1973
Vice President, General Foods Corp.
Grocery Manufacturers of America
1972–1978

*John L. Strubbe, Chairman 1973–1975
Vice President, Kroger Company
Supermarket Institute
1972–1975.

Wilbur Stump
Stump's Enterprises, Inc.
National Association of Retail Grocers of the United States
1972–1974

Donald K. Stunoff
Vice President, The Quaker Oats Co.
Grocery Manufacturers of America
1983–1985

William A. Sumner
Vice President, Bullock's
Distributor-at-Large Governor
1986–1992

Vincent H. Swoyer
Vice President, Corporate Systems, Sara Lee Corporation
Grocery Manufacturers of America
1989–1994

William Taubert
Vice President, Logistics, Hunt-Wesson Foods
Grocery Manufacturers of America
1975–1989

Steven Teachout
President, Canton N.A.
General Merchandise Manufacturer
1996–

Stephen Tecot
Chairman, Tecot Electric Supply Company
Industrial Governor
1989–

Joseph Thomas
Executive Vice President and CAO, KMart Corp.
Distributor-at-Large Governor
1988–1993

James C. Tuttle
Antitrust & International Counsel, KMart Corp.
Distributor-at-Large Governor
1983–1985

Harry Wade
Director of Works Methods, Winn-Dixie Stores, Inc.
Food Marketing Institute
1980–1985

*Robert B. Wegman, Chairman 1979–1981
Chairman of the Board, Wegman's Food Markets, Inc.
Food Marketing Institute
1977–1981

Richard Weis
Vice President, Management Information Systems, Richfood, Inc.
Cooperative Food Distributors of America
1980–1985

Bernard Weisberg
President, Chatham Supermarkets, Inc.
Supermarket Institute
1976–1978

Phil Woodman
President, Woodman's Food Markets, Inc.
National Grocer's Association
1992–

*Michael Wright, Chairman 1983–1985
President and COO, SuperValu Stores, Inc.
Food Marketing Institute
1981–1987

*Richard A. Zimmerman, Chairman 1989–1991
Chairman and CEO, Hershey Foods Corporation
Grocery Manufacturers of America
1985–1993

Chief Staff

Harold P. Juckett
Executive Vice President and CAO
1985–1994
President
1994–1996

Richard J. Mindlin
Executive Vice President & CAO
1978–1984

Thomas S. Rittenhouse
President & CEO
1997–

Appendix C
The U.P.C. Symbol[1]

The U.P.C. code numbering system consists of 12 numeric characters. The symbol also provides a 13-character format.

The standard symbol (a machine-readable version of the U.P.C. and other compatible codes) is in the form of a series of parallel light and dark bars of different widths and OCR-B numeric font equivalent, which hereinafter will be referred to as a "bar code symbol." (Not to be confused with the U.P.C. code, which is the numbering system that is represented by the symbol.) The basic characteristics of the symbol are as follows (see Figures 1 and 2):

- Series of light and dark parallel bars (30 dark and 29 light for any 12-character code) with a light margin on each side.
- Overall shape is rectangular.
- Each character or digit of a code is represented by 2 dark bars and 2 light spaces.
- Each character is made up of 7 data elements; a data element hereinafter will be called a "module."
- A module might be dark or light.
- A bar may be made up of 1, 2, 3 or 4 dark modules, as shown in Figure 2.

[1] U.P.C. Symbol Specification Manual, Copyright 1986, Uniform Code Council Inc., reprinted by permission.

Figure 1: U.P.C. Standard Symbol

Left 6 Characters of Code

Right 6 Characters of Code

Left-Hand
Guard Bars Pattern (101)

Tall Center
Bar
Pattern
(01010)

Modulo
Check
Character

Right-Hand
Guard Bar Pattern (101)

Number System
Character

Left Light Margin
Minimum 9 Modules Wide

Right Light Margin
Minimum 9 Modules Wide

Number System
Character

0

1 2 3 4 5 6 7 8 9 0

5

Modulo
Check
Character

Manufacturer
ID Number

Item
Number

Characters Per
OCR-B Font

(NOT TO SCALE)

Figure 2: Character Structure

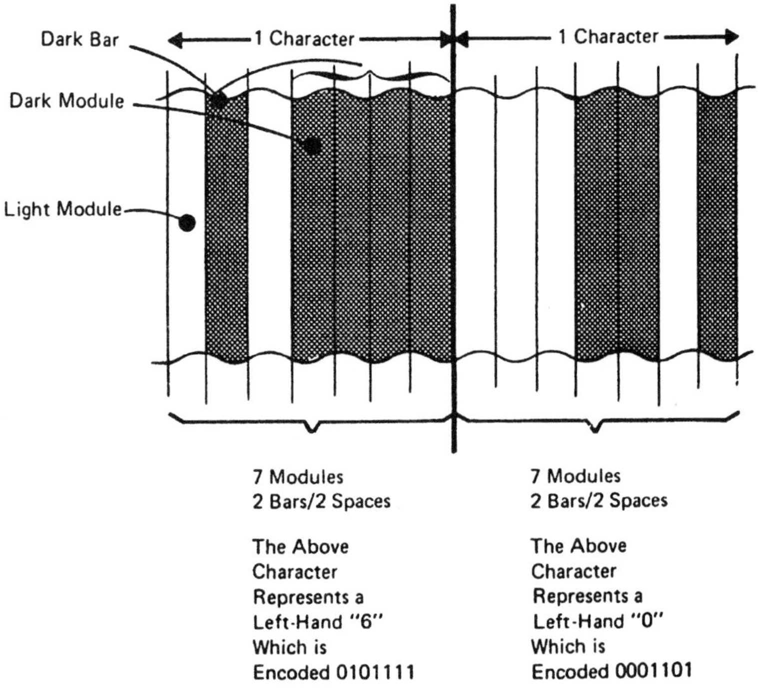

Dark Bar

Dark Module

Light Module

1 Character

1 Character

7 Modules
2 Bars/2 Spaces

The Above
Character
Represents a
Left-Hand "6"
Which is
Encoded 0101111

7 Modules
2 Bars/2 Spaces

The Above
Character
Represents a
Left-Hand "0"
Which is
Encoded 0001101

- Each character is independent.
- The symbol size is infinitely variable, to accommodate to the ranges in quality achievable by the various printing processes. That is, it can be uniformly magnified or reduced from the nominal size (defined later in this document) without significantly affecting the degree to which it can be scanned.
- The symbol is "wandable," which means a simple handheld device can be used to scan or read the symbol.
- Fixed-position scanners can be built to scan this symbol in an omnidirectional manner; that is, automatically read by a scanner when the symbol is drawn past the scanner in any orientation.
- The symbol prevents tampering. Unauthorized addition of lines is readily detectable by scanning devices. In the same way, poor printing will not result in scanning devices reading a wrong number. This is facilitated since the symbol has multiple error-detecting features which allow scanner designers to build equipment to automatically detect and reject a very poorly printed symbol or one that has been tampered with.
- The symbol also incorporates and presents the code number in a human-readable form. The symbol is designed to use methods consistent with printing practices in use throughout the converting industry(s).

How to Translate a Number
to its Equivalent Symbol Encodation

The symbol comprises a machine-readable bar code and the human-readable interpretation of that bar code. In addition to the information characters, the symbol includes other characters to identify the number system.

Several versions of the symbol are available. This section will describe the intended uses of, and differences between, these variations, as well as the organization and encoding of the machine-readable bar codes involved.

The two versions of the U.P.C. symbol relate to the following uses:

Version	Intended Use
A	*Regular version,* used to encode a 12 digit number, the first (high order) digit being the number system character, the next ten being information characters, and the last (low order) digit being the modulo check character.
E	*The zero-suppression version* of the symbol is included to facilitate source symbol-marking on packages that would otherwise be too small to include a symbol. This is achieved by encoding the symbol in a special way that leaves out some zeros that can occur in the U.P.C. code. For example, code 12300-00045 would be encoded in a symbol as 123453, effectively eliminating half of the area that would otherwise be required for the symbol. **NOTE:** Only number system character 0 symbols can be zero suppressed.

The format for the two versions varies as follows:

Version	Title	Format(s)
A	Regular	SXXXXX XXXXXC
E	Zero Suppression	XXXXXX[1]
	X = information character	
	S = number system character	
	C = modulo check character	

[1] Although explicit in the human readable form, the number system character is implicit in the bar code representation. Similarly, the modulo check character is implicitly encoded.

The number system character identifies 10 concurrent number sets which have been provided in the symbol. This approach is used to combine the various compatible codes with the U.P.C. code. The assignment of the number system characters is as follows:

Number System Character	Specified Use
0	Regular U.P.C. codes (Version A and E).
2	Random-weight items, such as meat and produce, symbol-marked at store level (Version A).
3	National Drug Code and National Health Related Items Code in current 10-digit code length (Version A). Note that the symbol is not affected by the various internal structures possible with the NDC or HRI codes.
4	For use without code format restriction and with check digit protection for in-store marking of non-food items (Version A).
5	For use on coupons (Version A).
6, 7	Regular U.P.C. codes (Version A).
1, 8, 9	Reserved for uses unidentified at this time.

The human-readable character identifying the encoded number system will be shown in the left-hand margin of the symbol as per Figure 1.

Regular Symbol (Version A)

The regular symbol normally contains dark bars and light spaces built up with nominal 0.0130-inch modules for the nominal-size symbol (Four characters involve "undersize" or "oversize" bars and spaces.) There are 113 modules in the regular symbol including 9 in the left margin and 9 in the right margin as shown in Figure 1.

When the modules are of nominal size, the regular symbol (including human-readable characters) will have an area of 1.4984 square inches including the light margins (1.469 × 1.020). The total symbol, however, may be larger or smaller than nominal, depending on the print quality of the printing process involved.

The determination of which modules are light and which are dark is given below. Starting at the left of the regular symbol following the light margin, it is encoded first with "guard bars," described below, followed by a number system character, followed by five U.P.C. characters on the left side of the center bars, and then with the remaining five U.P.C. characters on the right side of the center bars followed by a modulo-10 check character. Finally, the same guard bars are used at the right side, followed by the light margin. Individual bar code characters are easily identified. Note that each character on the left side of the center bars begins with a light space and ends with a dark bar. Correspondingly, characters on the right side of the center bars begin with a dark bar and end with a light space.

Dark modules represent 1's while light modules represent 0's. The number of dark modules per character on the left side is always 3 or 5 and the number is always 2 or 4 for right-hand characters. Encoding is identical for all characters on a given side of the symbol, whether the character is part of the U.P.C. number or is the number system Character or the modulo check character.

The first two bars at the left of the symbol and last two bars at the right of the symbol comprise the left and right guard bar positions, encoded 101.

The bars in the center comprise the fixed center bar pattern, encoded 01010.

Encodation for U.P.C. Characters, Number System Character and Modulo Check Character

The encodation for the left and right halves of the regular symbol, including U.P.C. characters, number system character and modulo check character, is given in the following chart, which is applicable to Version A. Note that the left-hand characters always use an odd number (3 or 5) of modules to make up the dark bars, whereas the right-hand characters always use an even number (2 or 4). This provides an "odd" and "even" parity encodation for each character and is important in creating, scanning and, decoding a symbol.

Decimal Value	Left Characters	Right Characters
	(Odd Parity—O)	(Even Parity—E)
0	0001101	1110010
1	0011001	1100110
2	0010011	1101100
3	0111101	1000010
4	0100011	1011100
5	0110001	1001110
6	0101111	1010000
7	0111011	1000100
8	0110111	1001000
9	0001011	1110100

Check Character Calculation

Digit positions are numbered from right to left in this algorithm so that the check digit position counts as position 1 and the number system character counts as position 12. For example, the U.P.C. number 012345-011238 would break out as:

Position	12	11	10	9	8	7	6	5	4	3	2	1
U.P.C. Number	0	1	2	3	4	5	0	1	1	2	3	?

Follow these steps to calculate the check character:

Step 1: Starting from position 2 of the number, add up the values in even numbered positions.
For the example:
$$3 + 1 + 0 + 4 + 2 + 0 = 10$$

Step 2: Multiply the result of step 1 by 3.
For the example:
$$10 \times 3 = 30$$

Step 3: Starting from position 3 of the number, add up the values of the digits in odd-numbered positions.
For the example:
$$2 + 1 + 5 + 3 + 1 = 12$$

Step 4: Add up the results of steps 2 and 3.
For the example:
$$30 + 12 = 42$$

Step 5: The check character is the smallest number that when added to the result obtained through step 4 gives a number that is a multiple of 10.
For the example:
$$42 + X = 50 \text{ (multiple of 10)}$$
$$X = 8$$

"8" is the number that when added to 42 results in a multiple of 10. Therefore, the check character is 8.

The human readable character identifying the encoded check character will be shown in the right-hand margin of the symbol as per Figure 1.

Note: The advantage of this method is that it can also be used to calculate check digits for EAN numbers.

Index

A&P, 41
academic governor, 124
accountants, 152, 239
A. C. Nielsen Co., 189–90
Adamy, Clarence "Clancy," xiii–
  xv, 42, 50, 55
Aders, Bob, 41, 43, 48, 262
Ad Hoc Committee
  approval of UGPIC, 47–48
  approval of U.P.C. symbol, 91–
    93
  assignment, 42–43
  chairmen, 40, 43
  choice of McKinsey as
    consultant, 44–47
  Code Management
    Subcommittee, 94–95, 96–97,
    118
  communication with FTC, 52–
    53, 54–55
  concerns about health risks of
    lasers, 21
  consumer concerns and, 50–51,
    125–26, 127
  contacts with other industries,
    83, 102–3
  coupon codes not addressed by,
    185
  efforts to expand acceptance of
    U.P.C., 97–98

expectations of, 48
Finance Committee, 119
formation, xiv–xv, 39–40
funding, 39–40, 54, 59–60, 119
guidance to Symbol
  Standardization Committee,
  58–59
importance of work, 46
meetings, 42–44, 46–47
members, 3–5, 40–42, 59, 102
Public Policy Committee, 26,
  126, 127, 128–29, 130, 255,
  264
recommendations for UCC
  dues, 119
reluctance to involve
  government, 51–53
responsibility for adoption of
  U.P.C., 54
subcommittees, 53
technical experts, 40–41, 47
UCC board of governors
  formed, 97
Administrative Systems Committee
  (GMA), xi–xii, 101, 105–6,
  163
Ahold A. V., 109, 195
AI. *See* Application Identifiers
AIM. *See* Automatic Identification
  Manufacturers

alcoholic beverages industry
  membership in UCC, 104
  proposed standard product
    code, 83, 102, 103
  representation on UCC board,
    111
  state liquor stores, 115, 151
  use of U.P.C., 115, 151
  wine, 115
Allais, David, 146
Allen, John, 26
Allumbaugh, Byron, 145, 224,
  226, 227, 229, 234, 247–48,
  258
American Meat Institute, 50
American National Standards
    Institute (ANSI)
  Board of Standards Review
    (BSR), 205
  Information Systems Standards
    Board (ISSB), 205–6, 208–9
  printed symbol quality
    standards, 231
  relationship with Ad Hoc
    Committee, 60
  relationship with UCC, 203–8
  standards process, 60–61
  X12, 168–69, 170, 171–72, 204
Andersen Consulting, 178–79, 240
Anker, 64
ANSI. See American National
    Standards Institute
antitrust laws, 51–53
apparel manufacturers, 16, 32–33
  See also textile industry
Application Identifiers (AI), 204,
  207, 234
Applied Image, Inc., 231
Arthur Andersen & Co., 43, 50,
  119–20, 121
Arthur D. Little, Inc., 164–65
associations,
  sponsoring, 228–29
  See also trade associations; and
    specific associations
auditors, outside, 152, 235, 239
Automatic Identification
    Manufacturers (AIM), 145, 209
automation of checkout counter:
  early demonstrations, 39, 108
  ergonomic issues, 236
  labor issues, 25–26
  research on, xii–xiii
  union fears of job losses, 124
  See also scanners

bar codes
  Code 128, 146, 229, 233–34
  development of, 89n
  uses, 9–10
  See also scanners; UCC–EAN
    Code 128; U.P.C. symbol
Battelle Institute, 72–73, 89, 106
Beinhorn, Leo, 132, 138, 149
Biermeier, Fritz, 58, 81, 104, 106
Bilgutay, Ilhan, 216–18
Bison, Henry, 55
Blackburn, Marsh, 158, 166, 167
Board of Governors (UCC)
  academic governor, 124
  committees, 145–46, 226–27
  consumer concerns and, 130
  contacts with other industries,
    116–17, 169–70, 177
  contract with DNB/DCI, 99–
    100, 131–32, 133, 136
  coupon issue, 185, 187, 190–91
  decisions on membership rules,
    100–101, 115–16
  decisions on U.P.C.
    administrative issues, 113–15
  decision to bring U.P.C.
    administration in-house, 112–
    13, 137–38, 148–49
  Executive Committee, 107, 109,
    232

expense reimbursements, 227–28, 248
Financial Advisory Committee, 225
focus on U.S. grocery industry, 176–77, 195
formation, 96–97
industrial governors, 175–78, 225
investment policies, 120, 152, 225–26, 256
lack of consumer representation, 125, 127, 130, 263
long-range planning, 177, 246, 268
McKinsey as executive secretary, 106–7
meetings, 111–12
members, 104–5, 107–8, 110–11, 150, 156, 167–68, 175–78, 235, 243
members listed, 269–79
objectives, 104
officer progression, 238–39
Operating Committee, 162, 224–25, 258
plan for symbol implementation, 101
public governors, 124–25, 128, 150, 228, 253
relations with ANSI, 168
relations with FTC, 102
terms of chairmen, 109, 243
trade association representation, 97, 104, 110–11, 166, 263
views on shipping container symbols, 134–35, 153, 229
Board of Standards Review (BSR; ANSI), 205
Boodman, David, 165
books, U.P.C. symbols on, 237

Booz Allen and Hamilton, 43
Brady, Tom, 233, 236, 245
Bristol Myers, 41, 102
Brous, Bill, 112
BSR. *See* Board of Standards Review
Butler, Fred, 41, 102
buyers, 10, 12–13
buying groups, 113

Campbell Soup, 225
Canada, Grocery Products Manufacturers of, 108
Carlson, David, 162
cash registers
electronic, 70, 73, 84
NCR, 69–70
tapes, 115, 123, 128
CFDA. *See* Cooperative Food Distributors of America
Charecogn, 67, 74, 76–77
check characters, 49, 288–89
checkout process
automation of, xii–xiii, 25–26, 39, 124, 236
impact of scanning, 108
Chernow, David, 111
Chicago, Department of Consumer Services, 130
Code 39, 146, 180, 204
Code 128, 146, 229, 233–34
See also UCC-EAN Code 128
Code Management Committee
decision on board structure, 96–97
decision to control manufacturer numbers only, 94–95
discussions of funding issue, 118
formation, 53
members, 53, 94
selection of service bureau, 95–96, 99

codes, product. *See* standard product codes; U.P.C.
Collin, Jean, 201, 234
Collins, Tom, 152, 235
commissaries, 179–80
Commission on Productivity, 102
complementary systems, 32–33
computers, 22, 242
  electronic cash registers, 70, 73, 84
  See also EDI (electronic data interchange)
consultants. *See* McKinsey & Co.
Consumer Federation of America, 128
consumer groups
  activism, 51
  distrust of industry, 128
  lack of representation on Ad Hoc Committee, 50–51
  lack of representation on UCC board, 125, 127, 130, 263
  opposition to item price removal, 26, 51, 68, 125–26, 128–29
  strength of, 96
  ties to labor unions, 124, 128
consumers:
  educating about scanning, 126
  predicted benefits of U.P.C., 115, 123–24, 130
  use of enhanced register tapes, 115, 123
converting industry, 141
Cooper, Ben, 175–76, 225
Cooperative Food Distributors of America (CFDA), xiii, 55, 97
cooperatives, 41
cost-benefit. *See* savings
Council for Periodical Distributors (CPDA), 114, 142, 156
country codes (EAN), 196–97, 199–200

coupons
  committee on, 185–89, 190, 214
  complexity of coding needed, 186, 188, 191
  development of add-on symbol for scanning, 146–47, 190–93
  doubling, 191
  Guideline 22, 186–88
  implementation of Guideline 22, 188–90, 191, 212, 215
  patent dispute, 211–15
  pressure to develop scanning mechanism, 114, 184–85
  tests of scanning, 213
CPDA. *See* Council for Periodical Distributors
Cracker Jack, 141
Crouse, Stuart, 181

data. *See* information
Data General, 76
Data Identifiers (DI), 204–5
Dayton (Ohio), 149, 159
DC (Distribution Code), 175
DCI. *See* Distribution Codes, Inc.
DeCA, 179–80
"Decision Making Procedures," 207, 233
Defense Logistics Agency (DLA), 182
Defense Personnel Supply Center, 244
Deloitte, Haskins and Sells, 225
Deloitte and Touche, 239
Department of Defense. *See* United States Department of Defense
DI. *See* Data Identifiers
Digital Equipment, 209
Distilled Spirits Institute, 83, 103
Distribution Code (DC), 175
Distribution Codes, Inc. (DCI), 101

administration of U.P.C., 131–33
communication with non-
    grocery industries, 103, 174
conflict with EAN, 138, 197
contract with UCC, 99, 131–32,
    133, 136
contract with UCC ended, 112–
    13, 117, 137–38, 149
costs, 131, 149
Distribution Code (DC), 175
newsletter, 132, 133, 136
offices, 136, 137–38
procedures for issuing
    manufacturer numbers, 100,
    105–6, 132
research on shipping container
    symbols, 134–35, 153
selected to administer UGPIC,
    95, 96
trademark application, 133–34
Distribution Number Bank
    (DNB). *See* Distribution
    Codes, Inc. (DCI)
Distribution Research and
    Education Foundation
    (DREF), 134, 153
distributors
automation of, 10–11
representatives on Ad Hoc
    Committee, 40
See also Cooperative Food
    Distributors of America
    (CFDA)
DLA. *See* Defense Logistics Agency
DNB (Distribution Number
    Bank). *See* Distribution Codes,
    Inc. (DCI)
DREF. *See* Distribution Research
    and Education Foundation
    drugs
manufacturers, 102, 106
National Drug Code (NDC), 49,
    102, 103

drug stores, U.P.C. scanning in,
    117
Dun & Bradstreet, 95, 96
Dunlop, John, 182
Dymo, 76

EAN (European Article
    Numbering Association)
alliance with UCC, 200, 201, 234
compatibility with U.P.C., 9,
    160, 196, 199–200, 266
conflict with DCI, 138, 197
country codes, 196–97, 199–200
development of standard code,
    108–9, 195–97
fees, 200, 202
organizational issues, 197
relations with UCC, 194–202,
    239, 257, 268
scanning issues in U.S., 198–99
Eberts, Marv, 104, 121
ECR. *See* Efficient Consumer
    Response
Eden, Murray, 88, 90
EDI (electronic data interchange)
benefits of, 10–12
development of, 163–65
education programs, 170–71
with food brokers, 240
standards for, 168–69, 172–73
user conferences, 172, 240
See also UCS; VICS
EDI Advisory Committee, 171,
    226, 227, 241, 242
Efficient Consumer Response
    (ECR) project, 172, 199, 242–
    43, 256–57
EFT (electronic funds transfer),
    164
electrical industry, use of
    Distribution Code (DC), 175
electronic data interchange. *See*
    EDI

electronic funds transfer. *See* EFT
Ellis, Gordon, 41–42, 44
"Environmental Guidelines," 64,
　65
Epley, Dennis, 201–2, 241
equipment manufacturers
　Automatic Identification
　　Manufacturers (AIM), 145,
　　209
　interest in scanner market, 82,
　　92–93
　opposition to U.P.C. symbol,
　　69–70
　relationship with UCC board,
　　106, 117
　symbol proposals, 56, 64, 74,
　　75–78, 86, 89–90, 92–93
　tests of proposed symbols, 64–
　　65, 68–69, 82
ergonomic issues, 236
Essarian, John, 77
Europe, scanning technology in,
　64, 74
European Article Numbering
　Association. *See* EAN
Exxon, 216

FACT. *See* Federation of
　Automated Coding
　Technologies
family codes, 186–88
federal government. *See* United
　States government
Federal Trade Commission (FTC),
　51
　relations with Ad Hoc
　　Committee, 52–53, 54–55
　relations with Symbol
　　Standardization Committee,
　　66–67
　relations with UCC, 102
　study of price scanning, 129–30
Federation of Automated Coding

Technologies (FACT), 204–5,
　206
Felter, Byron, 124–25, 130
film masters, of U.P.C. symbol,
　140–41
final system architecture study,
　159–60
Finance Committee, 119
Financial Advisory Committee,
　225
First National Stores, 253
Fleming Companies, 112
Flexible Packaging Association
　(FPA), 231
Flint, Wallace, xii, 95, 96, 99, 132
Focht, Sharon, 148, 157
food
　labeling regulations, 62, 86, 92,
　　237
　prices, 23–24
food brokers, 166, 240
Food and Commercial Workers
　Union, 124
Food and Drug Administration
　(FDA)
　food product labeling
　　regulations, 62, 86, 92, 237
　standard code systems, 49, 102
Food Marketing Institute (FMI)
　chairmen, 248
　reports on scanning
　　implementation, 159
　representation on UCC board
　　of governors, 111, 150, 162,
　　225
　staff support for UCC, 226
　U.P.C. problem reporting
　　service, 154, 234
Foote, Dick, 152, 239
Foreman, Carol Tucker, 128, 255
Fort Howard Paper Co., 108
FPA. *See* Flexible Packaging
　Association

Franz, Barry, 249–51
  on Coupon Committee, 186,
    249
  on Symbol Selection
    Committee, 57, 64, 72, 74,
    249
  as UCC board member, 110–11,
    112, 137, 150
  as UCC Treasurer, 154, 225,
    228, 239, 250–51, 258
FTC. *See* Federal Trade
  Commission

Gabor, Dennis, 21
Gallo wineries, 115
Galt, Bill, 57, 82–83
General Electric, 21
General Foods, 41, 58, 94
general merchandise, use of
  U.P.C., 117, 157–58, 169–70
General Merchandise and Apparel
  Implementation Committee
  (GMAIC), 169–70
General Mills, 41
General Services Administration
  (GSA), 182
Global Policy Committee,
  202
GMA. *See* Grocery Manufacturers
  of America
GMAIC. *See* General Merchandise
  and Apparel Implementation
  Committee
Gookin, R. Burt, 66, 251–53
  as chair of Ad Hoc Committee,
    40, 41, 43, 44, 46, 55, 59, 83,
    125–26
  as chair of UCC board, 111, 112,
    252
  meetings with FTC, 52
  as UCC board member, 110
governing board. *See* Board of
  Governors (UCC)

government. *See* United States
  government
Graphic Arts Technical
  Foundation, 72, 79
Greer, Tommy, 115–16
grocery industry
  briefings on U.P.C., 54, 55
  economic forces in 1970s, 23–
    24
  Efficient Consumer Response
    (ECR) project, 172, 199, 242–
    43, 256–57
  food brokers, 166, 240
  interest in EDI, 163
  labor costs, 24
  labor-management relations,
    24–27
  product proliferation, 13
  size in 1972, xi
  tests of symbol scanning, 68–69
  UCC board's focus on, 176–77,
    195
  wholesalers, xiii, 42, 50, 96, 97
  See also grocery retailers;
    manufacturers
Grocery Manufacturers of
  America (GMA)
  administration of UCS,
    165
  Administrative Systems
    Committee, xi–xii, 101, 105–
    6, 163
  funding of Ad Hoc Committee,
    39–40, 60
  interest in automated coupon
    redemption, 185
  interest in EDI, 240
  interest in shipping container
    symbols, 118
  opposition to item-pricing
    legislation, 126
  product code discussions, xiii
  representation on UCC board

Grocery Manufacturers (*cont.*)
of governors, 97, 104, 110–11,
150, 228
review of coupon validation
proposals, 187–89
Grocery Products Manufacturers
of Canada, 108
grocery retailers
cooperatives, 41
economics of scanning, 66–67
funding of Ad Hoc Committee,
54, 60, 119
implementation of scanning,
19, 108, 112, 115, 116, 126
implementation of U.P.C., 32
interest in EDI, 163–64
interest in standard product
codes, xiii, 31–32
lack of interest in automated
coupon validation, 188
representatives on Ad Hoc
Committee, 41–42
small, 66–67
specialty departments, 13, 16, 27
store sizes, 13, 27
tests of proposed symbols, 64–
65, 68–69, 71, 72, 76, 81, 213
tests of U.P.C. code, 100
transponders in, 34
use of product sales
information, 10–11, 12–13,
17, 114, 150–51
warehouse stores, 130
See also retailers; supermarket
chains; trade associations
GSA. *See* General Services
Administration
Guideline 22. *See* coupons

Haberman, Alan L., 253–55
as chair of Symbol Selection
Committee, 55, 57, 64, 72, 79,
82, 85, 88, 89, 90, 253, 254–55
on Finance Committee, 119
on UCC Board of governors,
104–5, 124, 128, 150, 253
Hackman, Dave, 95, 96
Harmon, Craig, 209–10
Harms, Jim, 201–2
Harrell, Gilbert, 26
Harvard Business School, 79, 246
Hayes, John, 40, 57, 64, 74–75, 132
hazardous materials, 182–83
Head, Bob, 64
Health Industry Business
Communications Council
(HIBCC), 179
health products
labeler identification code
(LIC), 243
manufacturers of, 102, 178
National Health Related Items
Code (NHRIC), 49, 102, 103
potential use of U.P.C., 243–44
Heijn, Albert, 109, 195, 196, 198
Hershey Foods, 220, 225
HIBCC. *See* Health Industry
Business Communications
Council
Highland Associates, 226
H. J. Heinz, 40
Hollis, Bill, 105
holography, 21, 64
Horizon Scan study, 178–79, 240,
244–45
Horwitz, Wayne, 26, 127
Hutt, Michael, 26
Hwang, Margaret, 32

IAPMO (International Association
of Plumbing and Mechanical
Officials), 219–22
IBM
Bilgutay allegations about, 217–
18
confidentiality requirements, 63

lasers, 21
as member of JTC1, 209
opposition to store tests of
symbols, 69, 70–72
symbol proposal, 56, 64, 74, 75,
76, 89–90, 93
ICAC. *See* Industrial Commercial
Advisory Committee
IDASC. *See* International Data
Applications and Standards
Committee
"Implementation Guide for New
Users," 235
Industrial Commercial Advisory
Committee (ICAC), 177–78,
179, 244
industrial companies
representation on UCC board,
175–78, 225
use of Distribution Code (DC),
175
use of U.P.C., 157–58
inflation, 23
information generated by
scanning
uses of, 10–11, 12–13, 17
value to retailers and
manufacturers, 114, 150–51
Information Systems Standards
Board (ISSB; ANSI), 205–6,
208–9
interleaved two of five (ITF)
shipping container symbol.
See shipping containers
Internal Revenue Service (IRS),
121–22
International Article Numbering
Association. *See* EAN
International Association of
Plumbing and Mechanical
Officials (IAPMO), 219–
22
International Data Applications

and Standards Committee
(IDASC), 201–2, 239
International Organization for
Standardization. *See* ISO
ISO (International Organization
for Standardization), 208
ISSB. *See* Information Systems
Standards Board
item price removal
consumer opposition to, 26, 51,
68, 125–26, 128–29
lack of consumer resistance in
tests, 68, 81
proposed laws to prohibit, 26,
126, 128–29
in warehouse stores, 130
ITF shipping container symbol. *See*
shipping containers

Jenkins, David B., 207, 225, 226,
233, 238, 242, 255–57
Jewel Food Stores, 73, 83–85
Johnson & Johnson, 104
Joint Industry Coupon
Committee, 191
Joint Labor Management
Committee of the Retail Food
Industry, 25–27, 127
JTC1, 208–10, 255
Juceam, Art, 104–5
Juckett, Harold P. (Hal), 257–59
administration of UCS, 157,
167, 169
education program on coupon
scanning, 189
hired by UCC, 157
meetings with government
agencies, 181–82
relations with EAN, 200, 201
relations with Mindlin, 157,
257–58
relations with STAC, 144–45,
147

Juckett (*cont.*)
relations with Wilson, 234
staff, 225, 259
as UCC administrator, 159, 162,
177, 219, 221, 224–25, 239
as UCC president, 243
visit to South Africa, 245
work with UCC board, 226,
227–28

Kane, W. J., 41, 42
Kaslow, Walter, 211–15
Keener, Dick, 167
Kelly, Paul, 165, 166
Kelman, Steve, 182
Kenwood (Ohio), Kroger
scanning test, 56, 68, 71, 76,
81, 213
Kiernan, Patrick, 228
KMart, 155–56, 225
Knauer, Virginia, 51
Koch, George, xiii–xv, 55
Koenig, Bob, 94, 134
Kornblau, Curt, 107–8, 119
Kozacik, Judy, 226
Kroger Company, 41, 94, 100, 110,
262
automated checkout counter
development, 43, 64
scanning test (Kenwood, Ohio),
56, 68, 71, 76, 81, 213
KSA. *See* Kurt Salmon Associates
Kurt Salmon Associates (KSA),
242, 244, 245

labeler identification code (LIC),
243
labels
FDA regulations, 62, 86, 92, 237
U.P.C. symbol placement, 67, 79–
80, 81, 83, 86, 87–88, 141, 143
labor
costs in grocery industry, 24

issues with automation, 25–26
relations with management, 24–
27
See also unions
Langan, John, 132, 138, 149
Larkin, Art, 41
lasers, 21, 91–92
Lauer, George, 90n
lawsuits. *See* legal issues
Leary, John, 209
Lee, Bob, 104
legal issues
abuses of U.P.C. system, 222–23
avoidance of lawsuits, 222–23
Bilgutay lawsuit, 216–18
coupon validation patent
dispute, 211–15
lack of patent for U.P.C. symbol,
77–78, 215–16
patent claimed for U.P.C.
symbol, 216–18
potential violations of antitrust
laws, 51–53
in symbol selection process, 62,
66–68, 77, 89
trademarks, 133–34, 219–22
LIC (labeler identification code),
243
liquor. *See* alcoholic beverages
industry
Litton, 64, 74, 76, 89–90, 92
Lloyd, Don, 41, 104, 110, 185, 186
lobbyists, of trade associations,
127–28, 129
Logan, Bill, 41
Logicon, Inc., 43
LOGMARS committee, 181–82

MacBain, Gavin, 41, 42, 55, 102
MacFarland, J. P., 41
Madison, Jesse, 130
MAD magazine, 117
Madsen, Earl, 41, 42

magazines
 add-on symbols for returns, 142
 U.P.C. coding of, 106, 114,
  156
Maginnis, Bill, 111, 153
Maiman, Theodore, 21
manufacturer codes (U.P.C.)
 decision to use, 49
 for general merchandise, 170
 issuance procedures, 85–86, 94–
  95, 100, 105–6, 113
 problems with, 154
 recalling, 158–59, 245–46
 trailing zeroes, 105
manufacturers
 adoption of U.P.C., 79, 85–86
 apparel, 16, 32–33
 benefits of automated coupon
  redemption, 184–85
 concerns with U.P.C. symbol,
  67–68
 costs of source-marking U.P.C.
  symbol, 62, 79–80, 81, 86, 87,
  91, 98
 drug industry, 102
 expectations for product sales
  information from retailers,
  114, 150–51
 government purchases from,
  180
 impact of U.P.C., 11–12
 increased acceptance of U.P.C.,
  98
 interest in EDI, 10–12, 163, 164
 interest in standard product
  codes, xiii, 31–32, 184
 product proliferation, 16
 relations with retailers, 30–32
 representatives on Ad Hoc
  Committee, 40, 41, 42
 textile, 169, 265–66
 See also equipment
  manufacturers; Grocery

Manufacturers of America
 (GMA)
Marsh's Supermarket (Troy,
 Ohio), 5, 103
Martin, Don, 104, 116, 117, 132,
 133
Martin, Ed, 231
Martin, Joseph, 52, 55
Mason, Earl, xiii–xv
Massachusetts Institute of
 Technology, 88
mass merchants, adoption of
 U.P.C., 5, 155–56
McGovern, Gordon, 224
McKinsey & Co.
 analysis of product code
  proposals, 45–46, 47, 50
 briefings on U.P.C., 54
 chosen as consultant to Ad Hoc
  Committee, 44
 economic studies of scanning,
  81, 116
 economic studies of source-
  marking, 62
 EDI proposal, 164
 end of relationship with UCC,
  234–35, 266–67
 as executive secretary of UCC
  Board, 106–7
 expertise in grocery industry,
  265
 legislative issues, 129
 predictions of UCC
  membership, 104, 111
 questions about role of, 158
 store tests and, 69, 72
 studies of shipping container
  symbols, 118, 135
 study of coupon coding, 185
 study of scanning economics in
  small stores, 66–67
 study of U.P.C. administration
  costs, 131, 149

McKinsey & Co. (*cont.*)
 study of U.P.C. final system
 architecture, 159–60
 work with EAN, 108–9, 195–96
 work with Symbol Committee,
 78
 work with textile industry, 169,
 265–66
McMorrow, Bob, 212–13, 215,
 216–17
McReady, Dick, 167
meat, U.P.C. coding of random-
 weight packages, 160
Messerli, Allen, 175–76, 177–78,
 180, 181–82, 225, 229
Mexic, Darryl, 215, 216–17
Mezines, Basil, 52, 54–55
Migros, 64, 74
Milgrom, Paul, 32
military. *See* United States
 Department of Defense
Mindlin, Richard J., 166, 259–60
 administration of UIC, 176
 administration of U.P.C., 112–
 13, 137, 138, 144, 148–49,
 151, 152, 155
 as co-chair of STAC, 139, 140,
 143–44
 relationship with Juckett, 157,
 257–58
mission statements (UCC), 112,
 117–18, 160–61, 177, 232,
 268
MIT (Massachusetts Institute of
 Technology), 88
Mosher, Walter, 178
Murray, Frank, 181

Nabisco Brands, 110
NACS. *See* National Association of
 Convenience Stores
Nader, Ralph, 96
NARGUS. *See* National Association

 of Retail Grocers in the
 United States
National-American Wholesale
 Grocers Association
 (NAWGA), xiii, 97, 112
National Association of
 Convenience Stores (NACS),
 228
National Association of Food
 Chains (NAFC), 77, 85
 briefings on U.P.C., 55
 discussions of standard product
 code, xi, xii, xiii–xv
 interest in shipping container
 symbol, 118
 lobbyists, 127–28
 opposition to item-pricing
 legislation, 126
 representation on UCC board
 of governors, 97, 104
 support of Ad Hoc Committee,
 39
 See also Food Marketing
 Institute (FMI)
National Association of Retail
 Grocers in the United States
 (NARGUS), xiii, 55, 97, 104
National Association of Wholesale
 Distributors (NAWD), 96, 132
National Association of
 Wholesalers (NAW), 50, 131
National Broiler Council, 235–36
National Bureau of Standards
 (NBS), 91, 102
 See also National Institute for
 Standards and Technology
 (NIST)
National Canners Association, 67–
 68, 79, 82–83
National Drug Code (NDC), 49,
 102, 103
National Flexible Packaging
 Association, 79, 80

National Food Brokers Association (NFBA), 166, 240
National Health Related Items Code (NHRIC), 49, 102, 103
National Institute for Standards and Technology (NIST), 146
  See also National Bureau of Standards (NBS)
National Retail Merchants Association (NRMA), 91, 116–17
  product codes, 83, 102, 117, 170, 203
National Soft Drink Association, 79, 83
National Stock Number (NSN), 180
Naval Supply Systems Command, 181, 182–83
NAW. *See* National Association of Wholesalers
NAWD. *See* National Association of Wholesale Distributors
NBS. *See* National Bureau of Standards
NCR
  Bilgutay allegations about, 217–18
  opposition to symbol development, 69–70, 82, 92, 259
  scanners, 70, 74–75, 92
  symbol proposal, 56, 64
NDC. *See* National Drug Code
Nelson, Tom, 41, 107, 119
network externalities, 27–30
Newspaper Advertising Bureau, 213
NFBA. *See* National Food Brokers Association
NHRIC. *See* National Health Related Items Code
Norris, Dick, 165

NRMA. *See* National Retail Merchants Association
NSN. *See* National Stock Number
number systems, of U.P.C., 102, 191, 285
nutrition labeling regulations, 62, 86, 92, 237

O'Connor, Mike, 50, 106
OCR-A, 117, 170, 203
Oddy, Bill, 104–5, 111, 149
Office of Management and Budget (OMB), 182
Olivetti, 64
OMB. *See* Office of Management and Budget Operating Committee, 162, 224–25, 258
Osborne, Andrew, 202

packages
  bottles, cans and glass, 82–83
  flexible, 79, 80, 231
  scanning problems, 142
  U.P.C. symbol placement, 67, 79–80, 81, 83, 86, 87–88, 141, 143
  See also source-marking
Paperboard Packaging Council, 67–68, 79, 80
paper industry, 108
patents
  claimed for U.P.C. symbol, 216–18
  for coupon-validation system, 211–15
  lack of for U.P.C. symbol, 77–78, 215–16
Paul, Sandy, 206, 209
Peck, Jerry, xiii–xv
Peet, Creighton, 64
Perkins, Don, 84
pharmaceuticals. *See* drugs

Pictorial Information Dissector and Analyzer. *See* PIDAS

PIDAS (Pictorial Information Dissector and Analyzer), 71–72

Pitney-Bowes-Alpex, 56, 74, 76, 92–93

Porter, Jim, 139, 140

post exchanges, 179–80

poultry, U.P.C. coding of, 235–36

Poultry and Egg Institute, 153

prices
    food, 23–24
    policies affected by technology, 34
    See also item price removal

printability gage, 140, 142–43

printing industry
    concerns about U.P.C. symbol, 110, 141, 143, 231
    relationship with UCC board, 106

Procter & Gamble, 12, 31, 150

produce, U.P.C. codes for, 161–62, 236

Produce Electronic Information Board, 236

Produceland. *See* produce

Produce Marketing Association, 161–62, 236

product codes. *See* standard product codes; U.P.C.

product proliferation, 13, 16

Progressive Grocer, 97

Project Info, 240

public governors, 124–25, 128, 150, 228, 253

Public Policy Committee, 26, 126, 127, 128–29, 130, 255, 264

QR. *See* Quick Response

Quick Response (QR), 170–71

radio frequency product identification (RFID), 245

Ralph's Grocery, 248

random weight products, U.P.C. coding of, 114, 153, 160, 235–36

Rawley, John, 232, 268

RCA
    scanning technology, 64
    symbol proposal, 74, 76, 82, 89–90
    symbol test in Kroger store, 56, 71, 213
    threat to leave market, 76, 82, 92

recordings, U.P.C. marking of, 117

Red Owl, 58, 104

register tapes, benefits of enhanced, 115, 123, 128

regulation
    food prices, 23–24
    of laser–emitting devices, 91–92
    nutrition labeling, 62, 86, 92, 237

Reidy, Bill, 163

Resources for Lawyers, 67, 77

Retail Clerks union, 125, 128, 236

"Retailer Guidelines on Relationships with Equipment Manufacturers," 64–65

retailers
    benefits of U.P.C., 11, 12–13
    book stores, 237
    changes in relationships with vendors, 10–12, 17, 30–32
    drug stores, 117
    increasing concentration of, 12–13
    mass merchants, 5, 155–56
    use of EDI, 10–12
    See also grocery retailers

RFID. *See* radio frequency product identification

Rich, Bob, 220
Roberts, John, 32
Robinson-Patman Act, xiii, 51
Roll, Ralph R., 169
Russell, Lawrence (Larry), 44,
  260–62
  EDI proposal, 164
  meetings with FTC, 52
  proposals to extend U.P.C. to
    other industries, 83
  as staff for UCC board, 106
  Washington strategy committee,
    55
  work with Ad Hoc Committee,
    46, 50, 54, 98, 101
  work with STAC, 139
  work on symbol, 48, 56, 63–64,
    67, 69, 86–87, 91
  work with Symbol Selection
    Committee, 58, 64, 68, 78, 80,
    84–85, 89, 249, 260–62
  work with UCC board, 100, 102
  work on U.P.C. implementation,
    105
Russia, coding authority, 242

Safeway, 74
Saint Louis Post Dispatch, 213
Satterfield, Carroll, 94
savings
  hard, 45–46, 65, 81, 89, 98, 116
  soft, 45–46, 50, 65, 81, 98, 117
  from standard product code,
    45–46, 50, 98, 117
  from symbol, 65, 81, 89, 116,
    117
  from UCS, 166
scanners
  ability to read EAN symbols,
    198–99
  accuracy, 126–27, 128, 129–30
  benefits to consumers, 128
  in book stores, 237

consumer education on, 126
cost of, 80–81
development of, 20–22, 64
economics of, in small stores,
  66–67
ergonomic issues, 236
first store using, 5, 103
implementation of, 19, 112,
  115, 116, 142
increased use of, 151, 159
information generated by, 10–
  11, 12–13, 17, 114, 150–51
Kroger test of, 68, 71
labor issues, 25–26
NCR, 70, 74–75, 92
productivity impact, 108
public policy issues, 125–26
small number of problems with,
  142, 143
tests in Europe, 64, 74
voice, 64
See also coupons; item price
  removal
Scanner Inc., 56, 74, 76
Schaeberle, Robert, 110, 112, 155
Schatz, Vern, 58, 73, 83
Schawlow, A.L., 21
Schenley, 111
Schnuck, Craig, 239n
Schubenel, Robert, 202
SCLMC. *See* Shipping Container
  Marking and Labeling
  Committee
Selvin, Peter, 221–22
Shaws, 225
Shipping Container Marking and
  Labeling Committee
  (SCMLC), 241
shipping containers
  adoption of symbol, 135, 154–
    55, 229
  ANSI approval of UCC
    standard, 207

shipping containers (*cont.*)
 bar codes on, 11
 development of symbols for,
  118, 134–35, 153
Shipping Container Symbology
 Study Group, 134, 135
SIL. *See* Standard Interchange
 Language
Singer, 74, 76, 92–93
SMI. *See* Supermarket Institute
Smith, Ron, 216
source-marking products
 cost of, 62, 79–80, 81, 86, 87,
  91, 98
 growth of, 98, 110, 117, 263–64
South African Article Numbering
 Association, 245
space shuttle, 10
sponsoring associations, 228–29
STAC. *See* Symbol Technical
 Advisory Committee
Standard & Poor's, 95, 96
Standard Interchange Language
 (SIL), 242
standard product codes
 alcoholic beverages, 102, 103
 benefits foreseen, xiii
 competing efforts, 50, 83, 102–3
 early discussions, xi–xii, xiii–xv
 global use, 9
 for health products, 49, 102,
  103, 243–44
 manufacturers' interest in, xiii,
  31–32, 184
 National Stock Number (NSN),
  180
 OCR-A, 117, 170, 203
 radio frequency product
  identification (RFID), 245
 retailers' interest in, xiii, 31–32
 savings from, 45–46, 50, 98, 117
 UCC-EAN Code 128, 146, 192–
  93, 204, 207

Uniform Industrial Code (UIC),
 175, 176, 178
 See also U.P.C.
standards
 benefits of, 31–32
 international, 208
 national, 207–8
 See also American National
  Standards Institute (ANSI)
Stokely, 104
Stop and Shop, 74
Stringer, Bob, 41, 44, 94, 96, 104,
 106, 109, 119, 134
Strubbe, John L. (Jack), 108, 262–
 64
 on Ad Hoc Committee, 41, 44,
  262–63
 as chair of UCC board, 106,
  109–10, 120, 125, 263
 on Code Management
  Committee, 94, 96, 97, 98,
  103
Stump, Wilbur, 104
supermarket chains
 implementation of scanning,
  151
 profitability in 1970s, 24
 representatives on Ad Hoc
  Committee, 41, 42
 use of U.P.C. symbols, 110
 See also grocery retailers
Supermarket Institute (SMI), 50,
 85, 106
 Albers Award, 66
 conventions, 53–54, 55, 79, 216
 expectations of Ad Hoc
  Committee, 48
 funding of Ad Hoc Committee,
  39
 representation on UCC board
  of governors, 97
 review of coupon validation
  proposals, 187

See also Food Marketing
    Institute (FMI)
Supertag, 245
Super Value Stores, 41, 94
suppliers. *See* manufacturers;
    vendors
Sweda, 56, 64, 74
Sweden, scanning test in, 64
Switzerland, scanning tests in, 64,
    74
symbol, U.P.C.. *See* U.P.C. symbol
"Symbol Evaluation Process," 64,
    65
Symbol Selection Committee. *See*
    Symbol Standardization
    Committee
Symbol Standardization
    Committee
  assignment, 58–59
  avoidance of ANSI, 60–61
  communication with public, 78–
    79
  consulting members, 69, 73–74
  decision on symbol, 87–93
  discussions of register tape,
    123
  "Environmental Guidelines,"
    64, 65
  formation, 53, 55
  legal concerns, 62, 66–68, 77,
    89
  meetings, 58, 60, 73–74
  members, 57–58, 69, 73
  relationship with Federal Trade
    Commission, 66–67
  relationships with trade
    associations, 79
  "Retailer Guidelines," 64–65
  Russell's work with, 260–62
  selection process, 60–62, 64, 65,
    66, 123–24
  "Symbol Evaluation Process,"
    64, 65

testing program, 68–71, 106
types of members, 73–74
Symbol Technical Advisory
    Committee (STAC)
  activities in 1980s, 144–46
  activities in 1990s, 146–47
  add-on symbol development,
    142, 146–47
  coupon validation issue, 187,
    192–93
  formation, 139–40
  meetings with board, 144
  members, 145
  mission, 139, 144–45
  printability gage issue, 140,
    142–43
  recommendations, 140–41,
    142–43, 146
  reporting relationship, 227
  shipping container symbol
    issue, 134
  subcommittees, 140, 141–42,
    144, 145
Symbol Location Guidelines
    manual, 143

Taubert, William, 111, 153, 165,
    169
tax status, of Uniform Code
    Council, 99, 119–20, 121–22,
    226
Technical Information,
    Education, and Update
    Service. *See* TIEUP
technology
  adoption of, 32–33
  computers, 22, 242
  future potential, 33–34
  holography, 21
  innovations related to U.P.C.,
    11–12
  studies of, 244–45
  transponders, 34

technology (*cont.*)
  See also EDI (electronic data
    interchange); scanners
technology industry
  interest in symbol development,
    62–64
  See also equipment
    manufacturers
Tecot, Steve, 176–78
Terry, Bill, 226
tests of proposed symbols, 56, 68–69
  evaluating, 65
  guidelines for, 59, 64–65, 69, 74
  importance of store tests, 72
  in Kroger store (Kenwood,
    Ohio), 56, 68, 71, 76, 81, 213
  laboratory, 72–73, 89, 106
  opposition to, 69–71
Texas Instruments, 56
textile industry, 169, 265–66
TIEUP (Technical Information,
  Education, and Update
  Service), 110, 111, 141
Townes, Charles, 21
trade associations
  early discussions of standard
    product codes, xi–xii, xiii–xv
  endorsement of U.P.C., 55
  lobbyists, 127–28, 129
  public policy issues, 125–26
  relations with UCC, 105, 106,
    111, 120, 121, 154, 228–29,
    232, 236, 263
  representatives on Ad Hoc
    Committee, 40
  representatives on UCC Board
    of Governors, 97, 104, 110–11
  UCC start-up money returned
    to, 120, 121, 232
  See also specific associations
trademarks
  application for, 133–34, 219,
    220–21

dispute over UPC, 219–22
  on register tapes, 115
translation, of U.P.C. codes to
  symbols, 283–89
transponders, 34
Tripartite Food Industry Wage
  and Salary Committee, 25
Troy (Ohio), Marsh's
  Supermarket, 5, 103
TRW, 56
Turner, Jim, 127
Tuttle, Jim, 156, 167
two dimensional symbology (2-D),
  33–34, 244–45

UCC (Uniform Code Council)
  accountants, 152, 239
  administration of EDI
    standards, 170, 172–73
  administration of UCS, 157,
    158, 166, 167–69, 173
  administration of UIC, 175,
    176
  administration of U.P.C., 3,
    112–13, 148–49, 155
  auditors, 152, 235, 239
  budgeting and project approval
    process, 224–25, 226, 267
  budgets, 119, 120, 149
  computer systems, 242
  "Decision Making Procedures,"
    207, 233
  education programs, 153, 154,
    157, 170–71, 189, 191
  endowment, 152, 250–51, 255–
    56
  expenses, 116, 121, 149
  formation, 98–99
  funding, 99–100, 118–19, 120–
    22, 152, 171
  membership fees, 97, 109–10,
    119, 121, 151, 155
  membership growth, 85–86,

101, 103–4, 108, 109, 111, 132, 151, 155–56, 170, 225

membership predictions, 104, 111, 152

membership rules, 100–101, 105, 108, 115–16, 151, 161, 223

mission statements, 112, 117–18, 160–61, 177, 232, 268

new member approval process, 238

offices in Dayton, 149, 159

procedures, 241

relations with ANSI, 203–8

relations with counterparts in other countries, 108, 242

relations with DNB/DCI, 99, 131–37

relations with EAN, 194–202, 239, 257, 268

relations with trade associations, 105, 106, 111, 120, 121, 154, 228–29, 232, 236, 263

responsibilities, 9

staff, 155, 157, 225, 233, 259

strategic plans, 232, 268

tax status, 99, 119–20, 121–22, 226

See also Board of Governors (UCC)

UCC-EAN Alliance, 200, 201, 234

UCC-EAN Code 128

adoption of, 146

ANSI approval of, 207

Application Identifiers (AI), 204, 207, 234

use for coupons, 192–93

use for health products, 243–44

UCS (Uniform Communications Standard)

administration of, 157, 158, 165, 166, 167–69, 173

compared to U.P.C., 165–66, 167

coordination with ANSI X12, 168–69, 170, 171–72, 204

development of, 165

growth of, 168, 171, 172, 225, 240–41

implementation problems, 169

potential savings, 166

revenues from, 167–68, 171, 172, 241

user conferences, 172, 240

See also EDI (electronic data interchange)

UGPCC (Uniform Grocery Product Code Council). *See* UCC (Uniform Code Council)

UGPIC (uniform grocery product identification code). *See* U.P.C. (Universal Product Code)

UIC. *See* Uniform Industrial Code

Uniform Code Council. *See* UCC

Uniform Communications Standard. *See* UCS

Uniform Grocery Product Code Council (UGPCC). *See* UCC (Uniform Code Council)

uniform grocery product identification code (UGPIC). *See* U.P.C. (Universal Product Code)

Uniform Industrial Code (UIC), 175, 176

subsumed into U.P.C., 178

Uniform Plumbing Code (UPC), 219–22

Uniform Product Code. *See* U.P.C. (Universal Product Code)

Uniform Product Code Council use of name, 109

Uniform Product Code Council
(*cont.*)
See also UCC (Uniform Code
Council)
unions
ergonomic concerns, 236
fears of job losses from
automation, 124, 125, 128
ties to consumer groups, 124,
128
See also labor
United States Department of
Defense, 179–80, 181–82, 209
United States government
Commission on Productivity,
102
Federal Trade Commission
(FTC), 51, 52–53, 54–55, 66–
67, 102, 129–30
Food and Drug Administration
(FDA), 49, 62, 86, 92, 102,
237
General Services Administration
(GSA), 182
Office of Management and
Budget (OMB), 182
regulation of food prices, 23–24
regulation of laser-emitting
devices, 91–92
reluctance of Ad Hoc
Committee to involve, 19–20,
51–53
use of U.P.C., 179–83, 244
United States Postal Service, 9
Universal Product Code. *See* U.P.C.
UP$, 115–16
UPC (Uniform Plumbing Code),
219–22
U.P.C. (Universal Product Code)
administration by DNB/DCI,
131–33
administration by UCC, 3, 112–
13, 139, 148–49, 155

administrative tasks, 94–95
analysis of alternatives, 45–46
ANSI approval of, 207–8, 238
benefits to retailers, 11, 12–13
capacity, 153, 158–60, 240
check characters, 49, 288–89
compatibility with drug and
health product codes, 102,
103
compatibility with EAN, 9, 160,
196, 199–200
decision on, 47–48, 53
efforts to expand acceptance of,
97–98, 100, 133
expansion to other industries,
83, 103, 116–17, 146, 157–58,
169–70, 174, 177–79, 229,
232
federal government use of, 179–
83
final system architecture study,
159–60
financing of management of,
95, 97
guide for new users, 235
hard savings, 45–46, 98
impact on manufacturers, 11–
12
implementation of, 19, 30, 50,
79, 100, 101, 110, 113–15, 115
for magazines, 106, 114, 142,
156
network externalities issue, 27–
30
number systems, 102, 191, 285
objectives, 45
in operation, 10, 12
opposition to, 50, 83–85
printed with symbol, 88
problem reporting, 153, 154,
159
for produce, 161–62, 236
public announcement of, 54–55

for random weight products, 114, 153, 235–36

for records and tapes, 117

selection of service bureau, 95–96

significance, 2, 10–20

skepticism about, 103–4

soft savings, 45–46, 50, 98, 117

store tests of, 100

structure, 3, 47, 49–50, 281–83

trademark issue, 133–34, 219–22

translation to symbols, 283–89

use by mass merchants, 5, 155–56

variation proposed to identify people, 156

Version A, 160, 284, 286–87

Version D, 160, 190–91, 192

Version E, 160, 284

widespread usage, 3–5

See also manufacturer codes; U.P.C. symbol

U.P.C. Advisory Committee, 226–27, 233, 241

U.P.C. symbol

add-on symbols, 142, 146–47

on books, 237

characteristics, 281–83

clear space, 142

concerns of manufacturers, 67–68

concerns with obsolescence, 85, 88

cost of source-marking, 62, 79–80, 81, 86, 87, 91, 98

criteria for selection, 86–87

decision to develop, 47–48

efforts to increase acceptance by grocer retailers, 110

failure to apply for patent, 77–78, 215–16

film masters, 140–41

first store to scan, 5, 103

growth of source-marking, 98, 110, 117, 263–64

human-readable number included in, 88

implementation of, 101, 108, 112

laboratory tests, 72–73, 89, 106

location on packages, 67, 79–80, 81, 83, 86, 87–88, 143

opposition to, 69–70, 83–85

patent dispute, 216–18

placement on multipack items, 141

in popular culture, 117

printability gage issue, 140, 142–43

printing issues, 110, 146, 231

print specifications, 72, 78, 80, 87, 91, 234

proposals, 62–64, 67, 68–69, 74, 75–78, 86, 87–91, 92–93

public-domain issue, 77–78, 215–16

requirements, 58, 65

savings predicted, 65, 81, 89, 116

selection process, 59, 60–62, 64, 65, 66, 123–24

shapes proposed, 72, 82, 88, 89–90

size, 81, 91

studies of economics of, 79–81

translating U.P.C. codes into, 283–89

truncation issue, 144

validation issue, 141, 146, 231

See also coupons; tests of proposed symbols

U.P.C. Technical Director, 233

US Brewers Association, 79, 83

User Conferences, UCS, 172, 240

US TAG (Technical Advisory Group), 209–10
US Trademark Association, 115

value codes, 186–89
variable data, standards for, 146, 233–34
variable weight products, U.P.C. coding of, 114, 153, 160, 235–36
vendors
    changes in relationships with retailers, 30–32
    use of EDI, 10–12
    See also manufacturers
Version A (U.P.C.), 160, 284, 286–87
Version D (U.P.C.), 160, 190–91, 192
Version E (U.P.C.), 160, 284
VICS (Voluntary Interindustry Communications Standards), 169, 170–71, 265–66
    administration by UCC, 170
    potential future technologies, 244
    proposed as ANSI standard, 204
    See also EDI
VISA, 156
voice scanning, 64
Voluntary Interindustry Communications Standards. *See* VICS

Waldbaum, Eric, 57, 64, 93, 249
Wal-Mart, 12, 31, 155
warehouse stores, 130
Washington strategy committee, 55
Wegman, Dan, 191

Wegman, Robert B., 126, 264–65
    as chair of Public Policy Committee, 264
    as chair of UCC board, 153–54, 155, 264
    fundraising effort, 60, 119, 264
Wegman's Super Markets, 60, 189, 264
Weil, David, 32
wholesalers, xiii, 42, 50, 96, 97
Wiesner, Jerome, 88
Willard Bishop Consulting, 235
Williams, Ted, 146, 229
Wilson, Thomas W., Jr., 44, 116, 265–67
    agreement with DCI on UIC, 175, 176
    billing practices, 158, 267
    departure from UCC, 234–35, 258, 266–67
    legislative issues, 127–28, 129
    meetings with FTC, 52
    predictions of UCC membership, 104
    on scanning accuracy, 126
    as staff for UCC board, 106–7, 143, 157, 161, 162, 177, 224, 226, 266
    view of UCS, 167, 169
    Washington strategy committee, 55
    work with Ad Hoc Committee, 83–84, 98, 185, 265
    work with EAN, 108–9, 160, 195–96, 197–98, 265
    work on symbol, 63–64, 89, 91
    work on U.P.C., 50, 54
    work on VICS standards, 265–66

winemakers, 115
Winn-Dixie, 58
WINS (public warehouse)
    standards, 170
Woodland, Joe, 90n
Wright, George, 176
Wright, Michael, 130
Wyman, James, 41, 42, 44, 55

X12 (ANSI), 168–69, 170, 171–72,
    204

Zaucha, Tom, 127–28
Zellweger, 64, 74, 92
Zimmerman, Richard A., 177, 201,
    220, 231–32, 234, 235, 267,
    268